W9-BKZ-997

the essential difference

books from

differences

series editors

NAOMI SCHOR

ELIZABETH WEED

the essential difference

edited by

NAOMI SCHOR

ELIZABETH WEED

Indiana University Press

Bloomington and Indianapolis

The editors wish to express
their gratitude to
Sheila Levrant de Bretteville
for her generous help with
the design of the new
differences *book series*
and to Jenny Anger
for her meticulous editing
of this first volume
in that series.

© 1994 by Brown University
and **d i f f e r e n c e s**
A Journal of Feminist Cultural Studies
All rights reserved
No part of this book may be reproduced
or utilized in any form or by any means,
electronic or mechanical, including
photocopying and recording, or by any
information storage and retrieval
system, without permission in writing
from the publisher. The Association of
American University Presses' Resolution
on Permissions constitutes the only
exception to this prohibition. The paper
used in this publication meets the
minimum requirements of American
National Standard for Information
Sciences—Permanence of Paper for
Printed Library Materials,
ANSI Z39, 48-1984.   ⊚™
Manufactured in the United States
of America

Library of Congress
Cataloging-in-Publication Data

The Essential Difference /edited by
Naomi Schor and Elizabeth Weed.
p.   cm. — (Books from Differences)
Includes bibliographical references
and index.
ISBN 0-253-35092-1 (cloth: alk. paper).—
ISBN 0-253-35093-X (pbk.: alk. paper)
1. Feminist Theory. 2. Sex differences
(Psychology) I. Schor, Naomi. II. Weed,
Elizabeth, date.   III. Series.
HQ1190.E87   1994   93-40428
305.42'01—dc20

    1 2 3 4 5 99 98 97 96 95 94

Contents

Introduction

*M*any moments in intellectual and political history can be defined by impassioned debates: the essentialism–anti-essentialism debates define '80s feminism and, in a broader framework, the politics of identity in which that feminism participates. And debates are either abandoned or generate or mutate into other debates: today's PC debates, for example, are not unrelated to the essentialism debates, insofar as anti-essentialism is a prime instance of politically correct thinking. Indeed, one of the most striking features of several of the pieces here, notably de Lauretis's, Spivak's, and my own, is their tone: sarcasm, cold fury, and contempt are some of the affective responses to the policing of feminism by the shock troops of anti-essentialism:

> *Here, not (say) in Italy, and now, not (say) in the '70s, the term* essentialism *covers a range of metacritical meanings and strategic uses that go the very short distance from convenient label to buzzword. Many who, like myself, have been involved with feminist critical theory for some time and who did use the term, initially, as a serious critical concept, have grown impatient with this word–essentialism–time and again repeated with its reductive ring, its self-righteous tone of superiority, its contempt for "them"–those guilty of it. (de Lauretis 1)*

> *What revisionism, not to say essentialism, was to Marxism-Leninism, essentialism is to feminism: the prime idiom of intellectual terrorism and the privileged instrument of political orthodoxy. Borrowed from the time-honored vocabulary of philosophy, the word essentialism has been endowed within the context of feminism with the power to reduce to silence, to excommunicate, to consign to oblivion. Essentialism in modern-day feminism is anathema. (Schor 42)*

> *What I am very suspicious of is how anti-essentialism,*
> *really more than essentialism, is allowing women to call names and*
> *congratulate themselves. . . .*
>
> *. . . I have to say that a lot of self-consciously anti-essentialist*
> *writing seems to me a bit useless and boring. . . . It's often very deriva-*
> *tive, resembling other and better models that are not as scared of*
> *essences. (Spivak 156, 171)*

But we are getting ahead of ourselves: what is essentialism, what anti-essentialism? At what point did the debate begin? In what context did the special issue of *differences*, which became this volume, come into being? The debate or at least its main terms have been around at least as long as second-wave feminism itself. It was first imported or smuggled into feminism along with Beauvoir's existentialism, though as Scholes pertinently observes there has been a significant shift since the time when existentialism was essentialism's binary opposite. In the essentialism debates, both existentialism and essentialism now find themselves yoked together in their counterposition to anti-essentialism.

> *Once upon a time, "essentialism" was opposed by an "existentialism"*
> *that emphasized the priority of actions over concepts in human affairs.*
> *The position that is now called "anti-essentialism," however, is just as*
> *opposed to existentialism as to the essentialism it claims to repudiate.*
> *(Scholes 127)*

This remapping is instructive, for it may be that in the future what now seems most radically disjoined, say essentialism and constructionism, will be conjoined and opposed to a third term as yet unknown but whose time will come.

Anti-essentialism, to the extent that we can proceed as though it speaks in a single voice–but, we shall see in a moment, that such is not the case–first became an issue in the conflict between Beauvoir and Beauvoirian "equality feminists" and the newer French "difference feminists" (Grosz), Hélène Cixous, Luce Irigaray, and others. Monique Plaza's critique of Irigaray, first published in Beauvoir's *Questions féministes*, can be seen in micro-historical terms as the opening salvo in a battle that extends far beyond the reception of Irigaray and

French feminism. But this history is a partial one; it needs to be supplemented by the helpfully contextualized version of events proposed by Teresa Brennan in her introduction to *Between Feminism and Psychoanalysis*, a collection of papers centrally concerned with the question of essentialism:

> *Initially in Britain, essentialist theories were criticized from a Marxist theoretical standpoint. This critique of essentialism was elaborated in the context of early 1970s shifts within received views on Marxism: a shift away from a "humanist" reading of Marx's theory of ideology towards the structuralist interpretation that criticized the early Marx on epistemological and related political grounds for his tacit reliance on the notion of a "human essence."* Where Marxism was allied with feminism, the critique of essentialism carried over. *(6–7; emphasis added)*

Given these two different but not incompatible accounts of the rise of anti-essentialism–Beauvoir was after all a Marxist and not a feminist when she wrote *The Second Sex*–it is perhaps no accident that of all the many books and articles directed against essentialism the book that more than any other brought the conflict first opposing two generations of French feminists to broader attention was Toril Moi's *Sexual/Textual Politics*. Appearing in 1985–a turning point in recent feminism criticism–the book, compact, cogent, readily accessible, widely circulated, written by a Beauvoirian socialist feminist, born and raised in Norway, and living and working in Britain, made (anti-)essentialism a household word.

In the wake of Moi's book, it became apparent that the discussion was spinning out of control, and some basic and patient reexamination of the terminology was urgently needed to save feminist theory from degenerating into unproductive name-calling and conceptual bankruptcy. Working independently in different cities, on far-flung campuses, two coasts, and at least two continents, several of the contributors to this volume began by going back to the dictionary; taking nothing for granted, they preface their discussions by asking what is essentialism? And the definitions offered here range from the relatively simple to the more complex. Both are necessary, for the relatively simple say what the more complex ones do not, namely that the fundamental issue is the body. As Rooney remarks, "The body is of course essentialism's great text . . ." (152):

> *. . . an essentialist in the context of feminism is one who instead of care-*
> *fully holding apart the poles of sex and gender maps the feminine onto*
> *femaleness, one for whom the body, the female body that is, remains, in*
> *however complex and problematic a way the rock of feminism. (Schor*
> *42–43; cf. Fuss on Scholes 99–100)*

The philosophical references range from Hegel to Locke, who emerges as the central purveyor of a viable redefinition of essence, with his distinction between nominal and real essence (de Lauretis, Fuss). This is how Fuss summarizes the Lockean distinction:

> *Real essence connotes the Aristotelian understanding of essence as*
> *that which is most irreducible and unchanging about a thing; nominal*
> *essence signifies for Locke a view of essence as merely a linguistic con-*
> *venience, a classificatory fiction we need to categorize and to label.*
> *(99)*

Clearly this distinction between a nominal essence, which is neither fixed nor singular, and a real essence, which is both, offers a tempting way out of the impasse created by the more primitive and intractable Aristotelian essential-ism, and de Lauretis is quick to make the most of it, arguing that since for most feminists the constructedness of gender and the historicity of patriarchy are axiomatic, "the 'essence' of woman that is described in the writings of so many so-called essentialists is not the *real essence*, in Locke's terms, but more likely a *nominal* one." And this nominal essence is more a utopian ideal than a "belief in a God-given or otherwise immutable nature of woman" (3).

However inviting this escape route may seem to the anti-anti-essentialist, it is not unproblematic from a theoretically pure anti-essentialist perspective: not only is it hard to maintain this distinction–as Fuss notes, "nominal essences are often treated by post-Lockians as if they were real essences" (100)–but it is hard to avoid the suspicion that just as in the view of strict constructionists (such as Judith Butler) the very distinction between sex and gender serves covertly to preserve the notion of a directly accessible nature/body, the distinction between nominal and real essences keeps alive the dream of an essentialism without a body, a language without a referent, or better, a referent outside of language. Here, however, the analogy between the two distinctions collapses because if there is one point on which there is wide agreement it is that real essentialism inheres in language and that further, as is becoming more apparent, anti-essentialism, in its zeal to jettison the body, tends toward an idealist view of language. In short it is anti-essentialism and not, as is often alleged, essentialism that fails to take into account the workings of language.

> *If to hold concepts in common is to essentialize, then language always essentializes. Whenever we speak or write, we are, willy nilly, essentialists. (Scholes 119)*

> *A critique of an essentialist vocabulary in feminist discourse can fall into an essentialist view of language, where words, disengaged from socio-historic relations, have fixed, inalterable meanings. (Rabine 136–37)*

The real/nominal distinction perpetuates the illusion that on the one hand there is such a thing as real essence, which anti-essentialism would contest, and that, on the other, there is a good and a bad essence, which essentialists would deny.

For all the appeals to philosophy, as Spivak notes in response to a question from Rooney, there is little connection between high philosophical essence and the discussions carried out in its name on other theoretical scenes; essentialism is not a "sexy" topic in the "house of philosophy," where it is "not taken seriously": "The question of anti-essentialism and essentialism is not a philosophical question; that's why there isn't any rebuttal from the house of philosophy" (160). But there is more than one house in philosophy, and in another, the very one where Spivak locates herself, which is the house that Jacques (Derrida) built, the house of deconstruction, the question of essence is taken very seriously, as we shall see in a moment.

Clearly, definitions are not sufficient to do the job of bringing some clarity and rigor to the debate; two other complementary gestures are enlisted here: on the one hand, the distinguishing of essentialism from other equally contested -isms (universalism, biologism, naturalism) with which it is all too often confused or lumped (Grosz), and, on the other, the disentangling of various strains within anti-essentialism which criticize essentialism as complicitous with patriarchy, naive realism, metaphysical thinking, false universalism (Schor). The net effect of this double gesture is perhaps paradoxical: it is to show that although essentialism is neither a universalism nor a biologism, it is not for all that a singular thing; to borrow the Lockean distinction discussed above, there is no real essence of essentialism, but a whole series of nominal essences, or in de Lauretis's terms, triangles.

The question then becomes why has anti-essentialism proceeded in this manner? Reductiveness and conflation are classical and effective polemical devices, but that does not suffice to account for the rhetorical heat of this particular debate. De Lauretis suggests several reasons—to which Spivak also makes reference—but one which at this point deserves particular attention is the following: the stakes of anti-essentialism are to secure feminism's place in male theory and recognition by it, notably the dominant male theory of the era, poststructuralism, which is most often to say, deconstruction. Anti-essentialism is the wages of academic legitimation. The fact that Moi chooses to end her book by a citation from Derrida is not lost on Scholes, for it marks the promotion of Derrida to the main guarantor of feminist anti-essentialism.

Two questions then arise: can there be an essentialist deconstruction? can there be an anti-essentialist feminism? (Fuss 101). Let us consider each question in turn. For at least two authors in this volume the question makes no sense: Scholes, for whom the pairing is oxymoronic, and Spivak, for whom, quite to the contrary, the two terms cannot be pulled apart. Far from being mutually exclusive, deconstruction and essentialism are, according to Spivak's authoritative analysis, bound up with each other. To use deconstruction as an instrument with which to bludgeon essentialism is to be insensitive to deconstruction's great respect for essentialism. Commenting on her own much cited statement to the effect that feminism must "take the risk of essentialism," Spivak says:

> So long as the critique of essentialism is understood not as an exposure
> of error, our own or others', but as an acknowledgement of the danger-
> ousness of what one must use, I think my revised statement—that we
> should consider how ourselves and others are essentialists in different
> ways—I think I would stand by it. The critique of essentialism should
> not be seen as being critical in the colloquial, Anglo-American sense of
> being adversely inclined, but as a critique in the very strong European
> philosophical sense, that is to say, as an acknowledgement of its useful-
> ness. (157)

> *... I would say that what deconstruction has taught me right*
> *from the beginning is the necessity of essentialism and how careful we*
> *must be about it. . . . So deconstruction also teaches me about the*
> *impossibility of anti-essentialism. . . . Deconstruction is not an essence. . . .*
> *Deconstruction itself can be an essentialism. (162–63)*

Citing Ruth Salvaggio's *Enlightened Absence* as an instance of "essentialist, humanist, deconstructivist feminism," Spivak concludes:

> *. . . it can certainly become a viewpoint in deconstruction, a description*
> *of what it is to be feminine, how the anti-essential feminine is the*
> *essence of the feminine. It can be an essentialism, I think; it doesn't*
> *come packaged with either one thing or the other. (163)*

Let us now move on to the second question: can there be an anti-essentialist feminism? Here we must shift the focus of our lexicographical inquiry and ask what then is feminism, what should it be? And how does the question of essence intersect with the question of feminism? De Lauretis is the first to pose the question by displacing the question of the *essence of the feminine* to that of the essence of feminism and its theory: ". . . feminist theory is all about an essential difference, an irreducible difference, though not a difference between woman and man, nor a difference inherent in 'woman's nature' (in woman as nature), but a difference in the feminist conception of woman, women, and the world" (1). And the "*essential* component" (Fuss 111) of feminist theory is "in a word," as all the contributors to this volume would, I think, agree, politics. Where they would disagree–and everything hinges on this disagreement–is on the order of events. As Rooney observes: "We seem to desire that what unites us (as feminists) pre-exist our desire to be joined: something that stands outside our own alliances may authorize them and empower us to speak not simply as feminists but as women, not least against women whose political work is elsewhere" (152). Do politics precede alliance (Fuss, Rooney) or does commonality ground politics (de Lauretis, Brennan, Braidotti in Brennan, Haraway cited by Fuss)? Put another way: can there be a feminist politics that dispenses with the notion of Woman? If essentialism stubbornly refuses to wither away, it is because, as Rooney recognizes, "it remains difficult to engage in feminist analysis and politics if not 'as a woman'" (152). And yet as Rooney goes on to say: "In reading the body, to find 'woman'; in 'women,' to secure feminism; to capture in a word the essence of a thing: essentialism is a dream of the end of politics among women, of a formal resolution to the discontinuity between women and feminisms" (152). To the extent that to be a feminist is to be committed to change through collective action, the issue of biological fixism is a red herring; what really matters is what the best strategy is for bringing about change. In the most current debates, Brennan suggests that this can be accomplished not merely by severing the spurious link between essentialism and fixism, but by going further and rethinking essence as a force for change and movement, as synonymous with empowering and dynamic identification rather than static and divisive identity ("Essence"). Nor is this an isolated gesture: in a similar move, Margaret Whitford argues that Luce Irigaray, long held to be the principal exemplar of what we might call negative essentialism, is on the contrary a feminist philosopher of change, a "kind of cultural prophet" (33).

At least two texts in the present volume give precise instantiations of "feminist essentialism," that is of a fully political "essentialist" practice. Both texts call into question the piety that essentialism is essentially conservative, reactionary, complicit with dominant groups, patriarchy's patsy. Context here is everything: contemporary French feminism cannot be understood without some knowledge of the history of French feminism, and similarly, contemporary Italian feminism cannot be understood without taking a specific situation into account. Thus Rabine's article shows that the Saint-Simonian women, pioneer nineteenth-century French proletarian feminists, used a form of essentialism, notably the equation between femininity and the maternal, to press their own claims to equality both with men and with bourgeois women:

> *Contemporary criticisms of essentialism see it as necessarily conservative, making feminists complicitous with an ideology of the dominant class and race. Yet the Saint-Simonienne strategy of changing all the structural relations around unchanging essence produces a different effect. In their situation, essentialism provides the only means available to speak against the dominant ideology of gender. (141)*

> *They [the young proletarian women] instead used this biology of difference to contest the very ideology of separate spheres and male supremacy it had been developed to serve. (134)*

> *The Saint-Simoniennes imitate not only a bourgeois ideal of feminine
> nature which they could never be seen as embodying, but also the mas-
> culine position which they had even less hope of occupying. (144–45)*

The second example is de Lauretis's presentation of Italian feminism, especially that theorized and practiced by the Milan Women's Bookstore collective. Central to the Italian feminists are the setting into place of a "genealogy of women" and the elaboration of an original woman-to-woman mentoring relationship, called "affidamento" (entrustment), that both work to facilitate woman's entry into and access to the symbolic order. Here again the seemingly essentialist moves–"the conception of sexual difference as 'originary human difference'" (27) –are not what they seem to be when taken out of context:

> *. . . this is not the sexual difference that culture has constructed from
> "biology" and imposed as gender, and that therefore could be righted,
> revisioned, or made good with the "progress of mankind" toward a
> more just society. It is, instead, a difference of symbolization, a different
> production of reference and meaning out of a particular embodied
> knowledge, emergent in the present time but reaching back to recognize
> an "image of the past which unexpectedly appears to [those who are]
> singled out by history at a moment of danger" ([Benjamin] 255). (27)*

As de Lauretis points out, Irigaray's influence has been decisive for the Italian feminists of the Milan Women's Bookstore collective. It is when they follow Irigaray in her retrieval of a primary being-woman and her call for female genealogies that these feminists run the greatest risk of essentialism (16).

In the great battle between essentialism and anti-essentialism, Irigaray is to essentialism what Derrida is to anti-essentialism, which means among other things that their complex texts have been ripped from their contexts and each in its different ways has been made to say what it never said. If, then, as we have seen above, essentialism inheres in deconstruction, so too does deconstruction inhere in essentialism, at least the alleged essentialism of Irigaray. It is then in the interest of all those who would promote some movement in this stagnant and "murky" (Braidotti, "Politics" 92) polemic to read both Derrida and Irigaray with a more exquisite attention to the nuances, the rhetorical gestures in their writings (see Spivak). Thus, as we see in Schor, Irigarayan mimesis is a profoundly Derridean notion, in that it is rent by an internal difference. Similarly, the notion that what Irigaray is all about is an unmediated access to the body is belied by her ambitious attempt to found an access to the symbolic for women that would not require their alienated subscription to the universal male standard (see Whitford).

The logical extension of feminist genealogy is separatism, and here we come to what is perhaps the rock of essentialism–which is not biologism–and it is here that the bond between de Lauretis and the Italian feminists she is representing and Irigaray stands out. Speaking of the different cultural meanings attached to the term *separatism* in Italian and North American feminist discourse, she writes:

> *Whence the different meaning and relative weight of the term*
> *separatism itself in feminist discourse in Italy and North America: there*
> *[Italy], it is mostly a "good" word, almost synonymous with feminism,*
> *and with positive connotations of intellectual and political strength for*
> *all feminists, regardless of sexual orientation or class differences. It*
> *lacks, in other words, most of the negative connotations that have ac-*
> *crued to separatism in this country and that, in my opinion, are due to*
> *more or less founded fears, on the part of feminists, of loss of profes-*
> *sional status, loss of heterosexist privilege, or loss of community*
> *identity. (19)*

This brings us at last to the text by Irigaray, which could only be described as essentialist (though nothing here about bodies and fluids, etc., the often derided thematics of Irigarayan essentialism) in that precisely it is concerned with communities, religious communities, that is, of women. Reviewing Elisabeth Schüssler Fiorenza's *In Memory of Her*, Irigaray dismisses the "equality feminism" that would consist in having women join the priesthood, be disciples of Jesus like any others, saying, "The important thing is for them to find their own genealogy, the necessary condition for their identity" (75). For women to have access to the divine, what they need is "a symbolic mother of daughters–woman-mother and lover . . ." (76). Here comes the crucial point: while Irigaray states in no uncertain terms–and anyone who knows anything about the cultural context of French feminisms knows that she means what she is saying–that she is for mixity, nevertheless (and here she even puts in a good word for Mary Daly), she can see the usefulness of separatism:

> *During this interim period, a considerable number of women refuse to confine themselves to male-female structures. And even if this withdrawal into same-sex groups does not accord with the liveliest and most creative engagement of human culture, those women's groups which have found no other solution to the problem should not be judged too quickly. . . . While I do not find myself in agreement with Mary Daly . . . I would not be so quick to dismiss her choice of communal sisterhoods as is Elisabeth Schüssler Fiorenza. . . . Personally I prefer to try everything in an effort to preserve the dimension of a sexual mix because that difference seems to me to safeguard those human limitations that allow room for a notion of the divine not defined as the result of a narcissistic and imperialistic inflation of sameness. What is more, both sexes need to form an alliance based on mutual respect; this is still far from happening. Meanwhile this detour through a separation of the sexes is preferable to discouragement, isolation, regression, and servitude. . . . So periods during which the sexes remain separate are necessary. (78–79)*

Thus we move from a notion of strategic essentialism to one of provisional separatism and this brings us to the final and largely unspoken reason for the demonization of essentialism: as de Lauretis points out, the "risk of challenging directly the social-symbolic institution of heterosexuality" (33). Though not all those one might list as belonging to the essentialist camp are openly lesbian (de Lauretis lists Adrienne Rich, Mary Daly, Catharine MacKinnon, Marilyn Frye, "occasionally Monique Wittig" [a sticky case; see Fuss]), nor are all lesbians pro-essentialism (the debate runs through lesbianism just as it does through feminism itself), there is no question but that the most submerged -ism in the demonized chain of -isms attached to essentialism is lesbian separatism or cultural feminism.

If this collection can be said to have sought to help defuse the debate not by promoting essentialism but merely by revisioning it, then it can be accounted a failure. Anti-essentialism in its positive form, constructionism, has won the day; and if essentialism is anathema, constructionism is dogma. At a time of proliferating subject positions, few are those (you can count them on one hand: Rosi Braidotti, Tania Modleski . . .) who chose to speak "as" essentialists (Miller ix-xvii). And yet the very multiplication of subject positions, carried out in the name of de-essentializing such massive monolithic categories as *women* or worse *Woman*, has gone hand in hand with the consolidation of an identity politics which in many respects reinscribes essentialism.

To undo Difference by multiplying differences is not necessarily to do away with Difference. Quite the contrary. It might be argued that the new particularism of identity politics is the half-life of essentialism. If essentialism has a foreseeable future then it lies first in the uneven developments of various identitarian communities–in this instance essentialism is viewed as a developmental stage of the (female, subaltern, etc.) subject. Second and more speculatively, it may consist in the increasingly and fashionable postmodern fragmentation of feminism–in this context essentialism would be viewed as an instrument for "gendering the universal" (Braidotti, "Female Feminist" 189–90) and, perhaps, for ensuring the very survival of feminism itself in this dizzying fin-de-siècle.

Works Cited

Benjamin, Walter. *Illuminations*. Trans. Harry Zohn. Ed. and intro. Hannah Arendt. New York: Schocken, 1969.

Beauvoir, Simone de. *The Second Sex*. Trans. H. M. Parshley. New York: Knopf, 1970.

Braidotti, Rosi. "On the Female Feminist Subject, or: From 'She-self to She-Other.'" *Beyond Equality and Difference: Citizenship, Feminist Politics and Female Subjectivity*. Ed. Gisella Bock and Susan James. London: Routledge, 1992.

_____. "The Politics of Ontological Difference." Brennan, *Between* 89–105.

Brennan, Teresa. "Essence against Identity." Forthcoming.

_____, ed. and intro. *Between Feminism and Psychoanalysis*. New York: Routledge, 1989.

Miller, Nancy K. *Getting Personal: Feminist Occasions and Other Autobiographical Acts*. New York: Routledge, 1991.

Modleski, Tania. *Feminism without Women: Culture and Criticism in a "Postfeminist" Age*. New York: Routledge, 1991.

Moi, Toril. *Sexual/Textual Politics: Feminist Literary Theory*. New York: Methuen, 1985.

Plaza, Monique. "'Pouvoir phallomorphique' et psychologie de 'la femme'; Bouclage patriarchal." *Questions féministes* 1 (1977): 91–119.

Salvaggio, Ruth. *Enlightened Absence: Neoclassical Configurations of the Feminine*. Urbana: U of Illinois P, 1988.

Schor, Naomi. "Previous Engagements: The Receptions of Luce Irigaray." *Engaging with Irigaray*. Forthcoming.

Whitford, Margaret. *Luce Irigaray: Philosophy in the Feminine*. New York: Routledge, 1991.

the essential difference

TERESA DE LAURETIS

The Essence of the Triangle or, Taking the Risk of Essentialism Seriously: Feminist Theory in Italy, the U.S., and Britain

*B*y pure coincidence, if there were such a thing, returning from a two-month stay in Italy where feminist theory was blooming more impressively than the spring, I happened upon two essays that refocused my reflection on the Anglo-American context of debate and steered it toward the theme of this issue. The discussion of the exciting recent work by Italian feminists on the constitutive role of sexual difference in feminist thought, which I hope to open up in the pages of this journal, will thus start out from the here and now of feminist theory in the United States and some considerations on the "essence" that is in question in both "essentialism" and "the essential difference."

I. Polemical Notes on Feminist Theory in the Anglo-American Context

Here, not (say) in Italy, and now, not (say) in the '70s, the term *essentialism* covers a range of metacritical meanings and strategic uses that go the very short distance from convenient label to buzzword. Many who, like myself, have been involved with feminist critical theory for some time and who did use the term, initially, as a serious critical concept, have grown impatient with this word–essentialism–time and again repeated with its reductive ring, its self-righteous tone of superiority, its contempt for "them"–those guilty of it. Yet, as the title of this special issue may wish to suggest, feminist theory is all about an essential difference, an irreducible difference, though not a difference between woman and man, nor a difference inherent in "woman's nature" (in woman as nature), but a difference in the feminist conception of woman, women, and the world.

For there is, undeniably, an essential difference between a feminist and a non-feminist understanding of the subject and its relation to institutions;

between feminist and non-feminist knowledges, discourses, and practices of cultural forms, social relations, and subjective processes; between a feminist and a non-feminist historical consciousness. That difference is essential in that it is constitutive of feminist thinking and thus of feminism: it is what makes the thinking feminist, and what constitutes certain ways of thinking, certain practices of writing, reading, imaging, relating, acting, etc., into the historically diverse and culturally heterogeneous social movement which, qualifiers and distinctions notwithstanding (e.g., Delmar), we continue with good reasons to call feminism. Another way to say this is that the essential difference of feminism lies in its historical specificity–the particular conditions of its emergence and development, which have shaped its object and field of analysis, its assumptions and forms of address; the constraints that have attended its conceptual and methodological struggles; the erotic component of its political self-awareness; the absolute novelty of its radical challenge to social life itself.

This is what is being addressed in the recent writings of some Italian feminist theorists, while their Anglo-American counterparts seem for the most part engaged in typologizing, defining, and branding various "feminisms" along an ascending scale of theoretico-political sophistication where "essentialism" weighs heavy at the lower end.[1] This is not to say that there should be no critique of feminist positions or no contest for the practical as well as the theoretical meanings of feminism, or even no appeal for hegemony by participants in a social movement which, after all, potentially involves all women. (There is plenty of that going on in Italy, as I will say later.) My polemical point here is that either too much or too little is made of the "essentialism" imputed to most feminist positions (notably those labelled cultural, separatist or radical, but others as well, whether labelled or not), so that the term serves less the purposes of effective criticism in the ongoing elaboration of feminist theory than those of convenience, conceptual simplification, or academic legitimation. Taking a more discerning look at "essentialism," therefore, seems like a very good idea.

Among the several acceptations of "essence" (from which "essentialism" is apparently derived) in the OED, the most pertinent to the context of use that is in question here are the following:

1. *Absolute being, substance in the metaphysical sense; the reality underlying phenomena.*

2. *That which constitutes the being of a thing; that 'by which it is what it is.' In two different applications (distinguished by Locke as* nominal essence *and* real essence *respectively):*

   a. *of a conceptual entity: The totality of the properties, constituent elements, etc., without which it would cease to be the same thing; the indispensable and necessary attributes of a thing as opposed to those which it may have or not. . . .*

   b. *of a real entity: Objective character, intrinsic nature as a 'thing-in-itself'; 'that internal constitution, on which all the sensible properties depend.'*

Examples of a., dated from 1600 to 1870, include Locke's statement in the *Essay on Human Understanding*: "The Essence of a Triangle, lies in a very little compass . . . three Lines meeting at three Angles, make up that Essence"; and all the examples given for b., from 1667 to 1856, are to the effect that the essence of a real entity, the "thing-in-itself," is either unknown or unknowable.

Which of these "essences" are imputed to feminist "essentialists" by their critics? If most feminists, however one may classify trends and positions–cultural, liberal, socialist, poststructuralist, and so forth–agree that women are made, not born, that gender is not an innate feature (as sex may be) but a sociocultural construction (and precisely for that reason it is oppressive to women), that patriarchy is historical (especially so when it is believed to have superseded a previous matriarchal realm), then the "essence" of woman that is described in the writings of many so-called essentialists is not the *real essence*, in Locke's terms, but more likely a *nominal* one. It is a totality of qualities, properties, and attributes that such feminists define, envisage, or enact for themselves (and some in fact attempt to live out in "separatist" communities), and possibly also wish for other women. This is more a project, then, than a description of existent reality; it is an admittedly feminist project of "re-vision," where the specifications *feminist* and *re*-vision already signal its historical location, even as the (re)vision projects itself outward geographically and temporally (universally) to recover the past and to claim the future. This may be utopian, idealist, perhaps misguided or wishful thinking, it may be a project one does not want to be a part of, but it is not essentialist as is the belief in a God-given or otherwise immutable nature of woman.

In other words, barring the case in which woman's "essence" is taken as absolute being or substance in the traditional metaphysical sense (and this may actually be the case for a few, truly fundamentalist thinkers to whom the term essentialist would properly apply), for the great majority of feminists the "essence" of woman is more like the essence of the triangle than the essence of the thing-in-itself: it is the specific properties (e.g., a female-sexed body), qualities (a disposition to nurturance, a certain relation to the body, etc.), or necessary attributes (e.g., the experience of femaleness, of living in the world as female) that women have developed or have been bound to historically, in their differently patriarchal sociocultural contexts, which make them women, and not men. One may prefer one triangle, one definition of women and/or feminism, to another and, within her particular conditions and possibilities of existence, struggle to define the triangle she wants or wants to be–feminists do want differently. And in these very struggles, I suggest, consist the historical development and the specific difference of feminist theory, the essence of the triangle.

It would be difficult to explain, otherwise, why thinkers or writers with political and personal histories, projects, needs, and desires as different as those of white women and women of color, of lesbians and heterosexuals, of differently abled women, and of successive generations of women, would all claim feminism as a major–if not the only–ground of difference; why they would address both their critiques or accusations and their demands for recognition to other women, feminists in particular; why the emotional and political stakes in feminist theorizing should be so high, dialogue so charged, and confrontation so impassioned; why, indeed, the proliferation of typologies and the wide currency of "essentialism" on one hand, countered by the equally wide currency of the term "male theory" on the other (e.g., Lugones and Spelman).

It is one of the projects of this paper to shift the focus of the debate from "feminist essentialism," as a category by which to classify feminists or feminisms, to the historical specificity, the essential difference of feminist theory itself. This will require engaging with some notion of essence, as in my metaphor of the essence of the triangle, and involve not just taking the risk of essentialism, but taking it seriously. To this end I first turn to the two essays mentioned at the outset, which prompted my reflection on the uses of "essentialism" in current Anglo-American feminist critical writing, Chris Weedon's

Feminist Practice and Poststructural Theory, published in London in 1987, and Linda Alcoff's "Cultural Feminism versus Post-Structuralism: The Identity Crisis in Feminist Theory," published in the Spring 1988 issue of *Signs*; then I will go on to reconsider essentialism and its risks in the context of contemporary Italian feminist thought.

The notion of an "essential womanhood, common to all women, suppressed or repressed by patriarchy" recurs in Weedon's book as the mark of "radical-feminist theory," whose cited representatives are Mary Daly, Susan Griffin, and Adrienne Rich. "Radical-feminist theory" is initially listed together with "socialist-feminist and psychoanalytic-feminist theories" as "various attempts to systematize individual insights about the oppression of women into relatively coherent theories of patriarchy," in spite of the author's statement, on the same page, that radical-feminist writers are hostile to theory because they see it as a form of male dominance which co-opts women and suppresses the feminine (6). As one reads on, however, socialist feminism drops out altogether while psychoanalytic feminism is integrated into a new and more "politically" sophisticated discourse called "feminist poststructuralism." Thus, three-fourths of the way through the book, one finds this summary statement:

> *For poststructuralist feminism, neither the liberal-feminist attempt to redefine the truth of women's nature within the terms of existing social relations and to establish women's full equality with men, nor the radical-feminist emphasis on fixed difference, realized in a separatist context, is politically adequate. Poststructuralist feminism requires attention to historical specificity in the production, for women, of subject positions and modes of femininity and their place in the overall network of social power relations. In this the meaning of biological sexual difference is never finally fixed. . . . An understanding of how discourses of biological sexual difference are mobilized, in a particular society, at a particular moment, is the first stage in intervening in order to initiate change. (135)*

There is more than simple irony in the claim that this late-comer, poststructuralist feminism, dark horse and winner of the feminist theory contest, is the "first stage" of feminist intervention. How can Weedon, at one and the same time, so strongly insist on attention to historical specificity and social–not merely individual–change, and yet disregard the actual historical changes in Western culture brought about in part, at least, by the women's movement and at least in some measure by feminist critical writing over the past twenty years?

One could surmise that Weedon does not like the changes that have taken place (even as they allow the very writing and publication of her book), or does not consider them sufficient, though that would hardly be reason enough to disregard them so blatantly. A more subtle answer may lie in the apologetic and militant project of her book, a defense of poststructuralism vis-à-vis both the academic establishment and the general educated reader, but with an eye to the women's studies corner of the publishing market; whence, one must infer, the lead position in the title of the other term of the couple, feminist practice. For, as the Preface states, "the aim of this book is to make poststructuralist theory accessible to readers to whom it is unfamiliar, to argue its political usefulness to feminism and to consider its implications for feminist critical practice" (vii). Somehow, however, in the course of the book, the Preface's modest claim "to point to a possible direction for future feminist cultural criticism" (vii) is escalated into a peroration for the new and much improved feminist theory called feminist poststructuralism or, indifferently, poststructural feminism.

In the concluding chapter on "Feminist Critical Practice" (strangely in the singular, as if among so many feminisms and feminist theories, only one practice could properly be called both feminist and critical), the academic contenders are narrowed down to two. The first is the poststructural criticism produced by British feminists (two are mentioned, E. Ann Kaplan and Rosalind Coward) looking "at the mechanisms through which meaning is constructed" mainly in popular culture and visual representation; the second is "the other influential branch of feminist criticism [that] looks to fiction as an expression of an already constituted gendered experience" (152). Reappearing here, the word "experience," identified earlier on as the basis for radical-feminist politics ("many feminists assume that women's experience, unmediated by further theory, is the source of true knowledge" [8]), links this second branch of feminist (literary) criticism to radical-feminist ideology. Its standard-bearers are Americans, Showalter's gynocritics and the "woman-centred criticism" of Gilbert and Gubar, whose reliance on the concept of authorship as a key to meaning and truth also links them with "liberal-humanist criticism" (154–55).

A particular subset of this–by now radical-liberal–feminist criticism "dedicated to constructing traditions" (156) is the one concerned with "black and lesbian female experience"; here its problems and ideological traps appear most clearly, in Weedon's eyes, and are "most extreme in the care of lesbian writing and the construction of a lesbian aesthetic" (158). The reference works for her analysis, rather surprisingly in view of the abundance of Black and lesbian feminist writings in the 1980s, are a couple of rather dated essays (Smith and Zimmerman) reprinted in a collection edited by Elaine Showalter and, in fact, misnamed *The New Feminist Criticism*. But even more surprisingly–or not at all so, depending on one's degree of optimism–it is again poststructuralist criticism that, with the help of Derridean deconstruction, can set all of these writers straight, as it were, as to the real, socially constructed and discursively produced nature of gender, race, class, and sexuality–as well as authorship and experience! Too bad for us that no exemplary poststructuralist feminist works or critics are discussed in this context (Cixous, Kristeva, and Irigaray figure prominently, but as psychoanalytic feminists earlier in the book).

Now, I should like to make it clear that I have no quarrel with post-structuralism as such, or with the fundamental importance for all critical thinking, feminist theory included, of many of the concepts admirably summarized by Weedon in passages such as the following:

> *For a theoretical perspective to be politically useful to feminists, it should be able to recognize the importance of the* subjective *in constituting the meaning of women's lived reality. It should not deny subjective experience, since the ways in which people make sense of their lives is a necessary starting point for understanding how power relations structure society. Theory must be able to address women's experience by showing where it comes from and how it relates to material social practices and the power relations which structure them. . . . In this process subjectivity becomes available, offering the individual both a perspective and a choice, and opening up the possibility of political change. (8–9)*

But while I am in complete agreement that experience is a difficult, ambiguous, and often oversimplified term, and that feminist theory needs to elaborate further "the relationship between experience, social power and resistance" (8), I would insist that the notion of experience in relation both to social-material practices and to the formation and processes of subjectivity is a feminist concept, not a poststructuralist one (this is an instance of that essential difference of feminism which I want to reclaim from Weedon's all-encompassing "post-structuralism"), and would be still unthinkable were it not for specifically feminist practices, political, critical, and textual: consciousness raising, the rereading and revision of the canon, the critique of scientific discourses, and the imaging of new social spaces and forms of community. In short, those very practices that Weedon allocates to the "essentialist" camp. I would also add that "a theory of the relationship between experience, social power and resistance" is precisely one possible definition of feminist, not of poststructuralist, theory, as Weedon would have it, since the latter does not countenance the notion of experience within its conceptual horizon or philosophical presuppositions; and that, moreover, these issues have been posed and argued by several non-denominational feminist theorists in the United States for quite some time: for example, in the works of Biddy Martin, Nancy K. Miller, Tania Modleski, Mary Russo, Kaja Silverman, as well as myself, and even more forcefully in the works of feminist theorists and writers of color such as Gloria Anzaldúa, Audre Lorde, Chandra Mohanty, Cherríe Moraga, and Barbara Smith.

So my quarrel with Weedon's book is about its reductive opposition–all the more remarkable, coming from a proponent of deconstruction–of a *lumpen* feminist essentialism (radical-liberal-separatist and American) to a fantom feminist poststructuralism (critical-socialist-psychoanalytic and Franco-British), and with the by-products of such a *parti-pris*: the canonization of a few, (in)famous feminists as signposts of the convenient categories set up by the typology, the agonistic narrative structure of its account of "feminist theories," and finally its failure to contribute to the elaboration of feminist critical thought, however useful the book may be to its other intended readers, who can thus rest easy in the fantasy that poststructuralism is the theory and feminism is just a practice.

The title of Alcoff's essay, "Cultural Feminism versus Post-Structuralism: The Identity Crisis in Feminist Theory," bespeaks some of the same problems: a manner of thinking by mutually oppositional categories, an agonistic frame of argumentation, and a focus on division, a "crisis in feminist theory" that may be read not only as a crisis *over* identity, but also as a crisis *of* identity, of self-definition, implying a theoretical impasse for feminism as a whole. The essay, however, is more discerning, goes much further than its title suggests, and even contradicts it in the end, as the notion of identity, far from fixing the point of an impasse, becomes an active shifter in the feminist discourse of woman.[2]

Taking as its starting point "the concept of woman," or rather, its re-definition in feminist theory ("the dilemma facing feminist theorists today is that our very self-definition is grounded in a concept that we must deconstruct and de-essentialize in all of its aspects"), Alcoff finds two major categories of responses to the dilemma, or what I would call the paradox of woman (406). Cultural feminists, she claims, "have not challenged the defining of woman but only that definition given by men" (407), and have replaced it with what they believe a more accurate description and appraisal, "the concept of the essential female" (408). On the other hand, the poststructuralist response has been to reject the possibility of defining woman altogether and to replace "the politics of gender or sexual difference . . . with a plurality of difference where gender loses its position of significance" (407). A third category is suggested, but only indirectly, in Alcoff's unwillingness to include among cultural feminists certain writers of color such as Moraga and Lorde in spite of their emphasis on cultural identity, for in her view "their work has consistently rejected essential-ist conceptions of gender" (412). Why an emphasis on racial, ethnic, and/or sexual identity need not be seen as essentialist, is discussed more fully later in the essay with regard to identity politics and in conjunction with a third trend in feminist theory which Alcoff sees as a new course for feminism, "a theory of the gendered subject that does not slide into essentialism" (422).

Whereas the narrative structure underlying Weedon's account of femi-nist theories is that of a contest where one actor successively engages and defeats or conquers several rivals, Alcoff's develops as a dialectics. Both the culturalist and the poststructuralist positions display internal contradictions: for example, not all cultural feminists "give explicitly essentialist formulations of what it means to be a woman" (411), and their emphasis on the affirmation of women's strength and positive cultural roles and attributes has done much to counter images of woman as victim or of woman as male when in a business suit; but insofar as it reinforces the essentialist explanations of those attributes that are part and parcel of the traditional notion of womanhood, cultural femi-nism may, and for some women does, foster another form of sexist oppression. Conversely, if the poststructuralist critique of the unified, authentic subject of humanism is more than compatible with the feminist project to "deconstruct and de-essentialize" woman (as Alcoff puts it, in clearly poststructuralist terms), its absolute rejection of gender and its negation of biological determinism in favor of a cultural-discursive determinism result, as concerns women, in a form of nominalism. If "woman" is a fiction, a locus of pure difference and resistance to logocentric power, and if there are no women as such, then the very issue of women's oppression would appear to be obsolete and feminism itself would have no reason to exist (which, it may be noted, is a corollary of poststructuralism and the stated position of those who call themselves "post-feminists"). "What can we demand in the name of women," Alcoff asks, "if 'women' do not exist and demands in their name simply reinforce the myth that they do?" (420).

The way out–let me say, the sublation–of the contradictions in which are caught these two mainstream feminist views lies in a "theory of the subject that avoids both essentialism and nominalism" (421), and Alcoff points to it in the work of a few theorists, "a few brave souls," whom she rejoins in developing her notion of "woman as positionality": "woman is a position from which a feminist politics can emerge rather than a set of attributes that are 'objectively identifiable'" (434–35). In becoming feminist, for instance, women take up a position, a point of perspective, from which to interpret or (re)construct values and meanings. That position is also a politically assumed identity, and one relative to their sociohistorical location, whereas essentialist definitions would have woman's identity or attributes independent of her external situation; however, the positions available to women in any sociohistorical location are neither arbitrary nor undecidable. Thus, Alcoff concludes,

> If we combine the concept of identity politics with a conception of the subject as positionality, we can conceive of the subject as nonessentialized and emergent from a historical experience and yet retain our political ability to take gender as an important point of departure. Thus we can say at one and the same time that gender is not natural, biological, universal, ahistorical, or essential and yet still claim that gender is relevant because we are taking gender as a position from which to act politically. (433)

I am, of course, in agreement with her emphases on issues and arguments that have been central in my work, such as the necessity to theorize experience in relation to practices, the understanding of gendered subjectivity as "an emergent property of a historicized experience" (431), and the notion that identity is an active construction and a discursively mediated political interpretation of one's history. What I must ask, and less as a criticism of Alcoff's essay than for the purposes of my argument here, is: why is it still necessary to set up two opposing categories, cultural feminism and post-structuralism, or essentialism and anti-essentialism, thesis and antithesis, when one has already achieved the vantage point of a theoretical position that overtakes them or sublates them?

Doesn't the insistence on the "essentialism" of cultural feminists reproduce and keep in the foreground an image of "dominant" feminism that is at least reductive, at best tautological or superseded, and at worst not in our interests? Doesn't it feed the pernicious opposition of low versus high theory, a low-grade type of critical thinking (feminism) that is contrasted with the high-test theoretical grade of a poststructuralism from which some feminists would have been smart enough to learn? As one feminist theorist who's been concurrently involved with feminism, women's studies, psychoanalytic theory, structuralism, and film theory from the beginning of my critical activity, I know that learning to be a feminist has grounded, or embodied, all of my learning and so en-gendered thinking and knowing itself. That engendered thinking and that embodied, situated knowledge (in Donna Haraway's phrase) are the stuff of feminist theory, whether by "feminist theory" is meant one of a growing number of feminist critical discourses–on culture, science, subjec-tivity, writing, visual representation, social institutions, etc.–or, more par-ticularly, the critical elaboration of feminist thought itself and the ongoing (re)definition of its specific difference. In either case, feminist theory is not of a lower grade than that which some call "male theory," but different in kind; and it is its essential difference, the essence of that triangle, that concerns me here as a theorist of feminism.

Why then, I ask again, continue to constrain it in the terms of essentialism and anti-essentialism even as they no longer serve (but did they ever?) to formulate our questions? For example, in her discussion of cultural feminism, Alcoff accepts another critic's characterization despite some doubt that the latter "makes it appear too homogeneous and . . . the charge of essentialism is on shaky ground" (411). Then she adds:

> *In the absence of a clearly stated position on the ultimate source of gender difference, Echols infers from their emphasis on building a*

> *feminist free-space and woman-centered culture that cultural feminists*
> *hold some version of essentialism. I share Echols's suspicion. Certainly,*
> it is difficult to render the views of Rich and Daly into a coherent
> whole without supplying a missing premise *that there is an innate*
> *female essence. (412; emphasis added)*

But why do it at all? What is the purpose, or the gain, of supplying a missing premise (innate female essence) in order to construct a coherent image of feminism which thus becomes available to charges (essentialism) based on the very premise that had to be supplied? What motivates such a project, the suspicion, and the inferences?

Instead of answering these questions from within the context of debate where they originate, let me move on and consider a practice of feminist thought that is rather distant from us both culturally and linguistically, and that is also distinct in its historical and political specificity from both Anglo-American and French feminisms while retaining, of course, significant connections with them.

II. A Feminist Theory of Social Practice: "The Practice of Sexual Difference" in Italy

Italian feminism (the word is strictly singular there, for all the variety of feminist positions and practices it covers) is virtually unknown here. With very few exceptions, its critical texts are not translated, discussed or cited by American or British (or French) feminists.[3] It would be obviously impossible in these pages–assuming it would ever be possible or desirable–to attempt even the concisest overview of its history. What I want to discuss, however, is one recent book that, in elaborating a critical theory based on the practice of sexual difference, also reconstructs *a* history of feminism in Italy from the particular location, the social and political situatedness, of its authors.

That this is only one possible history, one story that may be told out of the many documents and social memory of Italian feminism, and the experiential recollections of individuals and groups, is clearly stated in the book's title, *Non credere di avere dei diritti: la generazione della libertà femminile nell'idea e nelle vicende di un gruppo di donne*, which I translate "Don't Think You Have Any Rights: The Engendering of Female Freedom in the Thought and Vicissitudes of a Women's Group."[4] The partiality and situatedness of the book's theoretical and historical project are further emphasized by its attribution of authorship to the Milan Women's Bookstore (Libreria delle Donne di Milano), which one infers must be roughly coextensive with the "women's group" referred to in the subtitle, and are reiterated in the introduction:

> *This book is about the necessity to give meaning, exalt, and represent in words and images the relationship of one woman to another. If putting a political practice into words is the same thing as doing theory, then this is a book of theory, for the relationships between women are the substance of our politics. It is a book of theory, then, but interspersed with stories . . . tales of our practice, since theoretical reasoning customarily refers to things which already have a name, whereas here we are dealing, in part, with things that had no name. The events and ideas we recount took place between 1966 and 1986, mainly in Milan. They commonly go under the name of feminism. Now we would like to bring to light their actual meaning and therefore their name as well. That name is "genealogy." What we have seen taking shape, in the years and places indicated, is a genealogy of women, that is, a coming into being of women legitimated by the reference to their female origin.*
> *. . . We are not certain that the history reconstructed by this book will actually produce what we have sought, which is our inscription in a female generation. We do not exclude the possibility that, put to the test, our experience may turn out to be just one of the many historical vicissitudes of the fragile concept of woman. (9)*

The bold injunction of the title, "don't think you have any rights" (a phrase of Simone Weil's, cited in the epigraph), with its direct address to women and its unequivocal stance of negativity, sharply contrasts with the subtitle's affirmation of a freedom for women that is not made possible by adherence to the liberal concept of rights–civil, human, or individual rights–which women do not have *as women*, but is generated, and indeed engendered, by taking up a position in a symbolic community, a "genealogy of women," that is at once discovered, invented, and constructed through feminist practices of reference and address. Those practices, as the book later specifies, include the reading or rereading of women's writings; taking other women's words, thoughts, knowledges, and insights as frame of reference for one's analyses, understanding, and self-definition; and trusting them to provide a symbolic mediation between oneself and others, one's subjectivity and the world.

The word genealogy–whose root links it with gender, generation, and other words referring to birth as a social event–usually designates the legitimate descent, by social or intellectual kinship, of free male individuals. The intellectual and social traditions of Western culture are male genealogies where, as in Lacan's symbolic, women have no place: "Among the things that had no name [prior to feminist discourse] there was, there is, the pain of coming into the world this way, without symbolic placement" (10). In this sense, Virginia Woolf's "room of one's own" may not avail women's intellection if the texts one has in it are written in the languages of male tradition. A better image of symbolic placement (*collocazione simbolica*) is Emily Dickinson's room, as Ellen Moers describes it, filled with the insubstantial presence of women writers and their works–a symbolic "space-time furnished with female-gendered references" ("riferimenti sessuati femminili" [11]) which mediate her access to literature and poetry. Only in such a room may the woman "peculiarly susceptible to language" (as Adrienne Rich has put it) be able to find, or to look for, "*her* way of being in the world" (39). In other words, the women of Milan suggest, the conceptual and discursive space of a female genealogy can effectively mediate a woman's relation to the symbolic, allowing her self-definition as female being, or female-gendered speaking subject. And lest it be misconstrued, let me briefly say here, and expand on later, that this notion of genealogy is not limited to literary figures but reaches into relationships between women in everyday life.

Woolf, Dickinson, and especially Rich are major points of reference in the critical genealogy of feminism in Italy as elsewhere. And while the terms *symbolic, genealogy, freedom*, and others recast in the Milan book come from the philosophical tradition of Nietzsche, Lévi-Strauss, Beauvoir, Lacan, Kristeva, Irigaray, Foucault, etc., the sense of their recasting can be traced to Rich's 1971 essay "When We Dead Awaken: Writing as Re-Vision," which was published in Italian translation only in 1982.[5] In her reading of Rich over and against a comparably influential text in the male genealogy of poststructuralist criticism, Barthes's "The Death of the Author," Nancy K. Miller uses this very essay by Rich to argue for a double temporality of intellectual history unfolding concurrently, if discontinuously, in the "women's time" of feminist criticism and in the "standard time" of academic literary criticism. With regard to Rich's later work, however, Miller questions the "poetics of identity" grounded in a community of women exemplified by "Blood, Bread, and Poetry" (1983) and the limitations set to feminist theory by what she takes to be "a prescriptive esthetics–a 'politically correct' program of representation" (109–11). Instead, Miller proposes irony as a mode of feminist performance and symbolic production.

Now, there definitely is irony–no matter whether intended or not–in a theory of sexual difference such as the one proposed by the Italian feminists, that draws as much on the philosophical and conceptual categories of post-structuralism and the critique of humanism as it does on the classic texts of Anglo-American feminism–and recasts them all according to its partial, political project; an irony most remarkable here, in light of the categorical oppositions set up by Anglo-American feminists themselves between feminist theory and "male theory," America and Europe, or cultural feminism and post-structuralism, as discussed earlier. Miller, of course, makes no such gross generalizations; hers is a much more subtle perception of the complex temporality of historicity of discursive practices. But while both Miller and the authors of *Non credere* are feminist theorists fully conversant with post-structuralist critical thought, the latter trace their descent from Irigaray rather than Barthes. It is Irigaray's reading of woman's oblique, denied, repressed, unauthorized relationship to the symbolic order from Plato to Hegel and Lacan, that resonates, for the Italian theorists of sexual difference, with Rich's "peculiar keenness and ambivalence" to language, and motivates their shared political standing as (in Rich's words again) "disloyal to civilization." Here is, for example, another Italian feminist, the philosopher Adriana Cavarero, writing "Toward a Theory of Sexual Difference" in *Diotima*:[6]

> *Woman is not the subject of her language. Her language is not* hers. *She therefore speaks and represents herself in a language not her own, that is, through the categories of the language of the other. She thinks herself as thought by the other. . . . Discourse carries in itself the sign of its subject, the speaking subject who in discourse speaks himself and speaks the world starting from himself. There is thus some truth in man's immortality, which I mentioned earlier as a joke: in universalizing the finitude of his gendered being* [della sua sessuazione], *man exceeds it and poses himself as an essence that of necessity belongs to the "objectivity" of discourse. (Cavarero et al. 45, 49)*

The history of philosophy, she continues, records in various ways the finitude that the thinking subject carries in itself qua thinking being, but is extraordinarily blind to the finitude of its sexual difference. While it would have been possible to start from a dual conceptualization of being-man (*l'esser uomo*) and being-woman (*l'esser donna*) as originary forms of being, Western philosophy has started from the hypothesis of the one and from the assumption of a "monstrous" universal, at once neuter and male, whose embodiment in individuals of two sexes does not concern its essence as thinking being but remains external to it.

> *The task of thinking sexual difference is thus an arduous one because sexual difference lies precisely in the erasure on which Western philosophy has been founded and developed. To think sexual difference starting from the male universal is to think it as already thought, that is, to think it through the categories of a thought that is supported by the non-thinking of difference itself. (48)*

The question, for the feminist philosopher, is how to rethink sexual difference within a dual conceptualization of being, "an absolute dual," in which both being-woman and being-man would be primary, originary forms. This is a question that subverts the categories of Western thought which, precisely, elide sexual difference as primary–as "being there from the beginning" in both woman and man–and relegate it to the status of a secondary difference contained in the gender marking (*sessuazione femminile*) of the being-woman: "Woman is thus the repository of sexual difference, which constitutively belongs to her (and thus constitutes her) since the process of universalization has excluded it from the male" (62). It is a question quite similar to the one posed by Irigaray throughout her readings of Western philosophers in *Éthique de la différence sexuelle*, and similarly located, framed from inside the philosophical discourse they both mean to subvert. I will come back later to the notion of an originary or primary character of sexual difference and to the risk of essentialism that is taken there. For the moment, I return to the Milan Bookstore and its history of feminism, where the critical reflection on sexual difference has been going on since the early, activist days of the Women's Movement but, in the more self-reflexive writings of the '80s, has been taking shape as both a theory of sexual difference and a theory of social practice: the theory of that particular and specifically feminist practice now emerging in Italy, which is in fact referred to as *the practice of sexual difference* (*la practica della differenza sessuale*).

The first document of Italian feminism, in this history, was a manifesto issued in 1966 by a group known as Demau (acronym for Demystification of Patriarchal Authoritarianism). While centered on the contradictory position of women in society–which at the time and in the terms of its most progressive social thought, Marxism, was called "the woman question"–the Demau manifesto contained the suggestion that no solution could be found to the problem women pose to society as long as women themselves could not address the problem that society poses to women; that is to say, as long as the terms of the question were not reversed, and women were not the subject, rather than the object, of "the woman question." A further step in the development of what the Milan book calls "the symbolic revolution," namely, the process of critical understanding and sociocultural change whereby women come to occupy the position of subject, was the celebrated pamphlet by Carla Lonzi first published in 1970 with the title *Sputiamo su Hegel* (*Spit on Hegel*). Not coincidentally it is a philosopher, and a philosophy of history and culture, that are targeted in Lonzi's critique ("*The Phenomenology of Mind* is a phenomenology of the patriarchal mind"), rather than an anthropological or sociological notion of patriarchy, though she was not a philosopher but an art historian and later a feminist theorist whose influence on the development of Italian feminist thought has obviously continued long after her untimely death. Also not coincidentally, therefore, her writing resonates not only with Marx's *Communist Manifesto* but even more distinctly with the manifestoes of the Futurist movement, which ushered into Italy and into Europe the very image of a cultural revolution, the avant-garde, in the first two decades of this century.

The idea of women as a social subject, the "Subject Unexpected by the master-slave dialectic," recurs in Lonzi's impassioned pamphlet, as it did in the first feminist manifesto, their stylistic and ideological differences notwithstanding; but Lonzi articulates it further, in a dimension at once utopian, historical, and philosophical. "The unexpected destiny of the world lies in its starting all over with women as subjects," she wrote (60; qtd. in *Non credere* 29 et passim). Yet, with regard to the political strategies of feminism, she argued against equality and for difference:

> *Equality is a juridical principle . . . what is offered as legal rights*
> *to colonized people. And what is imposed on them as culture. . . .*
> *Difference is an existential principle which concerns the modes of being*
> *human, the peculiarity of one's experiences, goals, possibilities, and*
> *one's sense of existence in a given situation and in the situations one*
> *may envision. The difference between women and men is the basic*
> *difference of humankind. (20–21)*

Hence, feminism's fight for women's equality with men is misdirected since equality is "an ideological attempt to subject women even further," to prevent the expression of their own sense of existence, and to foreclose the road to women's real liberation. Evident in the above passages are the roots of the current concept of sexual difference as constitutive of one's sense and possibilities of existence. Elsewhere the ideal of a female symbolic or symbolic mediation is implied by negation ("the equality available today is not a philosophical, but a political equality"), and the necessity of a politics of radical separatism is adamantly asserted against the grain of the Marxist analysis of culture that has shaped all of Italy's recent social movements, the women's movement included: women, Lonzi states, who for two centuries have tried to express their demands by joining in the political demands of men, first in the French revolution and then in the Russian revolution, but obtaining only a subservient role, now see that "the proletariat is revolutionary with regard to capitalism, but reformist with regard to the patriarchal system" (29). "Women's difference is in their millenary absence from history. Let's take advantage of that difference. . . . Do we really want, after millennia, to share in the grand defeat of man?" (20).

During the '70s, the better part of Italian feminism took the latter road, a radical anti-institutional politics, even as large numbers of women continued to work within the parties of the Left for women's rights and social equality, achieving major social reforms such as the decriminalization of abortion in 1978. But even for those women (and they were many) who continued to be active in Left party and union politics, the development of a feminist consciousness took place in small women's groups, in the form of the separatist feminist practice known as *autocoscienza*; and because the two forms of activism were necessarily and strictly separated in time and place, not only during the first decade of the Movement but well into the '80s, Italian feminism was characterized by the widespread phenomenon of "the double militancy," a particular variant of what here was called "the double shift," with its distinctive contradictions and difficulties.

Autocoscienza (self-consciousness or consciousness of self, but the Italian word suggests something of an auto-induced, self-determined, or self-directed process of achieving consciousness) was the term coined by Carla Lonzi for the practice of consciousness-raising groups which Italian women adapted from North American feminism to suit their own sociocultural situation. "They were intentionally small groups, unattached to any larger organization, and consisting exclusively of women who met to talk about themselves or anything else, provided it was based on their own personal experience" (*Non credere* 32). And while this form of gathering could easily be grafted onto traditional cultural practices in a country more deeply conscious of gender and pervasively gender-segregated, yet more thoroughly politicized than the United States, the impact of this first, specifically feminist, political practice was perhaps stronger and ultimately more significant for the development of feminist theory in Italy than in North America.

Here, easier institutional access and a less gender-segregated history of white women in the public sphere (e.g., in education, social work, and what is now called pink-collar work) favored the diffusion, much earlier on, of the sites and modes of feminist consciousness. From the relatively private environment of small women's groups, feminism could move into more public ones like academic women's studies programs, publishing and media enterprises, social service and law firms, etc. Concurrently, a greater social and geographical mobility made life in separatist communities seem more of a realizable possibility than it ever could in Italy–or than it actually can be in the United States, for that matter. Whence the different meaning and relative weight of the term separatism itself in feminist discourse in Italy and North America: there, it is mostly a "good" word, almost synonymous with feminism, and with positive connotations of intellectual and political strength for all feminists, regardless of sexual orientation or class differences. It lacks, in other words, most of the negative connotations that have accrued to separatism in this country and that, in my opinion, are due to more or less founded fears, on the part of feminists, of loss of professional status, loss of heterosexist privilege, or loss of community identity.

In Italy, on the other hand, if it valorized women's interactions with one another and the sharing of personal experience by conferring upon the latter an unprecedented social significance and analytical power, nevertheless the relatively privatized practice of *autocoscienza* could not fulfill the need for immediate political effectivity in the larger world that was the goal of the Movement (and hence the practice of the double militancy); nor could it promote the public recognition of feminism as a critical analysis of society and culture, and not merely a narrowly political one. Above all, it could not envision (as the Milan book authors now can) a different symbolic order by reference to which women could be legitimated as women. Thus feminist thought "found itself in a bind: it needed conceptual tools to develop itself and its relation to the world but, wishing to guard its own authenticity, it could use none except *autocoscienza*. Which for many had become insufficient" (*Non credere* 41).

In a sense, it can be argued retrospectively, the "static" separatism of the small group practice that marked the Italian Movement in the '70s, in contrast with the more dynamic separatism (or "diffuse feminism") of the present day, reproduced and solidified the split between private and public existence typical of women's lives in general: a painful and contradictory rift between, on the one hand, the experience of a shared language and apprehension of female subjectivity and existence that occurred inside the Movement, and, on the other, the daily confirmation of its incompatibility with, its utter otherness and alienation from, all other social relations outside the Movement, where women's new critical knowledge–their "sense of existence" or their "ways of being in the world"–were neither legitimated nor recognized. And where, on the contrary, sexism and a pronounced disregard for feminism continued to pervade, as they still do, all social intercourse. Yet, I would suggest, that experience of a harsh and protracted separateness, of social-symbolic defeat–in the impossibility for women to achieve what Lonzi called "philosophical equality" and to gain self-representation in the established symbolic order–may be just what enabled the subjects of that experience to reach the present-day critical understanding of their own different subjecthood (the theory of sexual difference) and to attempt to define the modes of its possible existence, the ways of living it out in the practice of everyday life (the practice of sexual difference).

Eventually, then, under the pressure of its own contradictions, the practice of *autocoscienza* evolved into other, more open and conflictual practices that expanded or created new spaces of female sociality: cultural activities, parties, dances, conferences, journals, group holidays and travel, teaching, and direct contacts with feminists in other countries, notably the "Psychanalyse et Politique" group in France. This more dynamic and interactive, though no less separatist, mode of sociality and communication among women is regarded by the Milan authors as a breakthrough in the development of their theory of feminist practice. For among the results of the new practice of female relationships (*pratica dei rapporti tra donne*) was the necessity of coming to terms with the power and the disparity–the social and personal inequality–inherent in them, as well as with the erotic dimension of all relationships between women and *its* relation to power. This proved to be especially conflictual, indeed "scandalous," in view of the ethos of parity (equality among women), non-aggressivity, and sisterhood in oppression that had characterized the past practice and self-image of the Movement. Not surprisingly, these issues are still live as coals, and the views of the Milan authors very much contested.

A first formulation of the issues and perspective that inform the theory of the practice of sexual difference later developed in *Non credere di avere dei diritti* appeared in 1983 as a pamphlet of the Milan Bookstore publication, *Sottosopra* (*Upside Down*), entitled "Piú donne che uomini" ("More Women Than Men") but better known as "the green *Sottosopra*" from the color of its print, which by national consensus marked a definitive turning point for all Italian feminists, whatever their positions, pro or against or ambivalent about its authors' position.[7] Several years of intense debate ensued, in many Italian cities and with many groups representing various tendencies within the Movement. The debate has been rekindled since the publication of the book.

One of the major points at issue is the notion of entrustment (*affidamento*), a term proposed to designate a relationship between two women which, though recorded and variously accounted for in feminist and women's writings, had not yet been named or formally addressed in feminist theory. Briefly, the relationship of entrustment is one in which one woman gives her trust or entrusts herself symbolically to another woman, who thus becomes her guide, mentor, or point of reference–in short, the figure of symbolic mediation between her and the world. Both women engage in the relationship–and here is the novelty, and the most controversial aspect of this feminist theory of practice–not in spite, but rather because and in full recognition of the disparity that may exist between them in class or social position, age, level of education, professional status, income, etc. That is to say, the function of female symbolic mediation that one woman performs for the other is achieved, not in spite but rather because of the power differential between them, contrary to the egalitarian feminist belief that women's mutual trust is incompatible with unequal power.

Non credere questions this belief on the basis of the experience of social defeat and personal disempowerment that women in the Movement have admitted to, and that led to a weakening of energy, a levelling of women's fantasies, and a stifling of female desire ("within feminism, the politics of parity did not have a theoretical foundation but found nourishment in the weakness of female desire, in its reticence to expose itself, in its lack of symbolic authorization" [52]); and it forcefully argues that the disparity, which does exist in the world as constructed and governed by the male social inter- course, is invested in women by dint of their subjection to the institutions of the male social contract, i.e., by their being objects of the male symbolic ex- change. To confront that disparity and to practice it in the relationship of entrustment establishes the ground of a symbolic exchange between women, a female social contract whose terms can be defined autonomously from the male social contract.

> *To name the fact of disparity among women . . . meant to break out*
> *of the levelling of all women and their consequent subjection to the dis-*
> *tinctions imposed by male-directed thought according to its criteria*
> *and to the demands of men's social intercourse* [dei commerci tra
> uomini]. *It meant that exchange between women could and should be*
> *established [so that] from objects of exchange, as they were in the male-*
> *centered world, they can and must become subjects of exchange. (133)*

Only a generalized social practice of entrustment through disparity, the book implies, can change the affective contents, symbolic meaning, and social value of women's relations to one another and to themselves, and produce another structure of symbolic exchange and other practices of signification. But how can trust be given to the powerful (woman) when power has been the means of women's oppression, by other women as well as men?

The examples of the relationship of entrustment given in the intro- duction range from the biblical story of Naomi and Ruth to the relationships between H. D. and Bryher in Greece described in H. D.'s *Tribute to Freud,* between Virginia Woolf and Vita Sackville-West, Emily Dickinson and (the writings of) Elizabeth Barrett Browning, Mme du Deffand and Mlle de l'Espinasse, and from the "Boston marriages" back to the myth of Demeter and Persephone. What these have in common, besides the intimately complex and often erotic nature of the bond between the women, is the symbolic recognition, the value or valuation of human, gendered worth that each one is capable of conferring upon the other, their formal social differences notwithstanding. Though their roles and symbolic functions with respect to one another may have been as different as their social or personal powers, yet each woman of each pair validates and valorizes the other within a frame of reference no longer patriarchal or male-designed, but made up of perceptions, knowledges, attitudes, values, and modes of relating historically expressed by women for women–the frame of reference of what the book calls a female genealogy or a female symbolic. The recognition of mutual value is thus made possible by their inscription in a symbolic community for which the authors again borrow a phrase from Rich, "the common world of women" (and here Mlle de l'Espinasse serves as the negative example). But all this does not yet explain the concept of entrustment through disparity, in which consist the originality of this theory of sexual difference as well as its major difficulty, and on which are predicated two other crucial notions–the notions of female freedom (*libertà femminile*) and of the originary nature of sexual difference.

Again, this theory of sexual difference is also a theory of social practice, we must go back to the history of the women's group whose critical autobiography, as it were, is written in *Non credere*. By the early '80s, as women's politics had effectively pushed social legislation toward a degree of emancipation unprecedented in Italy, the process of women's assimilation into (male) society was well on its way, and the need for a discourse that could account for sexual difference by other concepts than victimization and emancipation was all the more urgently felt. The group began a project of reading literary works by women, especially novels, hoping to find in their contribution to Western culture some expression of "what culture does not know about women's difference. What that could be exactly, we could not know then, precisely because a 'language,' i.e., a symbolic structure of mediation was missing" (128).

Their method, therefore, was "experimental," from the perspective of literary criticism. Very simply, they treated the texts as they would have their own words, as parts of a puzzle to be solved by disarranging and rearranging them according to extratextual, personal associations and interpretations, and thus erasing the boundaries between literature and life. This practice of reading (based on the group's previous experience of a collective, wild form of psychoanalysis, which they named "the practice of the unconscious") led to a division in the group regarding the preferred writers and the contest of interpretations: some women, like their favorite writers, were seen as authoritarian "mothers" prevaricating over the preferences and interpretations of the others, who thus felt cast in the role of daughters. The admission of disparity among women–if only, in this case, in matters of literary authority or critical persuasiveness–was at first shocking but subsequently liberating.

> *We were not equal. . . . Naming the disparity present in the members of our group in effect freed us from the constraint of representing our relationships according to an abstract and non-gendered ideal of justice, and cleared from our minds not only the figure of such an ideal but also the feelings of guilt or resentment which that abstract, non-gendered authority had injected into our relationships. (131)*

And not by chance, the authors remark, the inequalities among the members of the group had emerged and were named in connection with the mother.

The next step, though not an easy one, was to understand that the source and point of reference of women's worth as female-gendered subjects was a female-gendered one; in other words, to understand that, while figures of authority such as God, the Father, the party, or the state delegitimate and erase all actual difference, a figure of female authorization or symbolic mediation is necessary to "legitimate female difference as originary human difference" (132). That figure, inscribed in the writings and words of other women, and embodied in the gestures and practices of female relationships in daily life, was named "the symbolic mother," the term signifying at once its power and capacity for recognition and affirmation of women as subjects in a female-gendered frame of reference, and its transcendence with regard to individual women's subjectivities and differences. "Our favorite women writers helped us to represent a female source of authority in conjunction with the expression of our differences. . . . Inscribed within the shared horizon of sexual difference, the words of all women could find affirmation, including the affirmation of their differences, without fear of self-destruction" (132).

As a theoretical concept, the symbolic mother is the structure that sustains or recognizes the gendered and embodied nature of women's thought, knowledge, experience, subjectivity, and desire–their "originary difference" and guarantees women's claim to self-affirmative existence as subjects in the social; an existence as subjects not altogether separate from male society, yet autonomous from male definition and dominance. As a guiding concept of feminist practice, in the relationship of entrustment, the notion of the symbolic mother permits the exchange between women across generations and the sharing of knowledge and desire across differences. It enables, as the book's authors put it, the alliance "between the woman who wants and the woman who knows" (148), that is to say, a mutual valorization of the younger woman's desire for recognition and self-affirmation in the world, and the older woman's knowledge of female symbolic defeat in the social-symbolic world designed by men. For there, the relation of daughter to mother is thought of as "natural, invested with affects and loaded with emotions, but without symbolic translation, i.e., without figures or rules" (155); whereas, in redefining the mother-daughter relationship as also a symbolic one, the concept of the symbolic mother extends it beyond the confines of the "natural" and the domestic to enable an alliance, a social contract between them. Without that social contract and the structure of symbolic mediation that supports it, no freedom or self-determination exists for women: "so long as a woman demands reparation, whatever she may gain, she will not know freedom" (156).

Freedom, however, is not understood in libertarian terms as freedom from all social constraint. On the contrary, the female freedom which the Milan group envisions for women entails a personal and social cost, a symbolic debt. For if, on the one hand, women owe nothing to men–since women's social survival has required the acceptance of both subordination and irresponsibility on their part, and hence, they state, "there is no social contract between women and men" (158)–it is not the case, on the other hand, that women owe nothing to no one, a belief fostered by the politics of victimization prevalent in the Movement. On the contrary, women owe women, and the price of female freedom is the symbolic debt each woman has toward other women, i.e., toward the symbolic mother.

> *The relationship of entrustment is a social relation, and we make it the*
> *content of a political project. The symbolic debt toward the mother is*

to be paid publicly, socially, before the eyes of everyone, women and
men . . . in the responsibility a woman assumes toward other women
because of her belonging to the female gender. (159–60)

Moreover, as the politically and consciously assumed practice of disparity brings to light the hidden or unconscious conflicts and emotions of the ancient (patriarchal) relationship with the mother, it opens up the possibility and the critical elaboration of new symbolic forms of female authority that can effectively legitimate a woman's subjecthood and thus render unto her not emancipation (under the law of the Father) but full social agency and responsibility as a woman. That is the meaning of the book's subtitle, the engendering of female freedom.

A freedom that, paradoxically, demands no vindication of the rights of woman, no equal rights under the law, but only a full, political and personal, accountability to women is as startlingly radical a notion as any that has emerged in Western thought. It is bound to appear reductive, idealist, essentialist, even reactionary unless one keeps in mind, first, the paradox on which it is founded and which has been the first task of feminist thought to disentangle–the paradox of woman, a being that is at once captive and absent in discourse, constantly spoken of but of itself inaudible or inexpressible, displayed as spectacle and yet unrepresented; a being whose existence and specificity are simultaneously asserted and denied, negated and controlled. And hence the task of feminist philosophy, as Cavarero puts it: "thinking sexual difference through the categories of a thought that is supported by the non-thinking of difference itself." Secondly, one should be mindful that this paradox is not solely discursive, but is grounded in a real contradiction for women in the world designed and governed by men, a conceptual and experiential contradiction in which women are necessarily caught as social beings, and which no other political or social thought but feminism has seen fit to consider. And thirdly, one cannot read the book and not be constantly reminded that its radical theory of sexual difference is historically and culturally located. The authors openly admit the limited, partial, and situated nature of their knowledge, embodied in the "vicissitudes," the history and the practices, of their group: "We see the necessity of entrustment because it appeared to us, but we cannot demonstrate it fully because our view is necessarily partial. To admit this does not weaken our arguments. It means that our arguments have been dictated in part [by] events that are not under our control but somehow favorable to us" (187–88).

The book's closing remark that female freedom comes about neither by historical necessity nor by pure chance, but by a kind of favor, of *kairós*, a particular historical convergence, suggests to me an unwonted connection. The concepts that articulate this theory of sexual difference (genealogy, symbolic mother, female freedom, female subject–terms drawn from Western critical discourse but drastically recast) and the original feminist practices which ground the theory and to which the theory gives formal expression (*autocoscienza*, entrustment, disparity, female relations) mark an epistemological rupture in the continuum of Western thought. This rupture, it seems to me, has the quality of that "leap in the open air of history" which, according to Benjamin, "blast[s] a specific era out of the homogeneous course of history," where the latter is understood as "progression through a homonogeneous, empty time" (263, 261).[8] Seen in this light, the conception of sexual difference as "originary human difference" proposed by *Non credere* and *Diotima* is less an essentialist–biological or metaphysical–view of woman's difference (from man) than a historical materialist analysis of "the state of emergency" in which we live as feminists. An emergency that, as Benjamin says of other oppressed and revolutionary classes, "is not the exception but the rule" (257). In other words, this is not the sexual difference that culture has constructed from "biology" and imposed as gender, and that therefore could be righted, revisioned, or made good with the "progress of mankind" toward a more just society. It is, instead, a difference of symbolization, a different production of reference and meaning out of a particular embodied knowledge, emergent in the present time but reaching back to recognize an "image of the past which unexpectedly appears to [those who are] singled out by history at a moment of danger" (255).

I offer that suggestion for further thought, and turn briefly to consider some of the responses, objections, and reverberations that the Milan book, like the green *Sottosopra* before it, sparked across the spectrum of Italian feminism. Though I cannot do justice to each argument, or to the specificity of the Italian situation, I think that the terms of the debate will give an idea of the seriousness of the risk taken by the authors of *Non credere*. From there I will come back to the questions raised in the first part of the essay.

III. Polemical Notes on Feminist Theory in Italy

The magnitude of the debate, and its repercussions at all levels of feminist politics, including the oldest and strongest women's organization in the Italian Communist Party (PCI), are evidence of the importance, timeliness, and theoretical strength of a feminist political theory based on a radical and uncompromisingly separatist stance. Which is also, of course, its major difficulty in obtaining consensus (let alone implementation) as a theory of political and social practice. The objections have ranged from the personal *ad foeminam* charges of authoritarianism, prevarication, and intellectual elitism brought against the authors by a subset of the Milan Bookstore collective itself (Lepetit et al.), to more general objections of political vanguardism and (bourgeois) class bias. However, this theory's unprecedented influence on progressive political thought, as represented by the second largest party of Italy, the PCI, is stated in no uncertain terms by Livia Turco and Rossana Rossanda in the first issue of *Reti,* a new cultural journal of communist women published in Rome by Editori Riuniti under the editorship of Maria Luisa Boccia. The terms feminist and feminism, sexual difference, female authorization, female reference, [symbolic] mediation, even female society ("La società femminile" is the amazing title of Boccia's editorial in the inaugural issue) recur throughout the journal, whose project is to elaborate the positions stated in the so-called Women's Charter (*Carta delle donne*), an official intervention by women members of the PCI in the direction of the party itself.

Reversing or subverting over sixty years of PCI theory and praxis on "the woman question," the Charter and the journal demand not only equality but also difference for women, insisting on the necessity for communist women to be both communists and feminists at once:

> *women are not a constituency to be added on [to party membership]*
> *but a different constituency, whose centuries-old history of difference,*
> *positively exploded in the past few years, entails a reconstitutive* self-
> consciousness *and thus a rethinking of the* entire *horizon and method*
> *of the party. . . . This is historically new, one of the problems facing a*
> *left-wing party today,*

writes Rossanda. But, she immediately adds, "the men of the party, who are still *the* party today," have not yet registered this fact or seen the necessity of a radical transformation of society that will prioritize the gendered subjects, rather than the objects, of social development (40–41). Then, addressing herself specifically to *Non credere*, Rossanda compares it with the political method implicit in the "Women's Charter": whereas the latter brings feminist issues and theory into direct confrontation with the party as the crucial political institution of Italian social life, the practice of entrustment is a simpler form of social relations, which shifts the emphasis away from the economic, the institutional, the mass levels, and toward an elitist, interest-group, and potentially hierarchical model of political practice based on diadic relationships between "female-gendered individuals" (*individui donne* [42]).

The interesting thing about Rossanda's article is not her ideological objection, which follows predictably from the historical contradiction of PCI women, as she herself describes it, unable to be both communists and feminists at once. It is rather her strategic move to grant political status to the theory of sexual difference, to take its feminist critical lesson to heart, and then to appropriate or absorb its conceptual novelty into her preferred position (the Charter's) while reducing the book's concept of a diffuse *social* practice of sexual difference to a *political* model, or "method," of narrow, personal, and hierarchical proportions. This strategy is not unique to her, though as a major figure of the Italian Left, Rossanda commands a higher degree of persuasiveness and national visibility than most of the other women who have publicly engaged in this debate (no man, to my knowledge, has done so).

Other objections have been less guarded and more impassioned, revealing their stakes in rather transparent ways. For example, Grazia Zuffa, also writing in *Reti*, laments the turn of feminism from the "'free' feminist politics" of the early *autocoscienza* groups to the current "necessary and thus obligatory" practice of disparity and symbolic mediation. The appeal of entrustment, she fears, is all too reminiscent of the appeal that the psychoanalytic relationship has on women, with its controlling definition of subjectivity. Isn't the symbolic mother really a projection of paternal authority vested in its familial enforcer, the social or real mother? That, one infers, would be bad enough. Worse still if the symbolic mother is the figure of a female social contract (as it indeed is), for then the whole theory is founded on a "radically separatist practice" and on refusing the male-female dialectic (or, as she awkwardly puts it, "on affirming the non dialectic with the masculine" ("nell'affermazione della non dialettica col maschile" [52])). Such "homosexual fundamentalism," she concludes, is a very long way and quite a different thing from "separatism as traditionally understood" in feminist politics. In other words, when the meaning of separatism shifts from the "traditional," socially innocuous, women's support group, in which women could let down their hair and commiserate with one another on personal matters, to a new social formation of women with no loyalty to men and intent on changing the world on their own–this is going too far.

Here we find ourselves on more familiar terrain, as Zuffa's homophobic sentiment lends itself easily to transcultural translation into Anglo-American feminism, where the term separatism has always carried the connotation she bluntly acknowledges, even as it is seldom stated in so direct a way as to reveal the heterosexual fundamentalism that motivates the objection. But unlike North America, where lesbianism has been a visible–if by no means unopposed or undivided–presence within the women's movement, and an acknowledged influence on the development of feminist thought, Italy has had no history of lesbian feminism, though it has a lesbian history that is now beginning to be told, and though lesbians have been active in the Movement all along as women and as feminists, if not as lesbians.[9] In a profoundly intelligent essay entitled "Doppio movimento" ("Double Movement"), published in a special issue of *DWF* on "Belonging" ("Appartenenza"), Ida Dominijanni does not so much object or adhere to the theory of sexual difference as take up its implications in her critical reading of the history (again, *a* history) of the Movement and the current stakes of feminism in Italy. And in one of the rare honest statements I have encountered in the pervasive silence that enshrouds lesbianism in Italian feminist writings, Dominijanni admits: "I will not even mention here [among the various forms of women's political identity or 'belonging'] the most unnamed of all belongings, if we can call it that: women's homosexual or heterosexual choice, on which Italian feminism has rightly chosen not to split itself, as happened in other countries, but which today is becoming a major cause of opacity in the theoretical and political debate" (25). And she goes on to another topic. But again extraordinarily, the same journal issue runs an article by Simonetta Spinelli, "Il silenzio è perdita" ("Silence Is Loss"), which argues for the necessity of coming out and theorizing lesbian identity and subjectivity as distinct from feminism. For the material specificity of lesbian desire and the embodied knowledges that can sustain a collective lesbian identity have remained "the unsaid of the Movement," as she puts it, and the price to lesbians has been the non-belonging to oneself as well as others, the loss of identity and finally of community (52).

Whether or not Italian feminists were right (as Dominijanni believes) in not splitting the Movement over what might well be called the lesbian question, Spinelli's intervention in the current debate on sexual difference hits very close to home when she indicts the inadequacy of a theory "that starts from me but in some oblique way also avoids me." Although she is not speaking directly about *Non credere*, a passage from the book actually sustains her objection: "Living in a community of women was an extraordinary experience, whose major revelation was the intense erotic charge that circulated in it. *It was not lesbianism, but female sexuality no longer imprisoned in masculine desire*" (*Non credere* 43; emphasis added). This is a troubled statement. What is meant by lesbianism, if it is not a female sexuality unfettered or autonomous from masculine desire and definition? Two are the possible readings of the statement.

One is that lesbianism is still understood in the terms of Havelock Ellis's sexology, as a form of sexual inversion whereby a woman would assume a masculine identification vis-à-vis her (female) sexual object choice. This is not only a pre-feminist notion that does not recognize lesbianism as a form of autonomous *female* sexuality (although it gained much credibility even among lesbians since its inscription in Radclyffe Hall's famous novel, *The Well of Loneliness*) but, more importantly, it is also a notion that would contradict the rest of the statement, for it forecloses the possibility of any form of female sexuality autonomous from the masculine. Havelock Ellis's definitions of homosexuality and inversion are in fact predicated on the male-centered conceptual structure that Irigaray cleverly called "hom(m)osexuality" or "sexual indifference," where "the object choice of the homosexual woman [can only be understood as] determined by a *masculine* desire and tropism" (Irigaray 99). The point of her pun was precisely to make visible the male-centeredness of the structure and its absolute negation of female sexuality in itself. (On the paradox of what I call *sexual (in)difference* and how it works in lesbian representation and self-representation, see de Lauretis).

The other, perhaps closer reading is the one suggested by Spinelli: that *Non credere's* conception of an autonomous female sexuality avoids lesbianism "in some oblique way," bypasses it, circumvents it, or disclaims it. In other words, one might ask more bluntly, is this a theory that dare not speak its name? Thus, Spinelli's essay is a powerful ironic counterpart to the homo-phobic objections that have met the Milanese proposal of a radically separatist social practice. For if that proposal does in fact articulate a position that we, here, might understand as lesbian feminism–however culturally, politically, and theoretically distinct from the North American variety–its dodging of the crucial questions of sexuality, fantasy, and the erotic in the definition of sexual difference all but drops the lesbian specification by the wayside.

To conclude, the risks involved in *Non credere's* effort to define female desire and subjecthood in the symbolic, without sufficient attention to the working of the imaginary in subjectivity and sexual identity, are many and great. As has been pointed out, it makes but little space for differences and divisions between–and within–women, and so tends to construct a view of the female social subject that is still too closely modeled on the "monstrous" sub-ject of philosophy and History. However, this is not a biological or metaphysical essentialism, but a consciously political formulation of the specific difference of women in a particular sociohistorical location where, for instance, race or color has not been at issue; and where, if sexuality is now emerging as an issue, it is not merely against, but in part owing to, the very strength of its theory of sexual difference.

As another contributor to the theory well said it, "by essential and orig-inary difference I mean that, for women, being engendered in difference [*l'essere sessuate nella differenza*] is something not negotiable; for each one who is born female, it is always already so and not otherwise, rooted in her being not as something superfluous or something more, but as that which she necessarily is: female" (Cavarero 180–81). If Cavarero's project of feminist philosophy can be rightly criticized for its unquestioning acceptance of the classic, unified subject of philosophy (see Braidotti), nevertheless the notion of essential and originary difference represents a point of consensus and a starting point for the Italian theory of sexual difference. And here as well, without this basic feminist assumption–basic, that is, to feminism as historically constituted at the present moment–the still necessary articulation of all other differences between and within women must remain framed in male-dominant and heterosexist ideolo-gies of liberal pluralism, conservative humanism, or, goddess forbid, religious fundamentalism.

One of the lessons I draw from this history of Italian feminism is this: if feminist theory remains unwilling to take the risk of essentialism seriously while continuing to gesture toward it from a respectable distance, call it post-structuralist/deconstructionist or communist or simply anti-essentialist, it will remain unable to be both feminist and poststructuralist, both feminist and communist, or both feminist and radical at once. And the question is, in that case, can it remain feminist?

Looking back to the first part of this essay and the questions left un-answered there, I would now suggest that what motivates the suspicion or the outright construction, on the part of Anglo-American feminists, of a fantom feminist essentialism, may be less the risk of essentialism itself than the further risk which that entails: the risk of challenging directly the social-symbolic in-stitution of heterosexuality. Which, at least in Italy, appears to be no easier said for lesbians than for heterosexual women. Here, however, the challenge has been posed, and most articulately by precisely those feminists who are then ac-cused of separatism in their political stance and of essentialism with regard to their epistemological claims. I do not think it is a coincidence.

That thinkers as diverse as Adrienne Rich, Mary Daly, Catharine Mac-Kinnon, Marilyn Frey, occasionally Monique Wittig (occasionally because her critical writings are more often referred to in the context of lesbian, not feminist, theory), and undoubtedly myself after this essay, can be lumped together as es-sentialists, and that no women of color usually appear either in this category or in its opposite, the anti-essentialists, suggests to me an unwillingness to con-front and come to terms with the stakes, indeed the investments that feminism may have in the heterosexual institution. I say an unwillingness, not to say a strategy of avoidance, a more or less conscious disavowal in the face of the diffi-culty that such a confrontation must present for all concerned. But then again, the next question goes, without that confrontation, can we remain feminists?

For feminism in the late 1980s, when gestures toward issues of race and sexuality are proferred in many quarters but all too often serve as a moral alibi to continue to do business as usual, that difficulty, too, may be non-negotiable–if it cost the dream of a common world of women, or of a mass base for feminist politics and theory. In the question of the essential difference of feminism as socio-historical formation, in the struggle to define the essence of the triangle, its risks and its future hang in the balance.

Notes

1   The typological project is central to, for example, Alice Echols, Alison Jaggar and Paula Rothenberg, Hester Eisenstein, Zillah Eisenstein, and more recently Chris Weedon and Michèle Barrett. In this proliferation of typologies, essentialism as the belief in "female nature" is associated with cultural feminism, "separatist" feminism, radical feminism (with qualifications), and occasionally liberal feminism, while socialist feminism and now post-structuralist or deconstructive feminism come out at the top of the scale. Third World feminism is also widely used as a term but seldom given official type status in the typologies. One exception is Jaggar and Rothenberg's anthology which, in its 1984 revised edition, adds the new category "Feminism and Women of Color" to the five categories of the 1978 edition of *Feminist Frameworks*: conservatism, liberalism, traditional Marxism, radical feminism, and socialist feminism. On their part, black, Latina, Asian, and other U.S. Third World feminists have not participated in the making of such typologies, possibly because of their ongoing argument with and ambivalence toward the larger category of "white feminism." And hence, perhaps, Jaggar and Rothenberg's respectful labelling of the new category "Feminism *and* Women of Color," suggesting distance between the two terms and avoiding judgment on the latter.

2   Since Alcoff refers extensively to my own work, this essay is in a sense a dialogue with her and with myself–that dialogue in feminist critical writing which often works as a variation of consciousness raising or better, its transformation into a significant form of feminist cultural practice, and one not always reducible to "academic" activity.

3   Two recent books have been published in the United States on Italian feminism (Chiavola Birnbaum; Hellman), and one in Britain on feminist film (Bruno and Nadotti). Also in Britain some extracts from a Milan Bookstore publication (Catalogue Editorial Collective) were recently edited and introduced by Rosalind Delmar, translator of the Italian classic feminist novel, Sibilla Aleramo's *A Woman*. An earlier article by Mary Russo is a rare example of American feminist theoretical writing dealing with the Italian women's movement in the '70s.

4   Since a forthcoming English version of *Non credere* is still in preparation, this title and all subsequent passages from the book are in my own translation. However, any act of translation is fraught with problems. The dense substratum of connotations, resonances, and implicit references that the history of a culture has sedimented into the words and phrases of its language is often simply untranslatable; thus the act of translation is often a rewriting of the original language (in this case, Italian) and a reconfiguration or interpretation of its plurivocal meaning by means of connotations and resonances built into the words and phrases of the second language (in this case, American English). I will try to account for my choices in the most glaring cases of untranslatability, and give the Italian in brackets, so as to make the extent of my interpretive rewriting as apparent as possible. For example, the subtitle of the book just cited presents several problems: 1) *generazione*, a word etymolo-

gically associated with gender and genealogy, usually corresponds to "generation" but I translate it as *engendering*, not only to strengthen the sense of an ongoing process rather than an achieved event, but also to convey the authors' idea that "female freedom" is only possible within a feminist consciousness of gender, a gendered consciousness. In fact, that idea, though clearly formulated in the book, is not conveyed as clearly by the Italian title because Italian does not normally use the word "gender" for the sex-based distinction between female and male, as English does. Instead, Italian uses *sesso*, "sex," and the adjective *sessuato/sessuata*, "sexed," where English would say "gendered," as in the phrase "gendered thinking" (*pensiero sessuato*) or "gendered subject" (*soggetto sessuato*). In this instance, then, the translation "the engendering of female freedom" actually renders the concept more precisely, or better conveys its complexity, than the Italian "la generazione (the generation) della libertà femminile." 2) Another problem is posed by the adjective *femminile*, which I translate as *female* although it also corresponds to the English "feminine." The latter, however, is strongly resonant with "femininity," the ideological construct of woman's "nature," which feminism has taken pains to deconstruct; alternatively, outside the context of feminist discourse, the phrase "feminine freedom" sounds rather like an advertisement for "personal hygiene" products. Thus, though I am fully aware of the biological connotations that hover around the term "female," I prefer to translate *libertà femminile* as *female freedom*: on balance, the risk of essentialism seems negligible in this instance.

5   See, for instance, the passage cited above about "the girl or woman who tries to write because she is peculiarly susceptible to language. She goes to poetry or fiction looking for *her* way of being in the world, since she too has been putting words and images together; she is looking eagerly for guides, maps, possibilities; and over and over in the 'words' masculine persuasive force' of literature she comes up against something that negates everything she is about: she meets the image of Woman in books written by men. She finds a terror and a dream, she finds a beautiful pale face, she finds La Belle Dame Sans Merci, she finds Juliet or Tess or Salomé but precisely what she does not find is that absorbed, drudging, puzzled, sometimes inspired creature, herself, who sits at a desk trying to put words together. So what does she do? What did I do? I read the older women poets with their peculiar keenness and ambivalence: Sappho, Christina Rossetti, Emily Dickinson, Elinor Wylie, Edna Millay, H.D." (39). The notions of a woman's relation to the symbolic marked by "peculiar keenness and ambivalence," of a female genealogy of poets, makers of language, and of their active role in mediating the young woman's access to poetry as a symbolic form of being (female being or being-woman) as well as writing (authorship, author-ity), are all there in Rich's passage, although the first two are stated, the last one only suggested by negation. Nearly two decades later, the Milan feminists turn the suggestion into positive affirmation.

6   Diotima, the collective author of the homonymous volume, is a "philosophical community" of academic feminists which has, however, some significant overlap with the more militant feminism of the Milan Libreria delle Donne. The members of the collective and authors of

Diotima are Adriana Cavarero, Cristiana Fischer, Elvia Franco, Giannina Longobardi, Veronica Mariaux, Luisa Muraro, Anna Maria Piussi, Wanda Tommasi, Anita Sanvitto, Betty Zamarchi, Chiara Zamboni, and Gloria Zanardo.

7   No individual authors' names appear in the pamphlet, or in *Non credere*, as customary in the Italian Movement practice of collective authorship, a practice no longer followed as strictly as it was in the '70s except by long-standing groups like the Milan Libreria delle Donne. Any Italian feminist, however, would be able to name at least some of the individuals in the group and knows that the authors of both the *Sottosopra verde* and *Non credere* include the two women most directly associated with the Libreria, Luisa Muraro and Lia Cigarini. For a full documentation of the Movement in Milan, see Calabrò and Grasso.

8   For this very interesting connection between radical feminist theory and Benjamin's "Theses on the Philosophy of History," I am indebted to the original work in progress of Kathy Miriam, doctoral candidate in History of Consciousness at the University of California, Santa Cruz.

9   A valuable contribution to the history of lesbian activism and its relation both to the women's movement and to the "diffuse feminism" of the '80s is Bianca Pomeranzi's "Differenza lesbica e lesbofemminismo," published in *Memoria*, a journal of women's history. But it is sadly remarkable that the most comprehensive and up-to-date account of lesbianism in Italy is a paper in English by Liana Borghi, Gloria Corsi, Simonetta Spinelli, and Alessandra Perini, "Italian Lesbians: Maps and Signs." Borghi is also the author of one of the first texts of lesbian fiction in Italy, a wonderful and funny novella, *Tenda con vista* (*Tent with a View*), published by Estro Editrice in Rome (one of the two lesbian small presses currently operating in Italy, the other being Felina Editrice). Estro is also the publisher of the major contribution to lesbian cultural history that has appeared in Italy, Rosanna Fiocchetto's *L'amante celeste: La distruzione scientifica della lesbica* (*Heavenly Lover: The Scientific Destruction of the Lesbian*). The only other lesbian publication is the monthly Bulletin of CLI (Collegamento fra le lesbiche italiane), a national organization based in Rome.

Works Cited

Alcoff, Linda. "Cultural Feminism versus Post-Structuralism: The Identity Crisis in Feminist Theory." *Signs: A Journal of Women in Culture and Society* 13.3 (1988): 405–36.

Aleramo, Sibilla. *A Woman.* Trans. Rosalind Delmar. Berkeley: U of California P, 1980.

Barrett, Michèle. "Some Different Meanings of the Concept of 'Difference': Feminist Theory and the Concept of Ideology." *The Difference Within: Feminism and Critical Theory.*

Ed. Elizabeth Meese and Alice Parker. Amsterdam: Benjamins, 1989. 37–48.

Benjamin, Walter. *Illuminations*. Trans. Harry Zohn. Ed. and Introduction Hannah Arendt. New York: Schocken Books, 1969.

Birnbaum, Lucia Chiavola. *Liberazione della donna: Feminism in Italy*. Middletown: Wesleyan UP, 1986.

Borghi, Liana. *Tenda con vista*. Rome: Estro, 1987.

_____, et al. "Italian Lesbians: Maps and Signs." *Homosexuality, Which Homosexuality?* Proc. of the International Conference on Gay and Lesbian Studies at the Free University of Amsterdam, 15–18 Dec. 1987: Amsterdam, 1987. 112–25.

Braidotti, Rosi. "Commento alla relazione di Adriana Cavarero." *La ricerca delle donne: Studi femministi in Italia*. Ed. Maria Cristina Marcuzzo and Anna Rossi-Doria. Turin: Rosenberg & Sellier, 1987. 188–202.

Bruno, Giuliana, and Maria Nadotti, eds. *Off Screen: Women and Film in Italy*. London: Routledge, 1988.

Calabrò, Anna Rita, and Laura Grasso, eds. *Dal movimento femminista al femminismo diffuso: Ricerca e documentazione nell'area lombarda*. Milan: Franco Angeli, 1985.

Catalogue [of the] Editorial Collective of the Women's Bookshop, Milan. "Writers and Readers." Ed. Rosalind Delmar. *Red Letters* 9 (n.d.): 17–34.

Cavarero, Adriana. "L'elaborazione filosofica della differenza sessuale." *La ricerca delle donne: Studi femministi in Italia*. Ed. Maria Cristina Marcuzzo and Anna Rossi-Doria. Turin: Rosenberg & Sellier, 1987. 173–87.

_____, et al. *Diotima. Il pensiero della differenza sessuale*. Milan: La Tartaruga, 1987.

de Lauretis, Teresa. "Sexual Indifference and Lesbian Representation." *Theatre Journal* 40.2 (1988): 155–77.

Delmar, Rosalind. "What Is Feminism?" *What Is Feminism: A Re-Examination*. Ed. Juliet Mitchell and Ann Oakley. New York: Pantheon Books, 1986. 8–33.

Dominijanni, Ida. "Doppio movimento." *DWF [DonnaWomanFemme]* 4 (1986): 25.

Doolittle, Hilda [H. D.]. *Tribute to Freud*. Boston: Godine, 1974.

Echols, Alice. "The New Feminism of Yin and Yang." *Powers of Desire: The Politics of Sexuality*. Ed. Ann Snitow, Christine Stansell, and Sharon Thompson. New York: Monthly Review, 1983.

_____. "The Taming of the Id: Feminist Sexual Politics." *Pleasure and Danger: Exploring Female Sexuality*. Ed. Carole S. Vance. Boston: Routledge, 1984.

Eisenstein, Hester. *Contemporary Feminist Thought*. Boston: Hall, 1983.

Eisenstein, Zillah. *The Radical Future of Liberal Feminism*. New York: Longman, 1981.

Fiochetto, Rosanna. *L'amante celeste: La distruzione scientifica della lesbica*. Rome: Estro, 1987.

Hall, Radclyffe. *The Well of Loneliness*. London: Hammond, 1956.

Haraway, Donna. "Situated Knowledges: The Science Question in Feminism and the Privilege of Partial Perspective." *Feminist Studies* 14. 3 (1988): 575–99.

Hellman, Judith Adler. *Journeys Among Women: Feminism in Five Italian Cities*. New York: Oxford UP, 1987.

Irigaray, Luce. *Éthique de la différence sexuelle*. Paris: Minuit, 1984.

———. *Speculum of the Other Woman*. Trans. Gillian C. Gill. Ithaca: Cornell UP, 1985.

Jaggar, Alison M., and Paul S. Rothenberg. *Feminist Frameworks: Alternative Theoretical Accounts of the Relations Between Women and Men*. New York: McGraw-Hill, 1984.

Lepetit, Laura, et al. *Una libreria e i suoi doni: Lettera aperta dalla Libreria delle Donne di Milano*. 1987.

Libreria delle Donne di Milano. *Non credere di avere dei diritti: La generazione della libertà femminile nell'idea e nelle vicende di un gruppo di donne*. Turin: Rosenberg, 1987.

———. "Più donne che uomini [More Women Than Men]." *Sottosopra* (Jan. 1983).

Lonzi, Carla. *Sputiamo su Hegel*. Milan: Scritti di Rivolta Femminile, 1974.

Lugones, María C. and Elizabeth V. Spelman. "Have We Got a Theory for You!: Feminist Theory, Cultural Imperialism and the Demand for 'the Woman's Voice.'" *Women's Studies International Forum* 6 (1983): 573–81.

Miller, Nancy K. "Changing the Subject: Authorship, Writing, and the Reader." *Feminist Studies/Critical Studies*. Ed. Teresa de Lauretis. Bloomington: Indiana UP, 1986. 102–20. Rpt. in Nancy K. Miller. *Subject to Change: Reading Feminist Writing*. New York: Columbia UP, 1988. 102–20.

Pomeranzi, Bianca. "Differenza lesbica e lesbofemminismo." *Memoria* 13 (1985): 72–78.

Rich, Adrienne. *On Lies, Secrets, and Silence: Selected Prose 1966–1978*. New York: Norton, 1979.

Rossanda, Rossana. "Politica: significati e progetti. Le diverse strade della Carta e dell'affidamento." *Reti: Pratiche e saperi di donne* 1 (1987): 39–44.

Russo, Mary. "The Politics of Maternity: Abortion in Italy." *Yale Italian Studies* 1.1 (1977): 107–27.

Showalter, Elaine, ed. *The New Feminist Criticism: Essays on Women, Literature, and Theory.* New York: Pantheon, 1985.

Smith, Barbara. "Toward a Black Feminist Criticism." 1977. Rpt. in Showalter 168–85.

Spinelli, Simonetta. "Il silenzio è perdita." *DWF [DonnaWomanFemme]* 4 (1986): 49–53.

Turco, Livia. "Una scelta di uguaglianza e differenza." *Reti: Pratiche e saperi di donne* 1 (1987): 4–6.

Weedon, Chris. *Feminist Practice and Poststructuralist Theory.* Oxford: Blackwell, 1987.

Zimmerman, Bonnie. "What Has Never Been: An Overview of Lesbian Feminist Criticism." 1981. Rpt. in Showalter 200–24.

Zuffa, Grazia. "Tra libertà necessità. A proposito di *Non credere di avere dei diritti.*" *Reti: Pratiche e saperi di donne* 1 (1987): 51–53.

This Essentialism Which Is Not One:
Coming to Grips with Irigaray

*A*s Jacques Derrida pointed out several years ago, in the institutional model of the university elaborated in Germany at the beginning of the nineteenth century no provision was made, no space allocated for the discipline of women's studies: "There was no place foreseen in the structure of the classical model of Berlin for women's studies" ("Women" 190).[1] Women's studies, a field barely twenty years old today, is a belated add-on, an afterthought to the Berlin model which was taken over by American institutions of higher learning. For Derrida the question then becomes: what is the status of this new wing? does it function merely as an addition, or rather as a supplement, simultaneously within and without the main building: "with women's studies, is it a question of simply filling a lack in a structure already in place, filling a gap?" (190). If the answer to this question were yes, then in the very success of women's studies would lie also its failure. "As much as women's studies has not put back into question the very principles of the structure of the former model of the university, it risks being just another cell in the university beehive" ("Women" 191). The question in other words is: is women's studies, as it has from the outset claimed to be, in some essential manner *different* from the other disciplines accommodated within the traditional Germanic institutional model of the university or is it in fact more of the same, different perhaps in its object of study, but fundamentally alike in its relationship to the institution and the social values it exists to enshrine and transmit. What difference, asks Derrida, does women's studies make in the university: "what is the difference, if there is one, between a university institution of research and teaching called 'women's studies' and any other institution of learning and teaching around it in the university or in society as a whole?" ("Women" 190). Derrida goes on to strongly suggest that in the accumulation of empirical research on women, in the tenuring of feminist scholars, in the seemingly spectacular success of women's studies, the feminist critique of the institution has been scanted. In the eyes of deconstruction women's studies *is* perilously close to becoming "just another cell in the academic beehive."

Derrida's account of the relationship of women's studies to the institution is perhaps not entirely fair, not sufficiently informed: women's studies–if one can generalize about such a vast and heterogeneous field–has been neither as successful nor as easily coopted as Derrida makes it out to be, no more or less so than deconstruction with which, as he points out, it is often linked by their common enemies. My concern, however, lies elsewhere: what I continue to find perplexing about Derrida's remarks, remarks that were made at a seminar given at Brown University's Pembroke Center for Teaching and Research on Women, is his failure to articulate the grounds on which women's studies would found its difference. My perplexity grows when I read in the published transcription of the seminar, which I both attended and participated in, the following:

> *This is a question of the Law: are those involved in women's studies– teachers, students, researchers–the guardians of the Law, or not? You will remember that in the parable of the Law of Kafka, between the guardian of the Law and the man from the country there is no* essential difference, *they are in oppositional but symmetric positions. We are all, as members of a university, guardians of the Law. . . . Does that situation repeat itself for women's studies or not? Is there in the abstract or even topical idea of women's studies, something which potentially has the force, if it is possible, to deconstruct the fundamental institutional structure of the university, of the Law of the university? (191–92; emphasis added)*

Is what Derrida is calling for then, that potentially deconstructive *something*, on the order of an essential difference? Is what he is calling for a women's studies that would be *essentially different* from its brother and sister disciplines? How, given the anti-essentialism of deconstruction, about which more in a moment, to found an essential difference between feminine and masculine guardians of the law? How can women's studies be essentially different from other disciplines in a philosophical system that constantly works to subvert all essential differences, all essentializing of differences?

These questions are of special concern to me because the conflict *within* the faculty of women's studies has from its inception been to a large extent a conflict–and a very violent one–over essentialism, and it is to this conflict that I want to turn in what follows. I will first consider the critiques of essentialism that have been advanced in recent years, then compare briefly Simone de Beauvoir and Luce Irigaray, the two major French feminist theoreticians, who are generally held to exemplify respectively anti-essentialist and essentialist positions. Finally, in the space I hope to have opened up for a new look at Irigaray, I will examine her troping of essentialism.

I. This Essentialism Which Is Not One

What revisionism, not to say essentialism, was to Marxism-Leninism, essentialism is to feminism: the prime idiom of intellectual terrorism and the privileged instrument of political orthodoxy. Borrowed from the time-honored vocabulary of philosophy, the word essentialism has been endowed within the context of feminism with the power to reduce to silence, to excommunicate, to consign to oblivion. Essentialism in modern-day feminism is anathema. There are, however, signs, encouraging signs in the form of projected books, ongoing dissertations, private conversations, not so much of a return of or to essentialism, as of a recognition of the excesses perpetrated in the name of anti-essentialism, of the urgency of rethinking the very terms of a conflict which all parties would agree has ceased to be productive.[2]

What then is meant by essentialism in the context of feminism and what are the chief arguments marshalled against it by its critics? According to a standard definition drawn from the *Dictionary of Philosophy and Religion*, essentialism is "the belief that things have essences." What then is an essence? Again from the same dictionary: "that which makes a thing what it is," and further, "that which is necessary and unchanging about a concept or a thing" (Reese 81, 80). Essentialism in the specific context of feminism consists in the belief that woman has an essence, that woman can be specified by one or a number of inborn attributes which define across cultures and throughout history her unchanging being and in the absence of which she ceases to be categorized as a woman. In less abstract, more practical terms, an essentialist in the context of feminism is one who instead of carefully holding apart the poles of sex and gender maps the feminine onto femaleness, one for whom the body, the female body that is, remains, in however complex and problematic a way the rock of feminism.

But, by defining essentialism as I just have have I not in turn essentialized it, since definitions are by definition, as it were, essentialist? Anti-essentialism operates precisely in this manner, that is by essentializing essentialism, by proceeding as though there were one essentialism, an essence of essentialism. If we are to move beyond the increasingly sterile conflict over essentialism, we must begin by de-essentializing essentialism, for no more than deconstruction *essentialism is not one*.[5] The multiplicity of essentialisms–one might, for example, want to distinguish French essentialism from the native variety, naive essentialism from strategic essentialism, heterosexual from homosexual–is revealed by the multiplicity of its critiques. Now most often these critiques are imbricated, so tightly interwoven in the space of an article or a book that they appear to form one internally consistent argument directed against one immutable monolithic position. And yet if one takes the trouble for purely heuristic purposes to disentangle the various strands of these critiques–I will distinguish four such critiques–it becomes apparent that they serve diverse, even conflicting interests and draw on distinct, often incompatible conceptual frameworks. However much in practice these critiques may overlap and intersect, when separated out they turn out to correspond to some of the major trends in feminist theory from Beauvoir to the present.

1. *The Liberationist Critique*: this is the critique of essentialism first articulated by Beauvoir and closely identified with the radical feminist journal, *Questions féministes*, which she helped found. "One is not born, but rather becomes a woman," Beauvoir famously declared in *The Second Sex* (249). This is the guiding maxim of the culturalist or constructionist critique of essentialism which holds that femininity is a cultural construct in the service of the oppressive powers of patriarchy. By promoting an essential difference of woman grounded in the body, the argument runs, essentialism plays straight into the hands of the patriarchal order, which has traditionally invoked anatomical and physiological differences to legitimate the socio-political disempowerment of women. If women are to achieve equality, to become fully enfranchised persons, the manifold forms of exploitation and oppression to which they are subject, be they economic or political, must be carefully analyzed and tirelessly interrogated. Essentialist arguments which fail to take into account the role of the socius in producing women are brakes on the wheel of progress.

2. *The Linguistic Critique*: this is the critique derived from the writings and seminars of Lacan and promoted with particular force by Anglo-American film critics and theoreticians, writing in such journals as *Screen, m/f*, and *Camera Obscura*. What the socius is to Beauvoir and her followers, language is to Lacan and Lacanians. The essentialist, in this perspective, is a naive realist who refuses to recognize that the loss of the referent is the condition of man's entry into language. Within the symbolic order centered on the phallus there can be no immediate access to the body: the fine mesh of language screens off the body from any apprehension that is not already enculturated. Essentialism is then in Lacanian terms an effect of the imaginary and it is no accident that some of the most powerfully seductive evocations of the feminine, notably those of Irigaray and Cixous, resonate with the presence and plenitude of the pre-discursive pre-Oedipal. In the symbolic order ruled by the phallus, "there is no such thing as The Woman" as Lacan gnomically remarks (144). What we have instead are subjects whose sexual inscription is determined solely by the positions they occupy in regard to the phallus, and these positions are at least in theory subject to change. The proper task of feminist theory is, however, not to contribute to changing the status of women in society–for the Law of the symbolic is posited as eternal–rather to expose and denaturalize the mechanisms whereby females are positioned as women.

3. *The Philosophical Critique*: the reference here is to the critique elaborated by Derrida and disseminated by feminist Derrideans ranging from Irigaray and Cixous to some of the major transatlantic feminist critics and theoreticians. Essentialism, in this view, is complicitous with Western metaphysics. To subscribe to the binary opposition man/woman is to remain a prisoner of the metaphysical with its illusions of presence, Being, stable meanings and identities. The essentialist in this scheme of things is not, as for Lacan, one who refuses to accept the phallocentric ordering of the symbolic, rather one who fails to acknowledge the play of difference in language and the difference it makes. Beyond the prisonhouse of the binary, multiple differences play indifferently across degendered bodies. As a strategic position adopted to achieve specific political goals, feminist essentialism has, however, its place in deconstruction.

4. *The Feminist Critique*: I have deliberately reserved this rubric for the only critique of essentialism to have emerged from *within* the women's movement. No proper name, masculine or feminine, can be attached to this cri-

tique as its legitimating source; it arises from the plurivocal discourses of black, Chicana, lesbian, first and third world feminist thinkers and activists. The recent work of Teresa de Lauretis, *Alice Doesn't*, and the edited volume of conference proceedings, *Feminist Studies/Critical Studies*, might, however, be cited as exemplifying this trend. Essentialism, according to this critique, is a form of "false universalism" that threatens the vitality of the newly born women of feminism. By its majestic singularity Woman conspires in the denial of the very real lived differences–sexual, ethnic, racial, national, cultural, economic, generational–that divide women from each other and from themselves. Feminist anti-essentialism shares with deconstruction the conviction that essentialism inheres in binary opposition, hence its displacement of woman-as-different-from-man by the notion of internally differentiated and historically instantiated women.[4]

Unlike deconstruction and all the other critiques of essentialism I have reviewed all too briefly here, the feminist is uniquely committed to constructing specifically female subjectivities, and it is for this reason that I find this critique the most compelling. It is precisely around the issues of the *differences* among as well as within women that the impasse between essentialism and anti-essentialism is at last beginning to yield: for just as the pressing issues of race and ethnicity are forcing certain anti-essentialists to suspend their critiques in the name of political realities, they are forcing certain essentialists to question their assertion of a female essence that is widely perceived and rightly denounced by minority women as exclusionary.

II. Beauvoir and Irigaray: Two Exemplary Positions

Quelle femme n'a pas
lu Le deuxième sexe?
(Irigaray, Je, tu, nous *9)*

The access of women to subjectivity is the central concern of the two major French feminist theoreticians of the twentieth century: Simone de Beauvoir and Luce Irigaray. Indeed, despite their dramatically opposed positions, both share a fundamental grounding conviction: under the social arrangement known as patriarchy the subject is exclusively male: masculinity and subjectivity are co-extensive notions. Consider these two celebrated assertions, the first drawn from Beauvoir's *The Second Sex*, the second, from

Irigaray's *Speculum*: "He is the Subject, he is the Absolute" (xix); "any theory of the 'subject' has always been appropriated by the 'masculine'" (133). Almost immediately the suspicion arises that though both are centrally concerned with the appropriation of subjectivity by men, Beauvoir and Irigaray are not in fact speaking about the same subject. Subjectivity, like essentialism, like deconstruction, is not one. There is a world of difference between Beauvoir's subject, with its impressive capitalized S, reinforced by the capitalization of Absolute, its homologue, and Irigaray's subject, with its lower case s and the relativizing quotation marks that enclose both subject and masculine.

Beauvoir's subject is the familiar Hegelian subject of existentialist ethics, a heroic figure locked in a life and death struggle with the not-self, chiefly the environment and the Other:

> *Every subject plays his part as such specifically through exploits or*
> *projects that serve as a mode of transcendence; he achieves liberty*
> *only through a continual reaching out toward other liberties. There is*
> *no justification for present existence other than its expansion into an*
> *indefinitely open future. Every time transcendence falls back into im-*
> *manence, stagnation, there is a degradation of existence onto the*
> *"en-soi"–the brutish life of subjection, to given conditions–and of liberty*
> *into constraint and contingence. This downfall represents a moral*
> *fault if the subject consents to it; if it is inflicted upon him, it spells frus-*
> *tration and oppression. In both cases it is an absolute evil. (xxviii)*

Subjectivity is for Beauvoir activity, a restless projection into the future, a glorious surpassing of the iterativity of everyday life. The dreadful fall from transcendence into immanence is woman's estate. Consigned by the masterful male subject to passivity and repetition, woman in patriarchy is a prisoner of immanence. Beauvoir's theory of subjectivity, thus, as has been often observed, dismally reinscribes the most traditional alignments of Western metaphysics: positivity lines up with activity, while passivity and with it femininity are slotted as negative. At the same time, however, Beauvoir's exemplary anti-essentialism works to break the alignment of the transcendent and the male; by leaving behind the unredeemed and unredeemable domestic sphere of contingency for the public sphere of economic activity women too can achieve transcendence. Liberation for women in Beauvoir's liberationist macronarrative consists in emerging from the dark cave of immanence "into the light of transcendence" (675).

Deeply implicated in the radical reconceptualization of the (male) subject that characterizes post-Sartrean French thought, Irigaray's subject is a diminished subject that bears little resemblance to the sovereign and purposeful subject of existentialist philosophy. For Irigaray–and this displacement is crucial–the main attribute of the subject is not activity but language. The *homo faber* that serves as Beauvoir's model gives way to *homo parlans*. Thus Irigaray's subject is for all practical purposes a speaking subject, a pronoun, the first person singular I. And that pronoun has under current social arrangements been pre-empted by men: "The I thus remains predominant among men" ("L'Ordre" 83). The much touted death of the subject–which can only be the male subject (Miller 102–20)–leaves Irigaray singularly unmoved:

> *And the fact that you no longer assert yourself as absolute subject does not change a thing. The breath that animates you, the law or the duty that lead you, are they not the quintessence of your subjectivity? You no longer cling to* [ne tiens pas à] *your "I"? But your "I" clings to you* [te tient]. . . . (Passions *101*)

For women to accede to subjectivity clearly means becoming speaking subjects in their own right. It is precisely at this juncture that the major difference between Beauvoir and Irigaray begins to assert itself, and once again I take them as representative of what Anthony Appiah has called the "classic dialectic": whereas for Beauvoir the goal is for women to share fully in the privileges of the transcendent subject, for Irigaray the goal is for women to achieve subjectivity without merging tracelessly into the putative indifference of the shifter. What is at stake in these two equally powerful and problematic feminist discourses is not the status of difference, rather that of the universal, and universalism may well be one of the most divisive and least discussed issues in feminism today. When Irigaray projects women as speaking a sexually marked language, a "parler femme," she is, I believe, ultimately less concerned with theorizing feminine specificity than with debunking the oppressive fiction of a universal subject. To speak woman is above all *not* to "speak 'universal'"; "No more subject which is indifferent, substitutable, universal" (*Parler* 9); "I have no desire to take their speech as they have taken ours, nor to speak 'universal'"(*Corps* 63–64).[5] For Beauvoir, on the other hand, it is precisely because women have been prevented from speaking universal, indeed because they have "no sense of the universal" that they have made so few significant contributions to the great humanist tradition. Mediocrity is the lot of those creators who do not feel "responsible for the universe" (671).

My task here is not to adjudicate between these two exemplary positions I am outlining, but to try to understand how starting from the same assumptions about women's exile from subjectivity, Beauvoir and Irigaray arrive at such radically different conclusions, and further to show that Irigaray's work cannot be understood without situating it in the relationship to Beauvoir's. In order to do so Beauvoir's and Irigaray's theories of subjectivity must be reinserted in the framework of their broader enterprises. Beauvoir's project throughout *The Second Sex* is to lay bare the mechanisms of what we might call, borrowing the term from Mary Louise Pratt, "othering" (139): the means by which patriarchy fixed women in the place of the absolute Other, projecting onto women a femininity constituted of the refuse of masculine transcendence. Otherness in Beauvoir's scheme of things is utter negativity; it is the realm of what Kristeva has called the abject. Irigaray's project is diametrically opposed to Beauvoir's but must be viewed as its necessary corollary. Just as Beauvoir lays bare the mechanisms of othering, Irigaray exposes those of what we might call by analogy, "saming." If othering involves attributing to the objectified other a difference that serves to legitimate her oppression, saming denies the objectified other the right to her difference, submitting the other to the laws of phallic specularity. If othering assumes that the other is knowable, saming precludes any knowledge of the other in her otherness. If exposing the logic of othering–whether it be of women, Jews, or any other victims of demeaning stereotyping–is a necessary step in achieving equality, exposing the logic of saming is a necessary step in toppling the universal from his/(her) pedestal.

Since othering and saming conspire in the oppression of women, the workings of *both* processes need to be exposed. And yet to date the articulation of these two projects has proved an elusive, indeed insuperable task for feminist theoreticians, for just as Beauvoir's analysis precludes theorizing difference, or rather–and the distinction is crucial–difference as positivity, Irigaray's proves incapable of not theorizing difference, that is difference as positivity. One of the more awkward moments in Beauvoir comes in the closing pages of *The Second Sex* when she seeks to persuade the reader that women's liberation will not signify a total loss of difference between men and women, for the entire weight of what precedes militates against theorizing a positive difference, indeed against grounding difference since both the body and the social have both been disqualified as sites of any meaningful sexual difference. Beauvoir gives herself away in these final pages when speaking of women's failure to achieve greatness in the world of intellect: "She can become an excellent theoretician, can acquire real competence, but she will be forced to repudiate whatever she has in her that is 'different'" (667). Similarly, by relentlessly exposing the mechanisms of saming, the economy of what she calls the "echonomy" of patriarchy, Irigaray exposes herself to adopting a logic of othering, precisely what has been called, her protestations notwithstanding, her essentialism.[6] What I am suggesting here is that each position has its own inescapable logic, and that that inescapability is the law of the same/other. If all difference is attributed to othering then one risks saming, and conversely: if all denial of difference is viewed as resulting in saming then one risks othering. In other words, it is as disingenuous to reproach Beauvoir with promoting the loss of difference between men and women as it is to criticize Irigaray for promoting, indeed theorizing that difference. And yet the logic I am trying to draw out of these two exemplary feminist discourses seems to have escaped Irigaray's most incisive critics who have repeatedly sought to sever her brilliant exposure of the specular logic of phallocentrism from her theorization of a specifically feminine difference. Toril Moi's formulation is in this regard typical:

> . . . *having shown that so far femininity has been produced exclusively in relation to the logic of the same, she falls for the temptation to produce her own positive theory of femininity. But, as we have seen, to define "woman" is necessarily to essentialize her.* (139)

My argument is *a contrario*: that Irigaray's production of a positive theory of femininity is not an aberration, a sin (to extend the theological metaphor), rather the logical extension of her deconstruction of the specular logic of saming. What is problematic about Irigaray's theorization of the feminine–which, it should be pointed out, is in fact only one aspect or moment of her work–is indicated by Moi's use of the word "positive." For finally the question posed by Irigaray's attempts to theorize feminine specificity–which is not to be confused with "defining" woman, a task she writes is better left to men–is the question of the difference *within* difference. Irigaray's wager is that difference can be reinvented, that the bogus difference of misogyny can be reclaimed to become a radical new difference that would present the first serious historical threat to the hegemony of the male sex. Irigaray's wager is that there is a *(la/une femme)* woman *in* femininity: "Beneath all these/her appearances, beneath all these/her borrowings and artifices, this other still sub-sists. Beyond all these/her forms of life or of death, still alive" *(Amante* 126). Mimesis is the term Irigaray appropriates from the vocabulary of philosophy to describe her strategy, transforming woman's masquerade, her so-called femininity into a means of reappropriating the feminine:

> *One must assume the feminine role deliberately. Which means already to convert a form of subordination into an affirmation, and thus to begin to thwart it. . . . To play with mimesis is thus, for a woman, to try to recover the place of her exploitation by discourse, without allowing herself to be simply reduced to it. It means to resubmit herself– inasmuch as she is on the side of the "perceptible," of "matter"–to "ideas," in particular to ideas about herself, that are elaborated in/by a masculine logic, but so as to make "visible," by an effect of playful repetition, what was supposed to remain invisible: the cover-up of a possible operation of the feminine in language. It also means to "unveil" the fact that, if women are such good mimics, it is because they are not simply resorbed in this function.* They also remain elsewhere. (This Sex 76)

Mimesis *(mimétisme)* in Irigaray has been widely and correctly interpreted as describing a parodic mode of discourse designed to deconstruct the discourse of misogyny through effects of amplification and rearticulation that work, in Mary Ann Doane's words, to "enact a defamiliarized version of femininity" (182). But there is yet another aspect of mimesis—a notoriously polysemic term[7]–which has been largely misread, and even repressed, because it involves a far more controversial and riskier operation, a transvaluation, rather than a repudiation of the discourse of misogyny, an effort to hold onto the baby while draining out the bathwater. For example, in *Le Corps-à-corps avec la mère,* Irigaray writes:

We are historically the guardians of the corporeal, we must not aban-
don this charge but identify it as ours, by inviting men not to make of
us their body, a guarantee of their body. (29)

Irigaray's use of the word mimesis mimes her strategy, bodies forth her wager, which might be described as an instance of what Derrida has termed pale-onymy: "the occasional maintenance of an *old name* in order to launch a new concept" (*Positions* 71). In the specific context of feminism the old mimesis, sometimes referred to as masquerade, names women's alleged talents at par-rotting the master's discourse, including the discourse of misogyny. At a second level, parrotting becomes parody, and mimesis signifies not a deluded mas-querade, but a canny mimicry. And, finally, in the third meaning of mimesis I am attempting to tease out of Irigaray's writings, mimesis comes to signify difference as positivity, a joyful reappropriation of the attributes of the other that is not in any way to be confused with a mere reversal of the existing phallo-centric distribution of power. For Irigaray, as for other new French anti-feminists, reversal–the coming into power of women which they view as the ul-timate goal of American-style feminists–leaves the specular economy she would shatter in place. The mimesis, as it were, a mimesis that recalls the original Platonic mimesis–does not signify a reversal of misogyny but an emer-gence of the feminine and the feminine can only emerge from within or beneath–to extend Irigaray's archeological metaphor–femininity, within which it lies buried. The difference within mimesis *is* the difference within difference.

III. Coming to Grips with Irigaray

Est-ce qu'il n'y a pas une fluidité
quelque déluge, qui pourrait ébranler
cet ordre social?
(Irigaray, Corps 81)
Où sont, au présent, les fluides?
(Irigaray, L'Oubli 35)

Few claims Irigaray has made for feminine specificity have aroused more virulent accusations of essentialism than her "outrageous" claim that woman enjoys a special relationship with the fluid. One of the earliest such assertions occurs in *This Sex Which Is Not One*, where in the heyday of "écriture féminine" Irigaray characterizes both women's writing and speech as fluid.

> *And yet that woman-thing speaks. But not "like," not "the same," not*
> *"identical with itself" nor to any x, etc. . . . It speaks "fluid."* (This Sex *111*)

So uncomfortable has this assertion made certain feminist theoreticians that they have rushed to ascribe it to Irigarayan mimicry as ironic
distancing, rather than to the positive form of mimesis I have delineated above:

> *Her association of femininity with what she refers to as the "real*
> *properties of fluids"–internal frictions, pressures, movement, a specific*
> *dynamics which makes a fluid nonidentical to itself–is, of course,*
> merely *an extension and a mimicking of a patriarchal construction of*
> *femininity. (Doane 104; emphasis added)*

And yet as Irigaray's linking up of feminine fluidity with flux, non-identity,
proximity, etc., indicates, the fluid is highly valorized in her elemental philosophy: "Why is setting oneself up as a solid more worthwhile than flowing as a
liquid from between the two [lips]" (*Passions* 18); "My life is nothing but the
mobile flexibility, tenderness, uncertainty of the fluid" (28).

Where then does this notion of the fluidity of the feminine, when not
the femininity of the fluid, come from? Undeniably it is appropriated from the
repertory of misogyny: "Historically the properties of fluids have been abandoned to the feminine" (*This Sex* 116). What is worse for the anti-essentialists, it
appears to emanate from an unproblematized reading out of the female body in
its hormonal instanciation. It is, indeed, triply determined by female physiology:

> *The anal stage is already given over to the pleasure of the "solid."*
> *Yet it seems to me that the pleasure of the fluid subsists, in women, far*
> *beyond the so-called oral stage: the pleasure of "what's flowing" within*
> *her, outside of her, and indeed among women. (*This Sex *140)*

> *The marine element is thus both the amniotic waters . . . and it is also,*
> *it seems to me, something which figures quite well feminine* jouissance.
> *(*Corps *49)*

The ontological primacy of woman and the fluid are for her one of the re-
presseds of patriarchal metaphysics; the forgetting of fluids participates in the

matricide that according to Irigaray's myth of origins founds Western culture: "He begins to be in and thanks to fluids" (*L'Oubli* 36).

Unquestionably then Irigaray's linking up of the fluid and the feminine rests on a reference to the female body.[8] The anti-essentialist would stop here, dismiss Irigaray's claims as misguided and turn away–and few of Irigaray's sharpest critics have bothered with the work published after 1977, which is to say the bulk of her writing.[9] In so doing they miss another and equally troublesome, but ultimately more interesting aspect of her work. And that is her reliance on the universe of science, notably physics (but also chemistry to the extent that the borders between them cannot always be clearly drawn) which enjoys a strange and largely unexamined privilege in Irigaray's conceptual universe.[10] Indeed, in her writings on the repressed feminine element of water the referential reality that Irigaray most ardently invokes to ground her assertions is not so much physiological as physical; it is on the rock of materialism and not of essentialism that Irigaray seeks to establish the truth of her claim. Thus, in an essay entitled "The Language of Man" she writes: "But still today this woma(e)n's language [*langage de(s) femme(s)*] is censured, repressed, ignored . . . even as the science of the dynamic of fluids already provides a partial interpretation of it" (*Parler* 290–91; see also 289). The real in Irigaray is neither impossible, nor unknowable: it is the fluid. Thus, further in the same essay, Irigaray insistently associates the fluid and the real, speaking of "the real of the dynamic of fluids" and "an economy of *real fluids*" (291).

Two remarks are in order here: first, given all that I have said before this new criticism of Irigaray may appear curious. But my desire in this paper is neither to "defend" Irigaray nor promote essentialism, but rather to de-hystericize the debate, to show how the obsessive focus on what is so loosely termed the *biological* has worked to impoverish the reading of as challenging and ambitious a thinker as is Irigaray. Second: there is, on the other hand, nothing particularly surprising from the perspective of anti-essentialism about the complicity of essentialism and scientism, in that both imply at least at some level a fundamental materialism. But because of the red flag (when it is not a red herring) of essentialism, the question of Irigaray's *mater*-ialism is never really addressed. It is as though certain feminists were more comfortable evacuating the body from the precincts of high theory–thereby, of course, reinforcing the very hierarchies they would dismantle–than carefully separating out what belongs to the body and what to the world of matter.

To say that science enjoys a special status in Irigaray's writings is not to say that science, the master discourse of our age, has escaped Irigaray's feminist critique. It has not. Laughter and anger are Irigaray's reactions to the supposed neutrality of scientific language, a form of writing which like all writing is inflected by gender but which more so than any other disclaims subjectivity. Science's failure to acknowledge the gendering of language results in its failures to adequately theorize that which it aligns with the feminine, notably the elements, notably the liquid. Thus, in "The 'Mechanics' of Fluids" Irigaray takes "science" to task for its failure to elaborate a "theory of fluids." And yet, in some of her more recent writings, while remaining highly critical of the ideology of science, she constantly invokes scientific theories as models, analogons for female sexuality. For example: rejecting as more adequate to male than to female sexuality the thermodynamic principles that underlie Freud's theory of libido, Irigaray writes:

> *Feminine sexuality could perhaps better be brought into harmony–*
> if one must evoke a scientific model–*with what Prigogine calls "dissi-*
> *pating" structures that operate via the exchange with the external*
> *world, structures that proceed through levels of energy. The organiza-*
> *tional principle of these structures has nothing to do with the search*
> *for equilibrium but rather with the crossing of thresholds. This would*
> *correspond to a surpassing of disorder or entropy without discharge.*
> *("Subject" 81; emphasis added)* [11]

Similarly, later in the same essay, Irigaray suggests that recent work in physics, as well as in linguistics, might shed light on the specificities of women's relationship to enunciation: "Some recent studies in discourse theory, *but in physics as well*, seem to shed light upon the locus from which one could or could not situate oneself as a subject of language production" (86; emphasis added). Whatever her questions to the scientists, and some of them–as in "Is the Subject of Science Sexed?"–are impertinent, Irigaray repeatedly attempts to anchor the truth of her theories in the latest scientific knowledge. She knows that scientific discourse is not neutral, but nevertheless she looks to it as the ultimate source of legitimation. Science is Irigaray's fetish.

Why then is science and especially physics privileged in Irigaray's writings? The answer emerges from a consideration of the pivotal role of Descartes in Irigaray's writings. As Moi has noted, the Descartes chapter in *Speculum* is located at the "exact center of the 'Speculum' section (and of the whole book). . . . Descartes sinks into the innermost cavity of the book" (131). This chapter is, as Moi further remarks, traditional at least in its presentation of the subject of the Cogito: the "I" of the Cogito is self-engendered, consti- tuted through a radical denial both of the other and of man's corporeal origins: "The 'I' thinks, therefore this thing, this body that is also nature, that is still the *mother*, becomes an extension at the 'I' 's disposal for analytical investigations, scientific projections, the regulated exercise of the imaginary, the utilitarian practice of technique" (*Speculum* 186). What is at stake here is the constitution of an ontology that excludes all considerations having to do with the physical world: "The same thing applies to the discussions of woman and women. Gynecology, dioptrics, are no longer by right a part of meta- physics–*that supposedly unsexed anthropos-logos whose actual sex is admitted only by its omission and exclusion from consciousness*, and by what is said in its margins" (*Speculum* 183). How surprising then to discover in *Éthique de la différence sexuelle* another Descartes, a Descartes whose treatise on the pas- sions of the soul contains the concept of admiration which fully realizes Irigaray's most cherished desire, the (re)connection of the body and the soul, the physical and the metaphysical:

> One must reread Descartes a bit and recall or learn how it is with movement in passions. One must meditate also on the fact that all philosophers–except for the most recent ones? why?–have always been physicists, have always rested their metaphysical research on or ac- companied it with the cosmological. . . . This cleavage between the physical sciences and thought doubtless represents that which threat- ens thought itself. (Éthique 75)

It is then in Descartes's treatise that Irigaray finds the alliance of the physical and the metaphysical, the material and the transcendental which rep- resents for her the philosophical ideal. Little matter that in elaborating his notion of admiration Descartes does not have sexual difference in mind: "Sexual difference could be situated here. But Descartes doesn't think of it. He simply asserts that what is different attracts" (*Éthique* 81); "He does not differentiate the passions according to sexual difference. . . . On the other hand he places admiration first among the passions. Passion forgotten by Freud? Passion which holds open a path between physics and metaphysics, corporeal impressions and movements toward an object be it empirical or transcendental" (*Éthique* 84). Thus in Irigaray, Descartes functions both as the philosopher who irrevocably sunders body from soul and the one who most brilliantly reunites them. Physics is here placed in service of Irigaray's radical materialism, her desire to return to a Presocratic (but also post-Nietzschean and -Bachelardian) apprehension of the four generic elements as foundational, which is–I repeat–not the same thing as essentialism.

But there is more: Irigaray's ultimate goal is not, so to speak, to put the physics back in metaphysics, but rather the ruining of the metaphysics of being through the substitution of a physics of the liquid for a physics of the solid. Heidegger names that moment in the history of philosophy when a possible questioning of the primacy of the solid remains earthbound, grounded in the very soil of metaphysics. The ruining of metaphysics is bound up with an anamnesis, a remembering of the forgotten elements:

> *Metaphysics always supposes, somehow, a solid earth-crust, from which a construction may be raised. Thus a physics which privileges or at least has constituted the solid plane. . . . So long as Heidegger does not leave the earth, he does not leave metaphysics. Metaphysics does not inscribe itself either on/in water, on/in air, on/in fire. . . . And its abysses, both above and below, doubtless find their interpretation in the forgetting of the elements which don't have the same density. The end of metaphysics would be prescribed by their reinvention in contemporary physics?* (L'Oubli *10*)

Finally, calling into question Irigaray's relationship to science returns us to the question of the institution, for what emerges from a reading of *Parler n'est jamais neutre* is that her interventions cannot be read without taking into account their institutional context. It is altogether striking in this regard to consider the difference between two of the most powerful essays in the volume, "The Misery of Psychoanalysis" and "Is the Subject of Science Sexed?" In the first of these essays, where Irigaray's addressees are the male guardians of the (Lacanian) psychoanalytic institution, her tone is from the outset self-assured, truculent, outraged. How different is the tone of her speech to the scientists. Addressing the members of the "Seminar on the history and sociology of scientific ideas and facts" of the University of Provence, Marseilles, Irigaray confesses to a rare attack of stage fright: "For a long time I have not experienced such difficulties with the notion of speaking in public" (74), she tells her audience. The problem is a problem of address: whereas the text to the analysis begins with a peremptory, "Messieurs les analystes," the speech to the scientists begins by interrogating the very act of address: "How does one talk to scientists?" (73).

Standing before the scientists Irigaray stands like a woman from the country before the law:

> *Anxiety in the face of an absolute power floating in the air, of an authoritative judgment: everywhere, yet imperceptible, of a tribunal, which in its extreme case has neither judge, nor prosecutor, nor accused. But the judicial system is in place. There is a truth there to which one must submit without appeal, against which one can commit violations . . . unwillingly or unknowingly. The supreme instance which is exercised against your will. (74–75)*

According to Derrida's reading of Kafka's parable there is no essential difference between the man from the country and the guardians of the law. Their positions in regard to the law are opposite but symmetrical: "The two protagonists are both attendant to the law but opposing one another" ("Devant" 139), writes Derrida. But what if the man from the country is replaced by a woman? Is there no essential difference between the woman from the country, here the feminist philosopher Luce Irigaray, and the guardians of the law, in this instance the scientists whose faculty is to a very large extent hegemonic in our universities today?[12] If the man from the country is replaced by a woman, can one so easily speak of positions that are opposite and *symmetrical* without risking relapsing into a logic of saming, precisely what Irigaray has called an "old dream of symmetry"?

There can be no easy answers to these questions which are immensely complicated by the very powerful interpretation Derrida has advanced of the law in Kafka's parable. If, however, Irigaray can be taken here as exemplifying the feminist intervention in the institution, then one can, however tentatively, discern the difference that women's studies can make: for instead of simply addressing the guardians of the law–if indeed any address is ever simple–Irigaray transforms the very conditions of the law's production and enforcement. In raising the question of the gender of the producers of knowledge, women's studies always involves a radical questioning of the conditions of the production and dissemination of knowledge, of the constitution of the disciplines, of the hierarchical ordering of the faculties within the institution. Further, by allying herself with the most radical elements in science, Irigaray points the way to what, paraphrasing Prigogine–who borrows the phrase from Jacques Monod–we might call a "new alliance" between women's studies and the law, one which would go beyond mere opposition. In other words, it is finally by insisting on the *dissymmetry* of the positions occupied by the guardians and the woman from the country in regard to the law, that women's studies, at least in its "utopian horizon," can never be "just another cell in the academic beehive."

What precedes is the revised text of a paper I delivered at a conference held at the University of Alabama, at Tuscaloosa, entitled, "Our Academic Contract: The Conflict of the Faculties in America." This conference has since achieved footnote status in the history of poststructuralism because it was on the occasion of this gathering that the scandal of Paul de Man's wartime journalism broke in the United States. I wish to thank Richard Rand for having invited me to participate in this event and Jacques Derrida for his response to my remarks, as well as for all his other gifts.

I also wish to thank the members of my feminist reading group– Christina Crosby, Mary Ann Doane, Coppélia Kahn, Karen Newman, Ellen Rooney–as well as Elizabeth Weed, Nancy K. Miller, and Kaja Silverman for their various forms of support and criticism.

Notes

1   When it was originally published in the Brown student journal, *subjects/objects*, in keeping with Derrida's wishes, the transcript of the seminar was prefaced by a cautionary disclaimer (reprinted in *Men in Feminism*) which I want to echo emphasizing the text's undecidable status, "somewhere between speech and writing," "authorized but authorless" (189). All references will be to the reprinted version of the text.

2   I refer here in turn to *Between Feminism and Psychoanalysis*, ed. Teresa Brennan, and Diana Fuss, *Essentially Speaking*, which started out as a dissertation at Brown University. The keynote to this new deal for essentialism was perhaps sounded in the footnote to a paper given at a recent feminist conference by Mary Russo who writes: "The dangers of essentialism in posing the female body, whether in relation to representation or to 'women's history' have been well stated, so well stated, in fact, that *anti-essentialism may well be the greatest inhibition to work in cultural theory and politics at the moment, and must be displaced*" (de Lauretis, *Feminist* 228; emphasis added).

3   Repeatedly in the course of an interview with James Creech, Peggy Kamuf, and Jane Todd, Derrida insists on the plural of deconstruction: "I don't think that there is something like *one* deconstruction"; ". . . it is difficult to define the *one* deconstruction [*la* déconstruction]. . . . Personally I would even say that its best interests are served by keeping that heterogeneity. . . ." ("Deconstruction" 4, 6). Finally, he concludes it is more accurate to speak of deconstructions than a singular deconstruction.

4   There is an extreme form of anti-essentialism, a candidate for a fifth critique, that argues that the replacement of woman by women does not solve but merely displaces the problem of essentialism. This is the position represented by Denise Riley who suggests in a chapter entitled, "Does Sex Have a History?": ". . . not only 'woman' but also 'women' is troublesome . . . we can't bracket off either 'Woman,' whose capital letter alerts us to her dangers, or the more modest lower-case 'woman,' while leaving unexamined the ordinary, innocent-sounding 'women'"(1). Cf. Donna Haraway who in her "A Manifesto for Cyborgs" remarks: "It is no accident that woman *disintegrates* into women in our time" (79; emphasis added). This is perhaps the place to comment on a critique whose conspicuous absence will surely surprise some: a *modern* Marxist critique of essentialism. I emphasize the word modern because of course Beauvoir's critique of essentialism in *The Second Sex* is heavily indebted to the Marxism she then espoused. Though the writings of Louis Althusser and Pierre Macherey, to cite the major Marxist theoreticians contemporaneous with Lacan and Derrida, inform some pioneering studies of female-authored fictions, they have not to my knowledge generated a critique of essentialism distinct from the critiques already outlined. This seeming absence or failure of a strong recent Marxist critique of essentialism is all the more surprising as clearly the critique of essentialism was at the outset appropriated by Beauvoir (and others) from Marxism. If Riley's book and Haraway's articles are at this point in time the only articulation we have of a post-modernist Marxist critique of essentialism then it might be said that for them the essentialist is one who has not read history.

5   Ironically, in rejecting the ideal of a universal subject in favor of a subject marked by the feminine, Irigaray has, like other bourgeois white feminists, only managed to relocate universality, to institute a new hegemony. The question that arises is: how to theorize a subjectivity that does not reinscribe the universal, that does not constitute itself by simultaneously excluding and incorporating others?

6   Irigaray's most explicit rejection of essentialism occurs in the "Veiled Lips" section of *Amante marine*, where she writes: "She does not for all that constitute herself as *one*. She

does not shut herself in [*se referme sur ou dans*] a truth or an essence. The essence of a truth remains foreign to her. She neither has nor is a being" (92). Irigaray's best defense against essentialism is the defiant plurality of the feminine; there can be no essence in a conceptual system that is by definition anti-unitary.

7 See Paul Ricoeur, "Mimesis and Representation," in *Annals of Scholarship*. Irigaray gives this polysemy full play, reminding us for example in a passage of *This Sex* that in Plato mimesis is double: "there is *mimesis* as production, which would lie more in the realm of music, and there is the *mimesis* that would be already caught up in a process of *initiation, specularization, adequation* and *reproduction*. It is the second form that is privileged throughout the history of philosophy. . . . The first form seems always to have been repressed. . . . Yet it is doubtless in the direction of, and on the basis of, that first *mimesis* that the possibility of women's writing may come about" (131). The question is, to paraphrase Yeats: how can you tell mimesis from mimesis?

8 In a brilliantly turned defense of Irigaray against her anti-essentialist critics, Jane Gallop cautions us against "too literal a reading of Irigarayan anatomy" (94). For example, when Irigaray speaks of the plural lips of the female sex, the word she uses, "lèvres," is a catachresis, an obligatory metaphor that effectively short-circuits the referential reading of the text: "Irigaray embodies female sexuality in that which, at this moment in the history of the language, is always figurative, can never be simply taken as the thing itself" (98). As brilliant as are Gallop's arguments against a naively referential reading of the Irigarayan textual body, in the end she recognizes that "the gesture of a troubled but nonetheless insistent referentiality" is essential to Irigaray's project of constructing a "non-phallomorphic sexuality" (99).

9 It is no accident that one of the most thoughtful and balanced recent articles on Irigaray is one which is based on a reading of her complete works, and not as many (though not all) of the highly critical analyses merely on the works currently available in translation; see Whitford.

10 On this point I would want to qualify Whitford's assessment of the place of science in Irigaray's discourse: "Her account of Western culture runs something like this. Our society is dominated by a destructive *imaginary* (whose apotheosis is the ideology of science elevated to the status of a privileged truth)" (5). My claim is that while condemning the imperialism of a neutered science, a science cut off from the life-giving female body, and which threatens us with "multiple forms of destruction of the universe" (*Éthique* 13; cf. the pronounced ecological strain in "Equal to Whom?" elsewhere in this volume), Irigaray continues to look to science as a locus of "privileged truth."

11 The reference here is to the Nobel prize–winning research by Ilya Prigogine on dissipative structures. For more on Prigogine's theories, whose influence on Irigaray has been significant, see Prigogine and Stengers. Shortly after I first presented this paper I received a letter from Katherine Hayles telling me that working out of the perspective of the relationship of

modern literature and science she had been struck "by certain parallels between the new scientific paradigms and contemporary feminist theory," notably that of Irigaray. I am most grateful to her for this precious confirmation of my argument.

12 The question of gender is raised by Derrida in his reading, but not as regards the "two protagonists." For Derrida what is problematic is the gender of the law, in German *das Gesetz* (neutral), in French *la loi* (feminine) ("Devant" 142).

Works Cited

Appiah, Anthony. "The Uncompleted Argument: Du Bois and the Illusion of Race." Gates 21–37.

Beauvoir, Simone de. *The Second Sex*. Trans. H. M. Parshley. New York: Knopf, 1970.

Brennan, Teresa, ed. *Between Feminism and Psychoanalysis*. New York: Routledge, 1989.

Christian, Barbara. "The Race for Theory." *Cultural Critique* 6 (1987): 51–63.

de Lauretis, Teresa. *Alice Doesn't: Feminism, Semiotics, Cinema*. Bloomington: Indiana UP, 1984.

_____, ed. *Feminist Studies/Critical Studies*. Bloomington, Indiana UP, 1986.

Derrida, Jacques. "Deconstruction in America: An Interview with Jacques Derrida." *Critical Exchange* 17 (1985): 1–33.

_____. "Devant lá loi." Trans. Avital Ronell. *Kafka and the Contemporary Critical Performance: Centenary Readings*. Ed. Alan Udoff. Bloomington: Indiana UP, 1987. 128–49.

_____. *Positions*. Trans. Alan Bass. Chicago: U of Chicago P, 1981.

_____. "Women in the Beehive: A Seminar with Jacques Derrida." *subjects/objects* 2 (1984): 5–19. Rpt. in *Men in Feminism*. Ed. Alice Jardine and Paul Smith. New York: Methuen, 1987. 189–203.

Doane, Mary Ann. *The Desire to Desire: The Woman's Film of the 1940s*. Bloomington: Indiana UP, 1987.

Fuss, Diana. *Essentially Speaking: Feminism, Nature and Difference*. New York: Routledge, 1989.

Gallop, Jane. "Lip Service." *Thinking Through the Body*. New York: Columbia UP, 1988. 92–99.

Gates, Henry Louis, Jr., ed. *"Race," Writing, and Difference*. Chicago: U of Chicago P, 1986.

Haraway, Donna. "A Manifesto for Cyborgs: Science, Technology, and Socialist Feminism in the 1980s." *Socialist Review* 80 (1985): 65–107. Rpt. in *Coming to Terms: Feminism, Theory, Politics.* Ed. Elizabeth Weed. New York: Routledge, 1989, 173–204.

hooks, bell. *Ain't I a Woman: Black Women and Feminism.* Boston: South End, 1981.

Irigaray, Luce. *Amante marine, de Friedrich Nietzsche.* Paris: Minuit, 1980.

_____. *Le Corps-à-corps avec la mère.* Montreal: Pleine Lune, 1981.

_____. *Éthique de la différence sexuelle.* Paris: Minuit, 1984.

_____. "Is the Subject of Science Sexed?" Trans. Edith Oberle. *Cultural Critique* 1 (1985): 73-88.

_____. *Je, tu, nous: Pour une culture de la différence.* Paris: Grasset, 1990.

_____. "L'Ordre sexuel du discours." *Langages* 85 (1987): 81–123.

_____. *L'Oubli de l'air chez Martin Heidegger.* Paris: Minuit, 1983.

_____. *Parler n'est jamais neutre.* Paris: Minuit, 1985.

_____. *Passions élémentaires.* Paris: Minuit, 1982.

_____. *Speculum of the Other Woman.* Trans. Gillian C. Gill. Ithaca: Cornell UP, 1985.

_____. *This Sex Which Is Not One.* Trans. Catherine Porter with Carolyn Burke. Ithaca: Cornell UP, 1985.

Lacan, Jacques. *Feminine Sexuality: Jacques Lacan and the école freudienne.* Ed. Juliet Mitchell and Jacqueline Rose. Trans. Jacqueline Rose. New York: Norton, 1982.

Miller, Nancy K. "Changing the Subject: Authorship, Writing, and the Reader." De Lauretis 102–20.

Moi, Toril. *Sexual/Textual Politics: Feminist Literary Theory.* London: Methuen, 1985.

Pratt, Mary Louise. "Scratches on the Face of the Country: Or, What Mr. Barrow Saw in the Land of the Bushmen." Gates 138–63.

Prigogine, Ilya, and Isabelle Stengers. *La Nouvelle alliance: Métamorphose de la science.* Paris: Gallimard, 1979.

Reese, William J. *Dictionary of Philosophy and Religion: Eastern and Western Thought.* Atlantic Highlands: Humanities, 1980.

Ricoeur, Paul. "Mimesis and Representation." *Annals of Scholarship* 2 (1981): 15–32.

Riley, Denise. *"Am I that Name?" Feminism and the Category of "Women" in History.* Minneapolis: U of Minnesota P, 1988.

Whitford, Margaret. "Luce Irigaray and the Female Imaginary: Speaking as a Woman." *Radical Philosophy* 43 (1986): 3–8.

LUCE IRIGARAY
TRANSLATED BY ROBERT L. MAZZOLA

Equal to Whom?

"Equal to Whom?" is ostensibly a review of Elisabeth Schüssler Fiorenza's 1983 work, In Memory of Her: A Feminist Theological Reconstruction of Christian Origins. *In her article, Irigaray makes use of the French translation by Marcelline Brun which appeared in 1986. Her "review" becomes an extension and further development of themes she has previously explored in other* Critique *articles: "Femmes divines" and "Les femmes, le sacré, l'argent." Readers as unacquainted with liberation theology as I was before undertaking to translate the present essay are referred to Schüssler Fiorenza's* Bread Not Stone: The Challenge of Feminist Biblical Interpretation *as well as to* In Memory of Her. *The former text makes explicit such vital notions as "women-church" (ekklesia gynaikon), the "household code," and "androcentrism" as they relate directly to a "hermeneutics of suspicion."*

I am grateful to Luce Irigaray for permission to translate her essay and have it appear in differences.

I would also like to thank Jeannette Ludwig of SUNY at Buffalo for her insightful reading of the first draft of this translation and for her many helpful suggestions. R.L.M.

I began reading Elisabeth Schüssler Fiorenza's *In Memory of Her* with astonishment and joy. At last something new on Christianity! Being a Christian (male or female) might no longer relate solely to the doctrines we have been taught most if not all the time and up until the present. This new dimension would stem from the fact–one among others if the phrase "among others" can still be used–that from the beginning of the Church, of the Christian community, women were equal disciples, "ministers" in their own right. They were not mere assistants, allowed to participate at designated moments in religious ceremonies, but actual celebrants, notably of the Eucharist, just as men and Jesus were.

When I think of all the arguments I have heard against the admission of women to the priesthood, Schüssler Fiorenza's views let in a breath of fresh air and a bit of spirit as well. Aren't these rational yokes precisely what bring about the paralysis of the slightest breath of spirit? As Kazantzaki's St. Francis of Assisi put it: the devil must be nowhere more in evidence than in Rome, given the number of religious purges that go on there.

What led Schüssler Fiorenza to this affirmation of the equality among the disciples of Jesus is a feminist critical approach to the establishment and interpretation of fundamental Christian texts and a feminist reconstruction of History. This means that we must interpret what we know of Christian order through a hypothesis of blanks, lacunae, overdeterminations, and persistent blindspots inherent in the patriarchal bias of History. That bias leaves its mark on the discernible historical facts and their practical outcome, as well as on theological truths and imperatives. The bias would be more Greco-Roman than Judeo-Christian. Doubtless Schüssler Fiorenza expresses some reservations concerning such theological expressions, but she speaks of the Jesus movement as "a Jewish movement that is part of Jewish history in the first century" (105). She also writes that "the praxis and vision of Jesus and his movement is best understood as an inner-Jewish renewal movement that presented an alternative option to the dominant [Greco-Roman] patriarchal structures rather than an oppositional formation rejecting the values and praxis of Judaism" (107).

I can find little with which to agree concerning these scissions for different reasons, notably the reduction of several periods in history to a *single* one and the possibility of conjoining and opposing them as a result of this a priori reduction. In reality there is no *one* Judaism and certainly no one Judeo-Christian tradition. As far as Judaism itself is concerned, it is divided into discrete eras, each with its particular characteristics. A re-reading of the Old Testament confirms the differences between Genesis and Exodus. Yet this is but a modest indication! Doesn't reducing Judaism to *one* amount to restricting the Israelites to a definition based on their reversals, limited to the horizon of their extinction, rather than affirming their complex history in which is situated, for example, the link between written law and God's disappearance from the field of human perception? According to that interpretation, Jesus would be the God present to the senses of living mortals, the divine made perceptible again through touch, sight, sound, and smell, possibly even taste mediated by smell and the fruits of the earth.[1] An amalgam of the very different epochs of the theophany runs the risk of falling into a state of fascination, a very ambiguous relationship to the Israelite and Christian peoples that is difficult for me to define. Such a reduction risks a progressive closing-off of the pathway to an understanding of those religious phenomena on which neither Jew nor Christian holds the monopoly. Moreover, how can one speak of the Judeo-Christian tradition without drawing extremely fine distinctions since the events in the life of Jesus do not generally carry the same meaning for Jews as they do for Christians? Doesn't this either force the hand of Judaism or else abolish Christianity? Doesn't it minimalize the gap between the divine which can be represented and those aspects of it which cannot? Either a *single* God or none? Doesn't it also overlook the difference in the languages used by these traditions and its impact on meaning, beyond the lack of homogeneity in the use to which these languages are put at various stages in their history? And further, doesn't this ignore the fact that Christianity is in principle not attached to an entire people and much more apolitical than Judaism, etc.?

Besides, what does it mean when Jews and Christians–supposedly less patriarchal or non-patriarchal–are set in opposition to the Greeks and Romans who, in their turn, are viewed as more patriarchal? The Greeks above all, but also the Romans, exhibit a non-patriarchal side to their histories; thus the ages of Aphrodite and the cult of Demeter were neither patriarchal nor simply mythical. They had their own institutions and singular laws, especially as concerned the ownership of property, the transmittal of names . . . and the relationship to the religious.[2] In the beginning divine truth was vouchsafed to women and passed on from mother to daughter. These ages of the divine accompanied the fertility of the earth, its flowers and fruit, and did not dissociate the human and the divine, body and mind, the natural and the spiritual. During those times love was respected in its corporeal manifestations, female fecundity took place both in and outside of marriage, and the public weal was the norm. It is certainly unrealistic to imagine that we could, by an act of determination, bring back the economy of such past eras; but it seems indispensable that we think of them as epochs that do not equate to chaos, to an archaic prehistory of myths and legends. Eras existed when female laws held sway and they possessed their own religions. To proceed to a feminist critical method and reconstruction of History would require close inspection of these women's reigns so as to interpret their qualities and characteristics in order also to come to an understanding of how and why those periods of history were censored by the phallocratic patriarchy, and what is left of them, etc. In any event, this sort of investigation into the nature of gynecocratic ages prohibits the kind of cultural opposition that Elisabeth Schüssler Fiorenza draws between the Judeo-Christian and the Greco-Roman. Such an investigation calls on us to question our Indo-European legacy, our links to the Orient, our relations to those areas of our civilization where the status of women, and men too for that matter, as divine are conceived of in different terms.

From the same perspective, I would question the female genealogy of Jesus, the importance of women in his life and his mysterious relationship with his father. Is Jesus the equivalent of the most radical entrenchment of the patriarchy, upheld by non-figurative writing? Does he represent an attempt at reconciling the Indo-European and Semitic traditions? Or does he claim to appropriate all such traditions to himself or sum them all up in his person? In Hölderlin's phrase, "Christ is the end." What remains is the unresolved problem of woman's divinity. Being a mother is but one possible mode of woman's service to Jesus; he lacks a wife. Defining her as the Church, as Israel is defined as the bride of Yahweh, is tantamount to saying that Christ is wed to his work alone, which is not the fulfillment of humanity but a model of the patriarchal and the phallocratic. And if Jesus is seen as the totality of Mankind understood generically, then he is both man and woman, a kind of androgyny. Mircea Eliade analyzes the myths of androgyny as Mephistophelean myths. Thus representing Christ, and by extension God, as human totality would confuse him with the Evil One or with an epoch that was in league with him.

But Jesus refuted the notion of himself as this totality when he affirmed that, in order for the spirit to come into the world, he must die. The accepted Church interpretation of Jesus often disregards the fact that he is a bridge. The unanswered question remains: A bridge from whom to whom? From what to what? And what becomes of him when he is locked into patriarchal archetypes with their imperatives of belief and their denegation of all mythology? Since both patriarchy and phallocracy represent myths in action, as do all cultures, doesn't denying this fact lead to a perversion of the spirit and to the cutting off of humanity from its most important realization?

Christian patriarchal order seems indeed nearer to gloomy and repressive reason than to a celebration of the joy of a human incarnation of the divine. Even the happy celebration of the Eucharist becomes an obligatory rite under the menace of sin. Nothing could be farther removed from Christ's invitation to share with him the fruits of the earth and to continue with this celebration after he is gone. It is true that Christ attracted the multitude without making demands upon them. Except in the case of those whom he had chosen as his disciples and who had accepted that role? And even from those . . . He demanded that they be available. With that said, those (men and women) who followed him did so of their own volition and not under the onus of a strict discipline. Those men and women who followed him also transgressed the interdictions of their society and culture rather than submit to the existing religious code. Thus Jesus instructed women and pagans, and preached in the open more often than in the temples. In any event, he didn't preach very much, nor did he spend much time poring over sacred texts. However, he did a lot of curing, consoled many, restored both the life of the body and of the spirit, and gave back dignity to those who had lost it, whether they were rich or poor. For Christ isn't just the Lord of the poor as today's preachers rather complacently tell us. He could use strong words to demonstrate his disapproval of the idolatry of the poor: "for you always have the poor with you . . . but me you do not always have." These are the words he offered about a woman who sprinkled perfume over him and whom Jesus's followers reproached for being "wasteful." This is what Schüssler Fiorenza evokes in *In Memory of Her*, sometimes more through her book's title than by virtue of its content. In this instance, Jesus very pointedly chose the woman and not the poor. Did he perhaps single out those (men and women) whom the patriarchy was oppressing?

Having said all that, woman's role in the Gospels really isn't as "central" as Schüssler Fiorenza would have us believe. It is Jesus himself who is at the center, surrounded by women, it's true. But it seems to me naive, demagogical (or maybe a mark of matriarchal acculturation) to say that women were "at the center" of Jesus's life. Yet neither were they excluded from most religious traditions. They took part in public and semi-private relations with Jesus, dinners among friends, festivals and the like. For the most part they were there when he preached and worked miracles; they were present in every aspect of his life: women were privately closer to Jesus than were other pagans. The manner in which women are described in the Bible is more characteristic of the Cult of Aphrodite than of that of Dionysus in which, generally speaking, women are exploited by the god.[5] Mary Magdalene is an example of this. I am not surprised that Luke's interpretation in the Gospel should confuse the woman Schüssler Fiorenza quotes at the beginning of her book with Mary Magdalene herself. Her anointment strikes me as a loving one. She loves Jesus as she attests in public and quite apart from marriage as in the non-Demeterian gynecocratic traditions. But is it a question of "propheticism" or memory? Does free love in its divine form come before or after Jesus?

In the same vein, can it be said that Jesus takes an interest in women because they are disenfranchised or because they are women? The angle of approach is different here, it seems to me. The fact that women turn out to be the poor in patriarchal and phallocratic regimes doesn't mean they got that way naturally as a result of their sex. That said, in women's time the money poor didn't exist. The only ones disenfranchised were those who had neither fruits nor vegetables and later, grain. Patriarchy and monetary poverty go hand in hand. Gynecocratic cultures succumb to this yoking only where they subsist as part of that patriarchy itself. From this perspective arises the question of Israel's history, fraught with cosmic catastrophes and continual famine through Exodus and Exile, and all the transformations that land has undergone relative to the fruitful earth. What is the significance of men's appropriation of the divine in relation to a respect for the earth, its culture, and world famine?

In this regard, how can we interpret the place of Jesus of Nazareth? His position is complex and contradictory. Attentive to the fruits of the earth to the point of becoming one with them, he nonetheless leads a semi-nomadic life and chooses for his disciples fishers, not gatherers or farmers. One thing is certain: his teachings cannot be reduced to those of one whose generosity toward the little people knows no bounds. Within these parameters, it is short work to classify Christianity as part and parcel of all the rest, a sort of good boy-bad boy socialism depending on the country, region, or culture in question.

Schüssler Fiorenza's position comes close to such a socio-economic appraisal of the Gospels. I think her interpretation is too reductive when it comes to the question of a possible theology of women's liberation. Women aren't just poor among the poor. As half of the human race, it is their exploitation that makes it possible to exploit others. This exploitation is primarily cultural and only secondarily socio-economic.

But is Christianity a religion based on a love of the poor and the hope of salvation for the ignorant? While far and away preferable to exploitation and disdain, these qualities of Christianity strike me as but one of its aspects or effects. It is the social outcome of the respect for the incarnation of all bodies (men's and women's) as potentially divine; nothing more nor less than each man and each woman being virtually gods. If Christ's redemption of the world lacks this meaning, then I see no other worthy of such historical loyalty.

However, this message, especially as it concerns women, is most often veiled, obscured, covered over. And while the message is certainly not explicit on all these points, that is no reason to pass over it in silence. There are times in the life of Jesus when his relations with women are quite clear. Thus his public following is made up equally of men and women. Aside from the twelve apostles, Jesus speaks to women just as much as to men, and in numerous instances the Gospels relate his public spiritual exchanges with women. He discusses truth with them and occasionally decides in their favor against the existing social order, particularly on the question of the "gentiles," as Schüssler Fiorenza points out. Certainly original with Christianity is the notion of gentiles (and perhaps it is women who represent their obscure paradigm) having access to the benefits of redemption. Thus Jesus instructs women, but he also listens to them and succumbs to the force of their confidence and faith, understood not as belief but as the power of affirmation, especially in matters of spiritual receptivity and sharing (Schüssler Fiorenza, *Memory* 140–54).

Contrary to the socio-cultural norms of his time, Christ approaches both women and men with the same freedom founded on wisdom rather than on logical reasoning. Read or reread the Gospels and try to find the logic of Jesus's words; he continually contradicts everything he says. Is this indicative of the impotence of an age in transition, or is it these contradictions that allow his message to rise above understanding? It's touching but also revolting to hear most priests argue over Christ's contradictions in the language of everyday rationality. The Good News turns to moral platitude or falls into a social bathos bearing little resemblance to the teachings of Jesus, as far as I can see. The irrational in Jesus leads to the liberation of the spirit, not to love, not to nothingness or the spiritual and mystical torture that probably originates in the stifling or paralysis of becoming, particularly along sexual lines.

On this point concerning contradiction, the course of Jesus's life appears close to the teachings of certain Indian sages, the Buddha, for example. They resemble one another on other points as well, including the fact that spiritual becoming and corporeal becoming are inseparable. Every stage in the life of Christ is noted and described in the Gospels as an event of the body: conception, birth, growth, fasting in the desert, immersion in the River Jordan, treks to the mountain or walks along the water's edge, meals, festivals, the laying-on of hands, the draining of physical strength after a healing, transfiguration, trials, suffering, death, resurrection, ascension. . . . His life cannot be reduced to speeches given in closed, airless structures, or to repetitive rituals and disincarnation, or to the unsaid, to abstractions of the flesh, or arguing fine distinctions in which the body is lost to lessons in tact. It cannot be reduced to moral injunctions or to debates among clerics. . . . Jesus disliked this. He said so. His words are in the Gospels. He made the point many times. Then why is there so much deafness? Why so many misunderstandings in handing down his story, his memory?

For me the best hypothesis here, the one most in keeping with the accounts of Jesus's life, is that women, who were his witnesses as much as men, were eliminated from all evidence relating to him. The history of the distancing of women from the announcement and sharing of the word and from the practice of the sacraments is patiently and informatively described by Schüssler Fiorenza in *In Memory of Her*. She discusses the first disciples' arguments on the subject and Peter's position in particular. She describes what things were like concerning women's rights and contributions within the missionary communities of Paul's time. She relates how women founded house churches and explains how women and men became the children of God through baptism, while circumcision separated the sexes as far as religion was concerned. And on this point, she recalls that becoming a Christian cannot correspond to racial, family, clan, or national rights, since it comes about as the result of the sacrament of baptism which is made available to all (men and women). And it is a baptism that assures individual salvation and access to a religious community. Schüssler Fiorenza distinguishes the theological rights and duties of Christ's male and female disciples from their evolution and transformation following the patriarchalization of the Church. And so on.

Schüssler Fiorenza recounts and explains many things which clarify the status of Christian theology today. I am giving only a very imperfect account of her book. Any cultivated person, but above all any evangelical community, ought to take the time to read *In Memory of Her*. Several hours spent reading her seem far more indispensable than attending some supplemental sermon which, according to the complaints of some clerics, no one (man or woman) understands anyway. It never occurs to these priests, who blame their parishioners for not listening, for their lack of attention and application, that the problem may lie in the image the preacher is projecting. It is true that these ignorant unfortunate Christians (men and women) find themselves in such a muddle of undifferentiated persons, intermediary personal pronouns and possessives, that it's no wonder they fail to know who is who, who is speaking to whom and about whom or what, with all those "ones," those "I" 's uttered in place of you, those "we" 's uttered instead of God, and so forth. Loss of identity is thereby assured, and I refuse to liken it to the communion of saints, if such a thing exists. This subjective dejection that quickly threatens the loss of all spiritual drive, is accompanied today for Christians by the prospect of "martyrdom," the need for a "baptism by blood," rather than by spirit, and announced on the occasion of John the Baptist's feast day.

None of this keeps them from preaching the Gospel in a neutral/neuter fashion on Christmas Day in Notre Dame. Indeed, the whole effect is one of great coherence. That Christmas sermon signed "Paris," based on an Evangelical text relating the childhood of Jesus, spoke of nothing else but the neutral incarnation of the word. I'm sure that the most advanced technocracy will have recognized in it the source and tone of its driving force. I'm certain, too, that cultivated (?) Parisians and carefree tourists from all nations can patronize a God one day a year. But is this about Jesus of Nazareth? And what modern turn of mind necessitates the selection of this particular text and sermon? I see two possibilities: the more or less conscious pressure brought to bear by women's liberation movements and the fear of offending the faithful of other traditions. Actually, at that crowded Christmas afternoon service in Notre Dame, no apparition occurred. There wasn't so much as a trace of the birth of God made man, and no incarnation save the choice of text, the voice of the preacher, and the congregation gathered there. No one and nothing else.

This is obviously scandalous from the point of view of a possible feminine or feminist theology. Women, already made submissive to God the Father and God made Man for centuries (sometimes under pain of a martyrdom inflicted by clerical authorities), find themselves by virtue of ecclesiastic decree, through whatever "good will," once again submitted to a neutral God. Up until now they haven't even been freed from motherhood, their only share in the redemption of the world. Out of the question to speak of their divinity as women. But also no images of the divine mother. No more incarnation either. Is this the work of science . . . or . . . ?

Is this how Christians see themselves as adults? Why invite the people to a celebration of the Eucharist on Christmas day if not to glorify the felt, the corporeal and fleshly advent of the divine, this coming, all the consequences of which theology seems far from understanding. Was it the calling of theology to turn away or mask the probing mind? Is that the Christian way?

As far as the neuter is concerned, who or what allows us to cancel out the difference between the sexes in a Catholic church today? Is this Paradise with no more men or women? It's a false impression. And may God or gods keep me (us) from its realization! And should most of the clergy refuse to acknowledge the importance of sexuality, it would only be fitting for them to give up on the theology of incarnation. Do you know of any asexual life? Just because the Patriarchy takes bets on a life after death and on the neutrality (neuterness) of the logos, doesn't mean that we should, in Christ's name, renounce our respect for life. Such a respect is integral to the witness he bore. Either his time is at an end, and so it's best not to continue exploiting him, even in his death, or else that time has barely come into its own as the result of an effacement of the sexual significance of his message. While other periods in history could afford to avoid that meaning, ours does so at the risk of sinking into absurdity and despair. The pathos of absurdity, so prized by the rich in our culture, leads whole peoples into a sort of profoundly depressing, really almost melancholy, state of unrest and aggression. Haven't they been deprived both of the organizing force of their own societies and of their God(s)? Have they concocted something better for their individual and collective well-being? Money? Apparently the masses are not satisfied with the substitution. A cultivation of the sexual, a spiritualization and divinization of the flesh, remain. Christ is the manifestation of only a part of this: he is God made man. But at least he's flesh and blood, living in the confines of a body and therefore sexual. He openly displays the sexual side of his relations with people. And while we know nothing of his private life, what is there about it that we ought to know? If it is true that certain sacred erotic models remove taboos surrounding sexuality and aid in its cultivation, should public teaching always be accompanied by some revelation of the instructor's private life? What perverseness, what lack of maturity, what childishness makes us want to witness the amorous behavior of those in authority in our society? By means of what narrow interpretation of the flesh do we underestimate instances of chastity as stages along the way to carnal wisdom? Apparently

Christ wasn't married. Are we sure that is all we know about it? Why do we want it to be so? Perhaps because we want to avoid the duties that go along with sexual responsibility. Isn't this because we see our relationship to sexuality, and to nature, as the last irreducible reality of our lives as human beings? Of course, this view of nature and sexuality is conditioned upon their realization, not as a destiny or a fault, but as a locus of creation, creation of ourselves as body and flesh.

So is that the reason we ask why Christ's sexuality should have been that of a married man? Isn't marriage, first and foremost, the affair of matriarchs and patriarchs? Isn't it a matter of goods and property rights, names and family privileges, with no necessary connection to the divine? And isn't this so even if matriarchal solutions generally seem closer to the divine than do others as a result of their respect for all life, nature, and truth? Besides, Jesus takes a stand concerning the institution of marriage when he considers the question of divorce and the resurrection of the dead (see pages 143–44 for Schüssler Fiorenza's comments on Mark 10.2–9 and 18–27). He does not call upon his followers to marry. Far from suggesting some more or less obscure and perverse chasteness, this lack of allegiance to the institution of marriage may be significant as a resistance to the patriarchal structures set into place at that time. It may also denote a wish to maintain the cult of Aphrodite, to draw one example from our cultural heritage. The cult could potentially be closer to the divine as it allows all (men and women) the possibility of celebrating their love without the need for human social contracts or even a dowry. Along those lines, Mary, Mother of Jesus, might represent Aphrodite, being pregnant outside of marriage and protected as such by the angels and birds of heaven. Other women–Mary Magdalene, the other Mary, etc.–are closer to the aphrodisiac traditions than to others. As for Jesus, he claims to bring the sword, or dissension, to the family (though not among all its members, it's true: the mother-son relationship seems to be spared this, a fact that Schüssler Fiorenza fails to mention [145–46]). However, their relationship is called into question as concerns Mary's privileged status as Jesus's mother vis-à-vis his other women disciples. This is a question which Schüssler Fiorenza does indeed point out (147). We should also recall that "fathers" are not part of Jesus's entourage, of his mixed "family of disciples" (147). This seems cruelly ironic, given that the history of the Church goes counter to this pattern as it ceaselessly (as Nietzsche has it?) covers over the meaning of Jesus's life.

The denegation of Christ's incarnation as a sexual being and the use to which that denial is put in the service of sexual hierarchization and exploitation seem to have blocked an understanding of that sexual nature and confined it to the province of the patricians and Pharisees. This is what I find most compelling in Schüssler Fiorenza's theological-historical argument. But, having said that, I think it's something else that interests me in part, namely the fact that a theology of women's liberation establishes as its priority not equal access to the priesthood, but rather an equal share in the divine. This means that what I see as a manifestation of sexual liberation is God made a couple: man and woman and not simply God made man.

Might Christ be the harbinger of this living reality? Why is his sexual incarnation denied or else treated on a human plane alone? To answer these questions, I would call upon the work done by Schüssler Fiorenza in *In Memory of Her* in order to formulate the hypothesis that this denial results from the exclusion of women from preaching the Gospels and from the priesthood. I believe that their lack of an "equal footing" among the disciples and their exclusion from the duties of preaching and the practice of the sacraments weigh heavily on the interpretation of the life of Jesus. At the very least the question has to be asked. Even if it should be necessary to redefine Christ as an exclusively patriarchal figure, it remains important to question why the Christian Church excluded women as ministers, if indeed they were excluded. Actually, this exclusion has been rationalized and has had a profound effect on the way the tradition has been handed down. Moreover, it has probably contributed to the cult of Christ's suffering, which has little to do with the life of Jesus of Nazareth apart from the accident of his passion and death. Jesus' life wasn't a particularly sad one, nor was it filled with drunkenness and debauchery as some would have us believe. His way of life approached wisdom.

That is to say, apart from his relation to the Father? But what does the Father mean to him anyway? And how could he have reconciled such an exclusive loyalty toward that patriarchal paradigm with his oddly liberal attitude toward women? Are we to suspect him of being Machiavellian? Because, after all, it is quite easy to dismiss him as his Father's son or as a member of a male trinity. Yet will that resolve the question of his incarnation? I think not. But I do believe that the question ought to be subjected to women's interpretation and considered a step toward becoming divine (for men and women). Otherwise Jesus truly does represent the realization of the Patriarchy, the appearance of the father's and the Father's power, the phenotype of a genotype glimpsed in the Word, since the father, unlike the mother, propagates outside himself and in a way that remains invisible. Thus, in order to affirm the reign of the father, it became necessary to eliminate the divine phenomenality of the daughter, of the mother-daughter couple, and lock it into the father-Father-son-Son genealogy and the triangle, father-son-holy spirit.

If this is the case, what interest can women have in being disciples or priests at all? The important thing is for them to find their own genealogy, the necessary condition for their identity. And saying that Jesus is the son of God-Sophia, as Schüssler Fiorenza has (134), doesn't suffice, or suffices only to confirm the end of gynecocratic genealogy, the son descended from the mother-daughter line. This being the case, it marks the appropriation of the daughter's divine status and of the mother-daughter relationship. This would mean that Jesus entrusts his mother to John and not to a woman at the moment of his death. Thus Jesus would stand for the erection of the system of patriarchal structures at the crossroads of the Greek and Semitic traditions at least. His defense at the hands of some American feminists would be rather comical! It is true that a great many European feminists know little of his life. They hope to be done with these religious traditions without having gauged their impact on the societies in which they live. They often imagine that equality in the workplace and in (neuter?) science will grant them sufficient status as subjects. This strikes me as quite an ingenuous error since they still lack what's needed to define their own socio-cultural identity. Many are ready to give up the little they have in order to bring about their neutralization by means of an identification with the generic masculine: they want to be "men" or "man." I wonder if something of this kind isn't secretly at work in Schüssler Fiorenza's book, given the short shrift she gives the divinization of sex in the history of Christianity.

The last chapter of *In Memory of Her* is a call for the overall reconciliation of women: Catholics, Jews, Mormons, black, white, or homosexual, which already takes into account a mixture of women's communities. But what is not clearly laid out is the conditions under which these "people of God" can get together. Though an appeal to the *ekklesia* of women is exciting, I am well enough acquainted with women's movements to know that they lack a rallying point. What they lack, at the very least, is the symbol of a divine mother. The so-called "people of God" are a people of men gathered in the name of the father, their father. What women need is a symbolic mother of daughters–woman-mother and lover–and not a mother of sons whose predications are defined by the incest taboo among others. Besides, women cannot make up their own communities removed from choices concerning History. This is why I don't believe that those women who reject the meaning of the incarnation of Christ are ready to come together in the name of sisterhood. And the same is true for those of other religions. In order for women truly to come together, there must be a reinterpretation of the meaning of all religious traditions and an examination of those which leave room for the genealogies of holy women.

Moreover, is it possible to put together the *ekklesia* of women as the "body of Christ"? Is this merely the manifestation of a zealous and pious desire? After all, Christ is not of our sex the way he is part of men's, of the people of men. And it is on selected numbers of them that the privilege of the ministry was conferred. This reality of a human and divine identity is in all likelihood the driving force behind centuries of religious law. Monotheistic religions speak to us of God the Father and God made man; nothing is said of a God the Mother or of God made Woman, or even of God as a couple or couples. Not all the transcendental fancies, or ecstasies of every type, not all the quibbling over maternity and the neutrality (neuterness) of God, can succeed in erasing this one reality that determines identities, rights, symbols, and discourse. It is for this reason that I've suggested that the divine incarnation of Jesus Christ is a partial one; a view which, in any event, is consistent with his own. "If I am not gone, the Paraclete cannot come." Why not? What coming of the Paraclete can be involved here, since Jesus is already the result of its work? We do not know the incarnation of the spirit, but the notion of a holy spirit as the pure product of patriarchal culture seems erroneous in view of Jesus's personality. His behavior toward women, in conjunction with his personal qualities, is evocative of a resistance to the patriarchy. Moreover, it is impossible for God to represent three instances of the masculine only as one aspect of the divine. That would be tantamount to ascribing divinity to men and the profane to women. This division, which certain men and women do not hesitate to consider the norm, has not always existed, nor has it always been the same. In the great Oriental traditions, a female trilogy exists alongside the male and, in their movements and their stability, neither one exists without the other.

However, insofar as a respect for the identity and dignity of women is concerned, two bridges must be established or re-established. One is the bridge consisting of the mother-daughter relation; the other is that of feminine identity. It is impossible to ask a woman to be holy, absolved of blame, as long as she is unable to recognize the potential holiness of her own mother. God made man or God the father are not enough to sanctify the female sex. All those women who have progressed by virtue of the risks and not merely the claims of women's liberation (starting with their own), understand the truth of this statement regardless of the difficulties and suffering it has imposed on them. But these trials are no longer synonymous with a collective pathos. They are born of women's need to be and remain vigilant, careful, and aware, in order to free their bodies and their sensibilities and make them accessible to the intellect and the spirit. It's the path we take "in memory of her" and, if possible, of him. This requires us to let go of those secondary benefits, those attachments and habits, that are correlates of the modus operandi of society as it now exists.

As things stand, how can we ask a priest to absolve us of a sin defined as such by a so-called Christian religion unless he himself is aware of the harm done to a woman who is preached to about God the Father and God made man alone, about a masculine Holy Spirit and about her function as the mother of sons. If today's Catholic religion involves only men and their mother-wives, perhaps it might make better sense to exclude from the churches those other women who cannot find any identity of their own there. Otherwise they ought to be advised that they have to find models for themselves other than those which have been proposed. They ought to be reminded that the Church may provide them with a possible stepping-stone but not with the truth. Without such warnings, welcoming them into the Church exposes their religious openness to constant frustration and a succession of pathological effects that result from it.

Why is it that Catholicism is not in accord with the conduct of Jesus Christ? Why does it provide such a minimal public presence to Mary, Mary Magdalene, Martha, and the others? As for Protestantism, what it allows women in the exercise of pastoral functions is annulled or revoked, at least in part, by the disappearance of anything representing holy women. Patriarchal religions are decidedly cunning! Confronted with the reality of all this, what sense does it make to speak of a woman sinner? Isn't this a designation more appropriate to men, since by definition it is they who practice exclusion and sacrifice and are therefore sinners? This in no way means that women are born saints. What it does signify is that their faults and shortcomings are first of all to be defined in relation to their bodies, their mothers' bodies and those of their daughter(s). One must first be a subject before being in a position to admit one's sins and seek repentance. In what way are women subjects in our cultures and religions? What words, images, or symbols allow women a social identity other than that of the mother of sons? And even this latter identity isn't freely chosen by women; it falls to them without any decision on their part, unless they kill their baby daughters. For centuries, in the religious communities we call our own, men have stayed pretty much to themselves. They define the systems of representation and exchange by and for themselves. And while women may possibly gain access to these systems, divine identity and divine rite are not accorded them. Should they demand their reinstatement in existing male communities, or does the future hold in store something newer than such "equality," since what does being equal mean as far as religion is concerned? Does it mean being equal to the other disciple, or to God? And how can woman be equal to that other when he is another sex?

In other words, can a claim to equality be acceptable without a fundamental respect for the subjective rights of both sexes, including the right to a divine identity? This would imply nothing more nor less than the remodeling of our culture so as to reconcile the reigns of women with patriarchal history. Only this historical synthesis (often defined as both prehistoric and historic) can reforge sexist hierarchies so as to bring about a cultural marriage between the sexes. All the rest can be tolerated in the interim only as a wish for the equal "redemption" of women and men. But equal means different and, once again not along the lines of the mother-son relation.

During this interim period, a considerable number of women refuse to confine themselves to male-female structures. And even if this withdrawal into same-sex groups doesn't accord with the liveliest and most creative engagement of human culture, those women's groups which have found no other solution to the problem should not be judged too quickly. Most misunderstanding and even provocation take place elsewhere! And isn't the Christian Church today, and for that matter society in general, part of the closed male order? While I do not find myself in agreement with Mary Daly, who often seems to me to lag behind what women might expect by way of a relationship to the divine, I would not be so quick to dismiss her choice of communal sisterhoods as is Elisabeth Schüssler Fiorenza. It may be that Mary Daly and others could do little else in their efforts to save their lives, their truth, and their own way. Personally I prefer to try everything in an effort to preserve the dimension of a sexual mix because that difference seems to me to safeguard those human limitations that allow room for a notion of the divine not defined as the result of a narcissistic and imperialistic inflation of sameness. What's more, both sexes need to form an alliance based on mutual respect; this is still far from happening. Meanwhile this detour through a separation of the sexes is preferable to discouragement, isolation, regression, and servitude. Besides, we still have everything to discover and rediscover about religion among women. So periods during which the sexes remain separate are necessary. Of course these separations cannot be controlled or recognized by men in the way traditional convents were. They must constitute moments of discovery and affirmation of the divine-made-woman (women).

In this regard, it is fitting to recall that in the early days of the Christian Church, communities of women would exclude men in order to pray and to celebrate certain rites dedicated in particular to the mother goddess. These women's communities served as "new families" and furnished "new mothers" to those women who suffered at the hands of their natural mothers (174). Today this task still seems more urgent, more divine, than the one that consists of simply obliging women to have one more child with no concern for their spiritual neglect or salvation.

Nonetheless, there's no question of a "leap" (24, 26) into another world but of discovering or rediscovering feminine identity by means of concrete instances rather than through "ecstasy." We don't have to become other than what we are. But we do have to mark out a qualitative threshold. For me the mark of that threshold is sexual difference. Within one sex it is usually the quantitative factor that holds sway. What we have to do is avoid the comparative mode through the perception, practice, and expression of our sexuality, our sensitivity, and our spirit by subjectivizing our relationships to mother, the universe, other women, and other men. Striking a blow against the mingling of the sexes is not enough to establish an identity. Such an identity risks falling into the trap of internalizing or continuing the internalization of the thing it claims to exclude. All sociological analyses, models, and techniques fail to provide access to such an identity. And this is why *In Memory of Her* disappointed me a little after having pleased me so much. I have to ask the woman who has given us such a work to excuse me. It can be of considerable use to those who hear its message. But sociology quickly bores me when I'm expecting the divine. She describes what already exists without inventing a new subjectivity which I don't believe can be reduced to a neat social effect. This is what certain men (and women) call my "ontological" side, most often without a clue as to what that means. A feminine identity brings ontology into question again, but it can define itself only by going back to that question. And though other social strategies are valuable and useful in part, they lack subjective dimensions for defining the relations to mother, to self, to the world and other living beings, to other subjects (men and women), to existing language and culture. What's at stake here is no stranger to Christianity. Jesus is given a Father and a mother (Mother?). He's the model man-son; he has a vision of the world; he furnishes the parameters of individual, social, and cultural identity. But for women that model is inadequate, because even if, as representative of the life of Jesus, it is not in opposition to them, it does not furnish them certain needed representations of themselves, of their genealogy, and of their relation to the universe or to others. Older religions offer them better examples of mother-daughter relationships, of the divinity of woman in her own sexual body, and of her relation to nature. For me, these form a radical dimension of women's religion which cannot be treated in simple sociological terms. Most societies, at least most societies among men, are organized against nature, in spite of nature, or by sacrificing nature, but not by remaining rooted in it and cultivating it. On this score communities of women are urgently needed. Mary Daly is right to be concerned with the cosmic dimensions of culture. And while I haven't read all she has written on the subject, I think it is more useful today to concern oneself with the vegetable than with the animal. This is, in any event, more closely in concert with women's traditions and their solutions for world salvation.

I think that any sermon on the salvation of the soul, on love of the poor, any so-called Eucharistic ritual, any Evangelical discourse that doesn't concern itself with saving the earth and its natural resources, is perverted. How can certain men and women repeat the words "This is my body, this is my blood" over the fruit of the earth without worrying about how long that earth will remain fruitful? What are these men and women talking about? There is a direct relationship between Jesus's words and the wheat and the fruit of the vine which serve life and are sufficient to it. At the moment of the Eucharist,

Jesus blesses and shares only what has ripened naturally and nothing that has been sacrificed. In so doing, he is perhaps re-establishing a bridge to those ancient traditions with which he keeps faith. Those traditions are often gynecocratic or matriarchal. Does he appropriate them to himself or act as their mediator? In any case, he respects them and hands them down to us as a legacy, a last sacrament.

Christianity isn't necessarily the religion of a single people. It isn't simply a social religion. It separates Church and State, but it cannot separate Jesus from nature, the divine from the corporeal, or the Eucharist from a respect for the earth. Unless, perhaps, *that* Jesus is sacrilegious. I believe it is the majority of his disciples, his male disciples, who are just that.

Notes

1 See Irigaray, "Epître aux derniers chrétiens" in *Amante marine* (175).

2 On this point, see the works of Johan Jacob Bachofen [Swiss philosopher, 1815–1887] which are invaluable for the information they provide. However, Bachofen's interpretation of the development of the patriarchy deserves to be questioned.

3 See "Quand naissent les dieux" in *Amante marine* (129–204).

Works Cited

Irigaray, Luce. *Amante marine, de Friedrich Nietzsche*. Paris: Minuit, 1980.

_____. "Egales à qui?" *Critique* 43.480 (1987): 420–37.

_____. "Femmes divines." *Critique* 41.454 (1985): 294–308.

_____. "Les femmes, le sacré, l'argent." *Critique* 42.467 (1986): 372–83.

Schüssler Fiorenza, Elisabeth. *Bread Not Stone: The Challenge of Feminist Biblical Interpretation*. Boston: Beacon, 1984.

_____. *En mémoire d'elle*. Trans. Marcelline Brun. Paris: du Cerf, 1986.

_____. *In Memory of Her: A Feminist Theological Reconstruction of Christian Origins*. New York: Crossroad, 1983.

ELIZABETH GROSZ

Sexual Difference and the Problem of Essentialism

*F*eminist theory is necessarily implicated in a series of complex ne-gotiations between a number of tense and antagonistic forces that are often unrecognized and unelaborated. It is a self-conscious reaction on the one hand to the overwhelming masculinity of privileged and historically dominant knowledges, acting as a kind of counterweight to the imbalances resulting from the male monopoly of the production and reception of knowledges. On the other hand, it is also a response to the broad political aims and objectives of feminist struggles. Feminist theory is thus bound to two kinds of goals, two commitments or undertakings that exist only in an uneasy and problematic re-lationship. This tension means that feminists have had to tread a fine line either between intellectual rigor (as it has been defined in male terms) and po-litical commitment (as feminists see it)–that is, between the risks posed by patriarchal recuperation and those of a conceptual sloppiness inadequate to the long-term needs of feminist struggles–or between acceptance in male terms and commitment to women's terms.

The ways in which feminists have engaged in the various projects of constructing or fabricating a knowledge appropriate to women–while keeping an eye on male academic traditions as well as on feminist politics–have left many open to criticism from both directions: from the point of view of mascu-line conceptions of theory evaluation, including notions of objectivity, dis-interested scholarship, and intellectual rigor, feminist theory is accused of a motivated, self-interested "biased" approach, in which pregiven commitments are simply confirmed rather than objectively demonstrated;[1] and from the point of view of (some) feminist "activists" feminist theory is accused of play-ing male power games, of participating in and contributing to the very forms of male dominance feminism should be trying to combat. It is not altogether surprising that underlying both criticisms is a common demand for a purity of position–an intellectual purity in the one case (a purity from social and political factors that mitigate or interfere with the goals of scholarly research) and a political purity in the other (a purity from the influence of patriarchal and masculinist values). Male-dominated theories require the disavowal of the sociopolitical values implicit in the production of all knowledges and the creation of a supposedly value-free knowledge, while feminist political purists require the disavowal of the pervasive masculinity of privileged knowledges and social practices, including feminist forms.

In spite of the sometimes puerile and often naive extremism of both types of objection, they do nevertheless articulate a real concern for feminist theory, highlighting an untheorized locus in its self-formation: by what criteria are feminists to judge not only male theory but also feminist theory? If the criteria by which theory has been judged up to now are masculine, how can new criteria be formulated? Can such criteria adequately satisfy the dual requirements of intellectual or conceptual rigor as well as political engagement? Is it possible to produce theory that compromises neither its political nor its intellectual credibility? In what ways is feminist theory to legitimate itself in theoretical and political terms? These questions are neither idle nor frivolous. They are of direct relevance to the ways in which feminist theory is assessed, and may help to clarify a number of issues that have polarized feminist theorists in unproductive ways.

In this brief note, I would like to use a major dispute between feminist theorists–the debate between so-called feminisms of equality and feminisms of difference–to raise the question of the dual commitments of feminist theory and the need to devise appropriate criteria for its assessment. Is the concept of sexual difference a breakthrough term in contesting patriarchal conceptions of women and femininity? Or is it a reassertion of the patriarchal containment of women? Is the concept essentialist, or is it an upheaval of patriarchal knowledges?

Essentialism and Its Cognates

Feminists have developed a range of terms and criteria of intellectual assessment over the past twenty or so years that aim to affirm, consolidate, and explain the political goals and ambitions of feminist struggles. These terms have tended to act as unquestioned values and as intellectual guidelines in assessing both male-dominated and feminist-oriented theories. Among the most frequent and powerful of these terms are those centered around the question of the nature of women (and men)–essentialism, biologism, naturalism, and universalism. While these terms are closely related to each other, sharing a common concern for the fixity and limits definitionally imposed on women, it is also important to be aware of the sometimes subtle differences between them in order to appreciate the ways in which they have been used by and against feminists. These terms are commonly used in patriarchal discourses to justify women's social subordination and their secondary positions relative to men in patriarchal society.

Essentialism, a term that is rarely defined or explained explicitly in feminist contexts, refers to the attribution of a fixed essence to women. Women's essence is assumed to be given and universal and is usually, though not necessarily, identified with women's biology and "natural" characteristics. Essentialism usually entails biologism and naturalism, but there are cases in which women's essence is seen to reside not in nature or biology but in certain given psychological characteristics–nurturance, empathy, supportiveness, non-competitiveness, and so on. Or women's essence may be attributed to certain activities and procedures (which may or may not be dictated by biology) observable in social practices, intuitiveness, emotional responses, concern and commitment to helping others, etc. Essentialism entails the belief that those characteristics defined as women's essence are shared in common by all women at all times: it implies a limit on the variations and possibilities of change–it is not possible for a subject to act in a manner contrary to her nature. Essentialism thus refers to the existence of fixed characteristics, given attributes, and ahistorical functions that limit the possibilities of change and thus of social reorganization.

Biologism is a particular form of essentialism in which women's essence is defined in terms of women's biological capacities. Biologism is usually based on some form of reductionism: social and cultural factors are the effects of biologically given causes. In particular, biologism usually ties women closely to the functions of reproduction and nurturance, although it may also limit women's social possibilities through the use of evidence from neurology, neurophysiology, and endocrinology. Biologism is thus an attempt to limit women's social and psychological capacities according to biologically established limits. It asserts, for example, that women are weaker in physical strength than men; that women are, by their biological natures, more emotional than men, and so on. Insofar as biology is assumed to constitute an unalterable bedrock of identity, the attribution of biologistic characteristics amounts to a permanent form of social containment for women.

Naturalism is also a form of essentialism in which a fixed nature is postulated for women. Once again, this nature is usually given biological form, but this is by no means an invariant. Naturalism may be asserted on theological or on ontological rather than on biological grounds. For example, it may be claimed that women's nature is derived from God-given attributes that are not explicable or observable simply in biological terms. Or, following Sartrean existentialism or Freudian psychoanalysis, there are, as it were, ontological invariants that distinguish the two sexes in, for example, the claim that the human subject is somehow naturally free or that the subject's social position is a function of his or her genital morphology. More commonly, however, naturalism presumes the equivalence of biological and natural properties.

While also closely related to essentialism, biologism, and naturalism, universalism need not be based on innate or fixed characteristics. It is usually justified in terms of some essential or biological characteristics, but universalism may be conceived in purely social terms. It refers to the attributions of invariant social categories, functions, and activities to which all women in all cultures are assigned. This may be the result of biology or ontology, but just as frequently it may reflect universal social or cultural requirements, such as the sexual division of labor or the prohibition of incest. Unlike essentialism, biologism, or naturalism, in which not only the similarities but also the differences between women may be accounted for (race and class characteristics can also be explained in naturalist, biologist, or essentialist terms), universalism tends to suggest only the commonness of all women at all times and in all social contexts. By definition, it can only assert similarities, what is shared in common by all women, and what homogenizes women as a category.

These four terms are frequently elided: each has commonly served as a shorthand formula for the others. In charging theories with these conceptual commitments, feminists assert that they are necessarily complicit in reproducing patriarchal values. In claiming that women's current social roles and positions are the effects of their essence, nature, biology, or universal social position, these theories are guilty of rendering such roles and positions unalterable and necessary and thus of providing them with a powerful political justification. They rationalize and neutralize the prevailing sexual division of social roles by assuming that these roles are the only, or the best, possibilities, given the confines of the nature, essence, or biology of the two sexes. These commitments entail a range of other serious problems: they are necessarily ahistorical; they confuse social relations with fixed attributes; they see these fixed attributes as inherent limitations to social change; and they refuse to take seriously the historical and geographical differences between women–differences between women across different cultures as well as within a single culture.

It is not surprising that these terms have become labels for danger zones or theoretical pitfalls in feminist assessments of patriarchal theory. One could be sure that the theories one analyzed were tinged with patriarchal values whenever a trace of them could be discerned. They are the critical touchstones of assessment, self-evident guidelines for evaluating patriarchal theories and the patriarchal residues or adherences of feminist theories. These terms seem unquestionably problematic; they indicate at least at first glance, a rare harmony between the principles of feminist politics and those of intellectual rigor, for they are problematic in both political and theoretical terms. Yet their value as criteria of critical evaluation for feminist as well as patriarchal theory is not as clear as it might seem.

Sexual Identity Sexual Difference

Among the most central and contested issues in contemporary feminist theory are the terms in which women's social, sexual, and cultural positions are to be understood. This kind of question is, moreover, crucially positioned at the heart of the conflict between feminist politics and the requirements of patriarchal knowledges. Is woman to be attributed an identity and sociocultural position in terms that make it possible for women to be conceived as men's equals? Or is woman's identity to be conceived in terms entirely different from those associated with and provided by men? This question implies two other related questions: are the frameworks of prevailing patriarchal knowledges capable of bestowing on women the same basic capacities, skills, and attributes they have posited for men? And if so, are these frameworks adequate for characterizing not only what women share in common with men (what makes both sexes human) but also what particularizes women and distinguishes them from men?

The positions of a number of pioneer feminists in the history of second-wave feminism, including, among others, Simone de Beauvoir, Betty

Friedan, Eva Figes, Kate Millett, Shulamith Firestone, and Germaine Greer, could be described as egalitarian. This broad position assumes that the liberation of women from patriarchal constraints entailed opening up social, economic, political, and sexual positions previously occupied only by men. These theorists in different ways believed that women have been unfairly excluded from positions of social value and status normally occupied by men. Women in patriarchy were regarded as socially, intellectually, and physically inferior to men, a consequence of various discriminatory, sexist practices, practices that illegitimately presumed women were unsuited for or incapable of assuming certain positions. This belief was fostered not only by oppressive external constraints but also by women's own compliance with and internalization of patriarchal sexual stereotypes.

Egalitarian feminists–among whom we should include, in spite of their differences, liberal and socialist feminists–were reacting to largely naturalist and biologist presumptions on which much of social and political theory is based. If it is in women's nature to be passive, compliant, nurturing, this is a "natural" index, guide, or limit to the organization of society. Defenders of patriarchal social order assume that social and cultural relations should conform and be conducive to "(human) nature." The goal is not an augmentation and reorganization of "nature" but simply its confirmation. The divisions and inequalities between the sexes were seen as the effects of a nature that should not be tampered with. This provides a ready-made justification for the most conservative and misogynist of social relations: they are treated as if they were the effects of nature alone.

Egalitarian feminists claim that women are as able as men to do what men do. The fact that women are not regarded as men's equals was, they claim, the result not of nature but of patriarchal ideologies, discriminatory socialization practices, social stereotyping, and role-playing. Women's social roles were, in other words, the result of culture, not nature, of social organization rather than biological determinants, and were thus capable of being changed. Indeed, if women's social roles are dictated by nature, feminism itself becomes impossible, for resistance to nature is, in one sense at least, impossible. Feminism is founded on the belief that women are capable of achievements other than those recognized and regarded by patriarchy, other than those to which women's "nature" has hitherto confined them.

As a category, women were consistently underrepresented in positions of social authority and status and overrepresented in socially subordinate positions. Girls systematically underachieve and are inadequately prepared for social success, while boys' social roles maximize their social potential. Feminism began largely as a struggle for a greater share of the patriarchal pie and equal access to social, economic, sexual, and intellectual opportunities. The early feminists of equality were bound up in what Julia Kristeva has called "the logic of identification," an identification with the values, norms, goals, and methods devised and validated by men. In its beginnings, the women's movement, as the struggle of suffragists and of existential feminists, aspired to gain a place in linear time as the time of project and history. In this sense, the movement, while immediately universalist, is also deeply rooted in the sociopolitical life of nations. The political demands of women; the struggles for equal pay for equal work, for taking power in social institutions on an equal footing with men; the rejection, when necessary, of the attributes traditionally considered feminine or maternal insofar as they are deemed incompatible with insertion in that historical–all are part of the logic of identification with certain values: not with the ideological (these are combatted, and rightly so, as reactionary) but, rather, with the logical and ontological values of a rationality dominant in the nation-state (Kristeva 18-19).

In place of the essentialist and naturalist containment of women, feminists of equality affirm women's potential for equal intelligence, ability, and social value. Underlying the belief in the need to eliminate or restructure the social constraints imposed on women is a belief that the "raw materials" of socialization are fundamentally the same for both sexes: each has analogous biological or natural potential, which is unequally developed because the social roles imposed on the two sexes are unequal. If social roles could be readjusted or radically restructured, if the two sexes could be resocialized, they could be rendered equal. The differences between the sexes would be no more significant than the differences between the individuals. These feminist arguments for an egalitarian treatment of the two sexes were no doubt threatening to patriarchs insofar as the sex roles the latter presumed were natural could be blurred through social means; women could become "unfeminine," men "unmasculine"; and the sovereignty of the nuclear family, marriage, monogamy, and the sexual division of labor would be undermined. Where it was necessary to recognize the changeable nature of sex roles and social stereotypes, as feminists of equality advocated, this was not, however, sufficient to ensure women's freedom from sexual oppression. The more successful egalitarian programs became, the more apparent it was that the political agenda included a number of serious drawbacks:

1. *The project of sexual equality takes male achievements, values, and standards as the norms to which women should also aspire. At most, then, women can achieve an equality with men only within a system whose overall value is unquestioned and whose power remains unrecognized. Women strive, then, to become the same as men, in a sense, "masculinized."*

2. *To achieve an equality between the sexes, women's specific needs and interests–what distinguishes them from men–must be minimized and their commonness or humanity stressed. (This may, for example, explain the strong antipathy to maternity among a number of egalitarian feminists,[2] a resistance to the idea that women's corporeality and sexuality make a difference to the kinds of consciousness or subjects they could become.)*

3. *Policies and laws codifying women's legal rights to equality–antidiscriminatory and equal opportunity legislation–have tended to operate as much against women as in their interest. Men, for example, have been able as much as women to use antidiscrimination or equal opportunity regulations to secure their own positions.*

4. *In this sense, equality becomes a vacuous concept insofar as it reduces all specificities, including those that serve to distinguish the positions of the oppressed from those of the oppressor. One can be considered equal only insofar as the history of the oppression of specific groups is effaced.[3]*

5. *Struggles for equality between the sexes are easily reduced to struggles around a more generalized and neutralized social justice. This has enabled a number of men to claim that they too are oppressed by patriarchal social role and are unable to express their more "feminine" side. The struggles of women against patriarchy are too easily identified with a movement of reaction against a gen-*

eral "dehumanization" in which men may unproblematically represent women in struggles for greater or more authentic forms of humanity.

6. *The project of creating equality between the sexes can be socially guaranteed, if it can, only in the realm of public and civic life. And even if some kind of domestic equality is possible, an equality at the level of sexual and particularly reproductive relations seems impossible insofar as they are untouched by egalitarianism.*

7. *Most significantly, even if the two sexes behave in the same ways, perform the same duties, and play the same roles, the social meanings of their activities remain unchallenged. Until this structure of shared meanings is problematized, equality in anything but a formal sense remains impossible.*

Try as it may, a feminism of equality is unable to adequately theorize sexual and reproductive equality. And this, in turn, results in its inability to adequately theorize women's specific positions within the social and symbolic order. Kristeva makes clear the link between sexual and symbolic functioning:

Sexual difference–which is at once biological, physiological, and relative to reproduction–is translated by and translates a difference in the relation of subjects to the symbolic contract which is the social contract: a difference, then, in the relationship to power, language and meaning. The sharpest and most subtle point of feminist subversion brought about by the new generation will henceforth be situated on the terrain of the inseparable conjunction of the sexual and the symbolic, in order to try to discover, first, the specificity of the female, and then, in the end, that of each individual. (21)

In opposition to egalitarian feminism, a feminism based on the acknowledgment of women's specificities and oriented to the attainment of autonomy for women, has emerged over the past ten years or more. From the point of view of a feminism of equality, feminisms of difference seem strangely reminiscent of the position of defenders of patriarchy: both stress women's differences from men. However, before too readily identifying them, it is vital to ask how this difference is conceived and, perhaps more important, who it is that defines this difference and for whom. For patriarchs, difference is understood in terms of inequality, distinction, or opposition, a sexual difference modeled on negative, binary, or oppositional structures within which only one of the two terms has any autonomy; the other is defined only by the negation of the first. Only sameness or identity can insure equality. In the case of feminists of difference, however, difference is seen not as difference from a pre-given norm but as pure difference, difference itself, difference with no identity. This kind of difference implies the autonomy of the terms between which the difference may be drawn and thus their radical incommensurability. Difference viewed as distinction implies the pre-evaluation of one of the terms from which the difference of the other is drawn; pure difference refuses to privilege either term.[4] For feminists, to claim women's difference from men is to reflect existing definitions and categories, redefining oneself and the world according to women's own perspectives.

The right to equality entails the right to be the same as men, while struggles around autonomy imply the right to either consider oneself equal to another or reject the terms by which equality is measured and to define oneself in different terms. It entails the right to be and to act differently. The concept of difference is used by a number of contemporary feminist theorists, including Luce Irigaray, Jane Gallop, and Hélène Cixous. It implies, among other things, the following:

1. *Difference suggests major transformation of the social and symbolic order, which, in patriarchy, is founded by a movement of universalization of the singular (male) identity. Difference cannot be readily accommodated in a system that reduces all difference to distinction and all identity to sameness.*

2. *Difference resists the homogenization of separate political struggles–insofar as it implies not only women's differences from men, and from each other, but also women's differences from other oppressed groups. It is not at all clear that, for example, struggles against racism will necessarily be politically allied with women's struggles or, conversely, that feminism will overcome forms of racist domination. This, of course, does not preclude the existence of common interests shared by various oppressed groups, and thus*

*the possibility of alliances over specific issues; it simply means that
these alliances have no prior necessity.*

3. *Struggles around the attainment of women's autonomy imply
that men's struggles against patriarchy, while possibly allied with
women's in some circumstances, cannot be identified with them. In
acknowledging their sexual specificity, men's challenge to patriarchy is necessarily different from women's, which entails producing an identity and sexual specificity for themselves.*

4. *The notion of difference affects women's definitions not only of
themselves but also of the world. This implies not only that social
practices must be subjected to feminist critique and reorganization
but also that the very structures of representation, meaning, and
knowledge must be subjected to a thoroughgoing transformation of
their patriarchal alignments. A politics of difference implies the
right to define oneself, others, and the world according to one's
own interests.*

The Difference That Makes a Difference

Feminists involved in the project of establishing women's sexual differences from men have been subjected to wide-ranging criticisms coming
from both feminist directions: they face the same general dilemma confronting
any feminist position which remains critical of the frameworks of patriarchal
knowledges yet must rely on their resources. From the point of view of traditional, male-governed scholarly norms, their work appears utopian, idealistic,
romantic, polemic, fictional–but above all, without substantial content or solid
evidence and justification. From the point of view of other forms of feminism–particularly from Marxist or socialist feminism–it appears essentialist
and universalist. In the one case, these feminists are accused of straying too far
from biological and scientifically validated information; and in the other, of
sticking too close to biological evidence. It seems that both these criticisms
misunderstand the status of claims made by feminists of difference, judging
them in terms inappropriate to their approach.

Charges of essentialism, universalism, and naturalism are predictable
responses on the part of feminists concerned with the idea of women's social

construction. Thus, any attempt to define or designate women or femininity is in danger of relying on commitments that generalize on the basis of the particular and reduce social construction to biological preformation. Any theory of femininity, any definition of woman in general, any description that abstracts from the particular historical, cultural, ethnic, and class positions of particular women, verges perilously close to essentialism. Toril Moi provides a typical response to a feminism of difference in her critique of Irigaray's notion of women or the feminine:

> . . . any attempt to formulate a general theory of femininity will be metaphysical. This is precisely Irigaray's dilemma: having shown that so far femininity has been produced exclusively in relation to the logic of the same, she falls for the temptation to produce her own positive theory of femininity. But, as we have seen, to define "woman" is necessarily to essentialize her. (139)

This, however, leads to a paradox: if women cannot be characterized in any general way, if all there is to femininity is socially produced, how can feminism be taken seriously? What justifies the assumption that women are oppressed as a sex? What, indeed, does it mean to talk about women as a category? If we are not justified in taking women as category, what political grounding does feminism have? Feminism is placed in an unenviable position: either it clings to feminist principles, which entail its avoidance of essentialist and universalist categories, in which case its rationale as a political struggle centered around women is problematized; or it accepts the limitations patriarchy imposes on its conceptual schemas and models and abandons the attempt to provide autonomous, self-defined terms in which to describe women and femininity. Are these the only choices available to feminist theory–an adherence to essentialist doctrines, or the dissolution of feminist struggles into localized, regional, specific struggles representing the interests of particular women or groups of women?

Posed in this way, the dilemma facing feminists involves a conflict between the goals of intellectual rigor (avoidance of the conceptual errors of essentialism and universalism) and feminist political struggles (struggles that are directed toward the liberation of women as women). But is this really a choice feminists must face? Is it a matter of preference for one goal over the other? Or can the linkages between theory and political practice be understood differently so that the criteria of intellectual evaluation are more "politicized" and the goals of political struggle are more "theorized"?

Gayatri Spivak sums up this dilemma well in her understanding of concepts and theoretical principles, not as guidelines, rules, principles, or blueprints for struggle but as tools and weapons of struggle. It is no longer a matter of maintaining a theoretical purity at the cost of political principles; nor is it simply a matter of the ad hoc adoption of theoretical principles according to momentary needs or whims. It is a question of negotiating a path between always impure positions–seeing that politics is always/already bound up with what it contests (including theories)–and that theories are always implicated in various political struggles (whether this is acknowledged or not):

> You pick up the universal that will give you the power to fight against the other side and what you are throwing away by doing that is your theoretical purity. Whereas the great custodians of the anti-universal are obliged therefore simply to act in the interest of a great narrative, the narrative of exploitation while they keep themselves clean by not committing themselves to anything. . . . [T]hey are run by a great narrative even as they are busy protecting their theoretical purity by repudiating essentialism. (Spivak 184)

The choice, in other words, is not between maintaining a politically pure theoretical position (and leaving the murkier questions of political involvement unasked) and espousing a politically tenuous one which may be more pragmatically effective in securing social change. The alternatives faced by feminist theorists are all in some sense "impure" and "implicated" in patriarchy. There can be no feminist position that is not in some way or other involved in patriarchal power relations; it is hard to see how this is either possible or desirable, for a purity from patriarchal "contamination" entails feminism's incommensurability with patriarchy and thus the inability to criticize it. Feminists are not faced with pure and impure options. All options are in their various ways bound by the constraints of patriarchal power. The crucial political questions are: which commitments remain, in spite of their patriarchal alignments, of use to feminists in their political struggles? What kinds of feminist strategy do they make possible or hinder? And what are the costs and benefits of holding these commitments? In other words, the decision about whether to "use" essentialism or to somehow remain beyond it (even if these extremes were possible) is a question of calculation, not a self-evident certainty.

In challenging the domination of patriarchal models that rely on essentialism, naturalism, biologism, or universalism, egalitarian feminists have pointed to the crucial role these assumptions play in making change difficult to conceive or undertake: as such, they support, rationalize, and underpin existing power relations between the sexes. But in assuming that feminists take on essentialist or universalist assumptions (if they do, which is not always clear) in the same way as patriarchs, instead of attempting to understand the ways in which essentialism and its cognates can function as strategic terms, this silences and neutralizes the most powerful of feminist theoretical weapons–feminism's ability to use patriarchy and phallocratism against themselves, its ability to take up positions ostensibly opposed to feminism and to use them for feminist goals.

> ... I think it is absolutely on target to take a stand against the discourses of essentialism, universalism as it comes to terms with the universal–of classical German philosophy or the universal as the white upper class male ... etc. but strategically we cannot. Even as we talk about feminist practice, or privileging practice over theory, we are universalizing. Since the moment of essentializing, universalizing, saying yes to the onto-phenomenological question, is irreducible, let us at least situate it at the moment; let us become vigilant about our own practice and use it as much as we can rather than make the totally counterproductive gesture of repudiating it. ... (Spivak 184)

In other words, if feminism cannot maintain its political purity from patriarchal frameworks, methods, and presumptions, its implication in them needs to be acknowledged instead of being disavowed. Moreover, this (historically) necessary binding of patriarchal terms is the very condition of feminism's effectivity in countering and displacing the effects of patriarchy: its *emersion* in patriarchal practices (including those surrounding the production of theory) is the condition of its effective critique of and movement beyond them. This emersion provides not only the conditions under which feminism can become familiar with what it criticizes but also the very means by which patriarchal dominance can be challenged.

Notes

This essay appeared previously in *Inscriptions* 5 (1989) and in *Feminist Knowledge: Critique and Construct*, edited by Sneja Gunew (New York: Routledge, 1990).

1   For an account of the challenges feminist theory has posed to male conceptions of objectivity, particularly in science, see Grosz and Lepervanche.

2   Kristeva makes this point forcefully in her analysis of the "two generations of feminists" outlined in her paper "Women's Time." She refers to Beauvoir's anti-maternal position, a position also analyzed in MacKenzie.

3   This is Kristeva's understanding of the effects of a fundamental egalitarianism; which produces, among other things, the oppressive structure of anti-Semitism: assimilationism entails the repression of the specific history of oppression directed toward the Jew. This is why Sartre's position in *Anti-Semite and Jew*, in spite of his intentions, is anti-Semitic. As Kristeva suggests: ". . . the specific character of women could only appear as nonessential or even nonexistent to the totalizing and even totalitarian spirit of this ideology. We begin to see that this same egalitarian and in fact censuring treatment has been imposed, from Enlightenment Humanism through socialism, on religious specificities and, in particular, on Jews" (Kristeva 21).

4   This difference between difference and distinction is suggested by Derrida in his conception of difference, which is partly based on his reading of Saussure's notion of pure difference in language. Although Derrida does not make use of this terminology himself, Wilden's careful gloss on these terms helps to clarify many of the issues at stake in Derrida's as well as in feminist conceptions of difference. See chapter 8 of Wilden.

Works Cited

Grosz, Elizabeth A., and Marie de Lepervanche. "Feminism and Science." *Crossing Boundaries: Feminisms and the Critique of Knowledges*. Ed. Barbara Caine, Elizabeth A. Grosz, and Marie de Lepervanche. Sydney: Allen, 1988. 5–27.

Kristeva, Julia. "Women's Time." *Signs: Journal of Women in Culture and Society* 7 (1981): 13–35.

MacKenzie, Catriona. "Simone de Beauvoir: Philosophy and/or the Female Body." *Feminist Challenges: Social and Political Theory*. Ed. Carole Pateman and Elizabeth Grosz. Boston: Northeastern UP, 1986. 144–56.

Moi, Toril. *Sexual/Textual Politics: Feminist Literary Theory*. New York: Methuen, 1985.

Sartre, Jean Paul. *Anti-Semite and Jew*. 1946. Trans. George J. Becker. New York: Schocken, 1965.

Spivak, Gayatri Chakravorty, with Elizabeth Grosz. "Criticism, Feminism, and the Institution." *Thesis Eleven* 10/11 (1984–85): 175–88.

Wilden, Anthony. *System and Structure: Essays in Communication and Exchange*. London: Tavistock, 1972.

Reading like a Feminist

Can social constructionism entirely dispense with the idea of essence? This is the central question I propose to address through a critique of the debates on gender and reading: what does it mean to read as a woman or as a man? When social constructionist theories of reading posit groups of gendered readers, what is it exactly that underwrites and subtends the notion of a class of women or a class of men reading? Precisely *where*, in other words, does the essentialism inhere in anti-essentialism? Although the present analysis focuses predominantly upon three recent pieces, Robert Scholes's "Reading like a Man," Tania Modleski's "Feminism and the Power of Interpretation," and Gayatri Spivak's "Subaltern Studies: Deconstructing Historiography" (*Other* 197–221), the dispute over "reading as woman" has a much longer history which includes Peggy Kamuf's "Writing like a Woman," Jonathan Culler's "Reading as a Woman," and, most recently, the many contributions to the controversial volume *Men in Feminism*. In the background of all these investigations lies the question of essentialism and the problem of the vexed relation between feminism and deconstruction. How and why have the current tensions between feminism and deconstruction mobilized around the issue of essentialism? Why indeed is essentialism such a powerful and seemingly intransigent category for both deconstructionists and feminists? Is it possible to be an essentialist deconstructionist, when deconstruction is commonly understood as the very displacement of essence? By the same token, is it legitimate to call oneself an anti-essentialist feminist, when feminism seems to take for granted among its members a shared identity, some essential point of commonality?

According to one well-known American critic, feminism and deconstruction are fundamentally incompatible discourses since deconstruction displaces the essence of the class "women" which feminism needs to articulate its very politics. The polarization of feminism and deconstruction around the contested sign of essence is perhaps nowhere so clear as in Robert Scholes's "Reading like a Man," a piece which seeks to disclose the often subtle and frequently suspect strategies which, in this instance, (male?) deconstructors employ to master feminism and to put it in its place. Jonathan Culler's "Reading as a Woman," a study which endorses the "hypothesis" (rather than the experience) of a woman reading,[1] is, for Scholes, a classic example of the way in which deconstruction's de-essentializing gestures are merely re-phallocentrizing appropriations in the end. Specifically, it is Culler's premature repudiation of "experience" as a legitimate ground of feminist interpretation which Scholes objects to and which becomes the critical spur for his own speculations on the role experience might play in "reading like a man." I find Scholes's careful critique of Culler's "Reading as a Woman" both incisive and enormously suggestive, but not entirely devoid of certain mastering strategies of its own. It is these strategies that I wish to discuss here, while declaring all the same my fundamental agreement with Scholes's basic premise that the relation between deconstruction and feminism is by no means unproblematic or uncomplicated. The most serious (but also the most intriguing) problem with this essay is that it leaves the feminism/deconstruction binarism firmly in place–it reinforces and solidifies their antithesis in order to claim that deconstruction is bad for feminism. To secure this moral judgment, the hybrid positions of deconstructive feminism and feminist deconstruction are glossed over, rejected from the start as untenable possibilities–untenable because feminism and deconstruction are "founded upon antithetical principles: feminism upon a class concept and deconstruction upon the deconstructing of all such concepts" (208).

Everything hinges here, as Scholes himself is quick to point out, on the notion of "class." What he objects to, specifically, is deconstruction's rejection of what W. K. Wimsatt, following Locke, calls "nominal universality" (208), that is, nominal essence. In *An Essay Concerning Human Understanding*, Locke makes the crucial distinction between what he calls "real" versus "nominal" essences. Real essence connotes the Aristotelian understanding of essence as that which is most irreducible and unchanging about a thing; nominal essence signifies for Locke a view of essence as merely a linguistic convenience, a classificatory fiction we need to categorize and to label.[2] When feminists today argue for maintaining the notion of a *class* of women, usually for political purposes, they do so, I would suggest, on the basis of Locke's nominal essence. It is Locke's distinction between nominal and real essence which allows us to work with the category of "women" as a *linguistic* rather than a natural kind, and for this reason Locke's category of nominal essence is especially useful for anti-essentialist feminists who want to hold onto the notion of women as a group without submitting to the idea that it is "nature" which categorizes them as such. Scholes believes that feminism needs to hold onto this "linguistic/logical" (207) idea of a class of women in order to be effective. I would not disagree. I would, however, wish to point out that nominal essences are often treated by post-Lockians as if they were real essences, and this is what I perceive to be the main point of vulnerability in "Reading like a Man."

While still subscribing to the "linguistic/logical" dimension of class, Scholes later goes on to endorse "the ability of women to be conscious of themselves as a class . . . bound by a certain shared experience" (212–13). What, then, does the category "experience" signify for Scholes? "Whatever experience is," he concludes, "it is not just a *construct* but something that *constructs*" (215). This definition sounds remarkably similar to Locke's description of "real essence" as the "something I know not what" which nonetheless determines the "what" of who we are. And what is it, exactly, that constitutes that "certain shared experience" which allows women "to be conscious of themselves as a class"? Could it be that which Scholes reprimands Culler for eliding, precisely that which Culler (in Scholes's opinion) rashly jettisons from consideration in his deconstructive third moment: namely, "the bodily experience of menstrual flow" (211)? Of course, not all females, in fact, menstruate. It may well be that Scholes wishes us to think of "experience" in the way Teresa de Lauretis suggests: "an on-going process by which subjectivity is constructed semiotically and historically" (*Alice* 182). But what distinguishes Scholes's understanding of experience from de Lauretis's is the former's hidden appeal to referentiality, to (in this case) the female body which, though constructed, is nonetheless constructed *by its own processes*, processes which are seen to be real, immediate, and directly knowable.[3] Bodily experiences may seem self-evident and immediately perceptible but they are always socially mediated. Even if we were to agree that experience is not merely constructed but also itself constructing, we would still have to acknowledge that there is little agreement amongst women on exactly what constitutes "a woman's experience." Therefore we need to be extremely wary of the temptation to make substantive claims on the basis of the so-called "authority" of our experiences. "No man should seek in any way to diminish the authority which the experience of women gives them in speaking about that experience" (217–18), Scholes insists, and yet, as feminist philosopher Jean Grimshaw rightly reminds us, "experience does not come neatly in segments, such that it is always possible to abstract what in one's experience is due to 'being a woman' from that which is due to 'being married,' 'being middle class' and so forth" (85). In sum, "experience" is rather shaky ground on which to base the notion of a class of women. But if we can't base the idea of a class of women on "essence" or "experience," then what can we base it on? Before tendering a possible answer to what is admittedly a vexing and frustrating question, much more needs to be said by way of rounding out my critique of Scholes's "Reading like a Man."

By taking as his model of feminism a humanist or essentialist version, and by reading deconstruction as fundamentally anti-essentialist, Scholes forecloses the possibility of both an anti-essentialist feminism and an essentialist deconstruction. But recent work in feminist theory suggests that not only are these positions possible, they can be powerfully displacing positions from which feminists can speak. To take the first instance, an anti-essentialist feminism, Monique Wittig rejects unequivocally the idea of a "class of women" based on shared (biological) experience and bases her feminism on the deconstructive premise that, in Derrida's words, "woman has no essence of her very own" (31). To take the second instance, an essentialist deconstruction, Luce Irigaray bases her feminism on the bodily metaphor of "the two lips" in order to construct and *deconstruct* "woman" at the same time; for Irigaray, the very possibility of a radical deconstruction is based on the simultaneous displacement and *redeployment* of essentialism–a "thinking through the body."[4] Such "hybrid" instances in feminist theory suggest that Scholes's feminism/deconstruction binarism is ultimately more harmful than helpful. It leads, for example, to such baffling statements as "feminism is right and deconstruction is wrong" (205). Mastery, in Scholes's work, operates along an ethical axis: feminism is disappropriated from deconstruction so that its alleged moral superiority might be protected from the ill repute and questionable designs of its powerful (male?) suitor, deconstruction. What we see in this piece is a curious form of critical chivalry; feminism, I would submit, has become the angel in the house of critical theory.

But who is this errant knight dedicated to saving feminism, and from what country does he heed? What language does he speak? Does Scholes speak, read, or write as a woman or as a man? The final lines provide the answer we have all been waiting for:

> *We are subjects constructed by our experience and truly carry traces of that experience in our minds and on our bodies. Those of us who are male cannot deny this either. With the best will in the world we shall never read as women and perhaps not even like women. For me, born when I was born and living where I have lived, the very best I can do is to be conscious of the ground upon which I stand: to read not as but like a man. (218)*

The distinction between the similes "as" and "like" is nothing short of brilliant, but does not answer a far more interesting question, a question which, through a series of rather nimble acrobatic maneuvers of his own, Scholes manages to side-step: namely, does he read as or like a *feminist*? It is the very slippages between "woman," "women," "female," and "feminist" throughout the text that permits the writer to defer the question of reading as or *like* a feminist–the question, in other words, of *political identification*. I read this piece like a feminist; what it means to read as or even like a woman I still don't know.

Scholes is not alone in his repudiation of Culler's alleged deconstructionist appropriation of feminism. Tania Modleski, in her "Feminism and the Power of Interpretation: Some Critical Readings" also takes Culler to task for "being patriarchal just at the point when he seems to be the most feminist," that is, at the point "when he arrogates to himself and to other male critics the ability to read as women by 'hypothesizing' women readers" (133). What allows a male subject to read as a woman is the displacing series of repetitions which Culler adapts from Peggy Kamuf's "Writing like a Woman": "a woman writing as a woman writing as a woman. . . ." But, to Modleski, the deconstructionist definition of a woman reading (as a woman reading as a woman . . .) simply opens a space for male feminism while simultaneously foreclosing the question of real, material female readers: "a genuinely feminist literary criticism might wish to repudiate the *hypothesis* of a woman reader and instead promote the 'sensible,' visible, actual female reader" (133). While I am not contesting that there are certainly "real," material, gendered readers engaged in the act of reading, I nonetheless stumble over the qualifier "genuinely":

what is it, exactly, that might constitute for Modleski a "genuinely feminist literary criticism"?

Read alongside Scholes's "Reading like a Man," Modleski's "Feminism and the Power of Interpretation" proposes an answer that should perhaps not surprise us: "the experience of real women" (134) operates as the privileged signifier of the authentic and the real. Experience emerges to fend off the entry of men into feminism and, further, to naturalize and to authorize the relation between biological woman and social women: "to read as a woman in a patriarchal culture necessitates that the *hypothesis* of a woman reader be advanced by an *actual* woman reader: the female feminist critic" (133–34). Like Scholes, Modleski can appeal to experience as the measure of the "genuinely feminist" only by totally collapsing woman, female, and feminist and by prefacing this tricky conflation with the empirical tag "actual." Modleski objects to Kamuf's and Culler's ostensible position that "a 'ground' (like experience) from which to make critical judgments is anathema" (134). If this were an accurate assessment of Kamuf's and Culler's positions I might be inclined to agree, but the poststructuralist objection to experience is not a repudiation of grounds of knowing per se but rather a refusal of the hypostatisation of experience as *the* ground (and the most stable ground) of knowledge production. The problem with categories like "the female experience" or "the male experience" is that, given their generality and seamlessness, they are of limited epistemological usefulness. When Modleski does some hypothesizing of her own and presents us with her fictional "case of a man and a woman reading Freud's text," and when she informs us that "the woman, accustomed to the experience of being thought more sensual than intellectual, must certainly respond to it differently from the man," what "woman" and what "man" is she talking about? Can we ever speak so simply of "the female reader" or "the male reader" (133), "the woman" and "the man," as if these categories were not transgressed, not already constituted by other axes of difference (class, ethnicity, nationality . . .)? Moreover, are our reading responses so easily predictable, so readily interpretable?

Both Modleski and Scholes are right to insist that critical interpretation has everything to do with power. Why, then, do I find Modleski's eloquent concluding invocation of "female empowerment" so distinctly *disempowering*? Her words are strong, emphatic, a political call to arms: "the ultimate goal of feminist criticism and theory is female empowerment. My particular concern here has been to empower female readers of texts, in part by rescuing them from the oblivion to which some critics would consign them" (136). Perhaps what is discomforting is the singular, declarative, and prescriptive tone of this guideline for political action. But it is more than a question of tone. Exactly which readers is Modleski speaking for, to, and about? Does she propose to rescue *all* female readers, including "third world" readers, lesbian readers, and working-class readers? Are not some female readers *materially* more empowered than others, by virtue of class, race, national, or other criterion? For that matter, are not *some* female readers more empowered than *some* male readers? Do these more privileged readers need to be "rescued"? Modleski seems to be as committed as Scholes to saving feminism from the appropriative gestures of men (even well-intentioned ones): "feminist criticism performs an escape act dedicated to freeing women from *all* male captivity narratives, whether these be found in literature, criticism, or theory" (136). Though "Feminism and the Power of Interpretation" presents itself as a materialist investigation of "reading as woman," no allowance is made for the real, material differences between women. In the end, this materialist piece is curiously a-materialist in that the differences between women which would de-essentialize the category of Woman are treated, by their very own omission, as *immaterial.*

All of this brings me to a possible way to negotiate the essentialist dilemma at the heart of these theories of "reading like a man" (Scholes), "reading as a woman" (Culler), or reading like a "female feminist critic" (Modleski). It is by no means insignificant that nearly every piece in the volume *Men in Feminism*, of which Scholes's "Reading like a Man" is one of the more noteworthy contributions, manifests a preoccupation with the question of place, specifically with the problem of where men stand in relation to feminism. Paul Smith wishes to claim for men the privileged space of displacement, usually reserved in deconstruction for Woman, in order to mark the difference of feminism, the subversive presence within. Stephen Heath speculates that the obsession with place is a male obsession with decidedly phallic overtones: are men "in" or "out" of feminism? Still others, Cary Nelson and Rosi Braidotti, suggest that men have no place (or at the very least no *secure* place) in feminism; according to this line of thinking, men may need feminism but feminism doesn't need men.[5] While place emerges as the recurrent theme that pulls together the twenty-four disparate essays which comprise *Men in Feminism,* I am also struck by how many of these articles inevitably come round to the question of essence, eventually invoke essentialism as the real impediment to theorizing men "in" feminism. An unarticulated relation between essence and place seems to motivate each piece. While it is no doubt imperative to continue to investigate the place of essence in contemporary critical discourse, perhaps we should be interrogating not only the place of essentialism but the essentialism of place; one question might provide us with a gloss on the other. The remainder of this article will demonstrate that the essentialism in "anti-essentialism" inheres in the notion of place or positionality. What is *essential* to social constructionism is precisely this notion of "where I stand," of what has come to be called, appropriately enough, "subject-positions."

To understand the importance of place for social constructionist theory, we must look to Jacques Lacan's poststructuralist psychoanalysis. Lacan's return to Freud is, above all, a project which seeks to reclaim the place of subjectivity as a destabilizing and decentering force from the work of ego psychologists who, through their unquestioned allegiance to Western humanism, seek to re-encapsulate the subject within a stationary, traditional Cartesian framework. It is during the "pre-subject's" passage from the Imaginary into the Symbolic that the child, under the threat of castration, recognizes the different sexed subject-positions ("he," "she") and finally assumes one.[6] It is especially significant that throughout his work Lacan always speaks in terms of the *place* of the subject. His subversive rewriting of Descartes's "I think, therefore I am" (*cogito ergo sum*) as "I think where I am not, therefore I am where I do not think" provides a good case in point (*Écrits* 166). The emphasis in Lacan's anti-cogito falls on the "where"; the question "who is speaking" can only be answered by shifting the grounds of the question to "where am I speaking from?" But it is important to remember that the place of the subject is nonetheless, ultimately, unlocalizable; were we able to fix the whereabouts of the subject in a static field of determinants, then we would be back in the realm of ego psychology. What is important about Lacan's emphasis on *place* is that thinking in terms of positionality works against the tendency of concepts such as "subject" or "ego," or "I" and "you," to solidify. The "I" in Lacanian psychoanalysis is always a precarious and unstable place to be– "intolerable," in fact, in one critic's estimation (Gallop, *Reading* 145).

Another recurrent emphasis in Lacan's work, useful for our purposes here, is his insistence on the *construction* of the subject's sexuality rather than the *de facto* assignation of a sex at birth. Lacan teaches us in "The Meaning of the Phallus" that we assume our sex, "take up its attributes only by means of a threat"–the threat of castration (*Feminine Sexuality* 75). It is because the birth of the subject does not coincide with the biological birth of the human person (Freud's fundamental insight into the problem of sexuality) that Lacan can speak in "The Mirror Stage" of "a real *specific prematurity of birth* in man" (*Écrits* 4). Jane Gallop describes our delayed entry into subjectivity this way: "the child, although already born, does not become a self until the mirror stage. Both cases are two-part birth processes: once born into 'nature,' the second time into 'history'" (*Reading* 85). The 'I,' then, is not a given at birth but rather is constructed, assumed, taken on during the subject's problematic entry into the Symbolic. Lacan's focus on the complex psychoanalytic processes which participate in the constitution of the subject is, of course, a pre-eminently anti-essentialist position and, as we shall see, it has profound implications for the way in which we think about the subject who reads and the subject who is read.

I turn now to the theory of subject-positions most recently deployed, to brilliant effect, by Gayatri Spivak in her work on the subaltern. Spivak borrows and adapts her theoretical terminology not from Lacan but from Michel Foucault, although Lacan's theory of subjectivity is everywhere in the background here. It is in *The Archaeology of Knowledge* that Foucault elaborates his own notion of subject-positions as one of the four fundamental components of "discursive formations." Recognizing this obvious debt to Foucault, it is equally important to situate Spivak's turn to subjectivity in the context of her interest in the Subaltern Studies group, a Marxist historical collective devoted to the project of exposing and undermining the elitism which characterizes traditional approaches to South Asian culture.[7] Spivak's main critique of Subaltern Studies is, in fact, the classic critique generally levelled against materialists–namely, a failure to address adequately questions of subjectivity. Although deconstructivist in their goal to displace traditional historiography, the members of Subaltern Studies nevertheless rely on certain humanist notions such as agency, totality, and presence. Spivak's "Subaltern Studies: Deconstructing Historiography" is a sharp and discerning reading of the way in which the collective's entire attempt to "let the subaltern speak" falls prey to a positivistic search for a subaltern or peasant consciousness, which, in Spivak's opinion, can never be ultimately recovered.[8] What is strikingly different about Spivak's reading of Subaltern Studies is that she does not dismiss their essentialism out of hand. In

fact, she reads the collective's humanist ambitions to locate a subaltern consciousness as "a *strategic* use of positivistic essentialism in a scrupulously
visible political interest" (205). Wittingly or unwittingly, Subaltern Studies *de-
ploys* essentialism as a provisional gesture in order to align themselves with the
very subjects who have been written out of conventional historiography:

> *Although the group does not wittingly engage with the poststructur-
> alist understanding of "consciousness," our own transactional reading
> of them is enhanced if we see them as* strategically *adhering to the
> essentialist notion of consciousness, that would fall prey to an anti-
> humanist critique, within a historiographic practice that draws many
> of its strengths from that very critique. . . . If in translating bits and
> pieces of discourse theory and the critique of humanism back into an
> essentialist historiography the historian of subalternity aligns himself
> to the pattern of conduct of the subaltern himself, it is only a progres-
> sivist view, that diagnoses the subaltern as necessarily inferior, that
> will see such an alignment to be without interventionist value. Indeed it
> is in their very insistence upon the subaltern as the subject of history
> that the group acts out such a translating back, an interventionist
> strategy that is only partially unwitting. (206–207)*

Spivak's simultaneous critique and *endorsement* of Subaltern Studies's
essentialism suggests that humanism can be activated in the service of the
subaltern; in other words, when put into practice by the dispossessed themselves, essentialism can be powerfully displacing and disruptive. This, to me,
signals an exciting new way to rethink the problem of essentialism; it represents an approach which evaluates the motivations *behind* the deployment of
essentialism rather than prematurely dismissing it as an unfortunate vestige of
patriarchy (itself an essentialist category).

I do, however, have some serious reservations about treating essentialism as "a strategy for our times" (207). While I would agree with Spivak
that a provisional return to essentialism can successfully operate, in particular
contexts, as an interventionary strategy, I am also compelled to wonder at what
point does this move cease to be provisional and become permanent? There is
always a danger that the long-term effect of such a "temporary" intervention
may, in fact, lead once again to a re-entrenchment of a more reactionary form

of essentialism. Could it be that the calls, such as Spivak's, for a strategic essentialism might be humanism's way of keeping its fundamental tenets in circulation at any cost and under any guise? Could this be "phallocentrism's latest ruse"?[29] It may well be a ruse, but in the end I would agree that the risk is worth taking. I cannot help but think that the determining factor in deciding essentialism's political or strategic value is dependent upon who practices it: in the hands of a hegemonic group, essentialism can be employed as a powerful tool of ideological domination; in the hands of the subaltern, the use of humanism to mime (in the Irigarayian sense of "to undo by overdoing") humanism can represent a powerful displacing repetition. The question of the permissibility, if you will, of engaging in essentialism is therefore framed and determined by the subject-positions from which one speaks.

We return, then, to Foucault's poststructuralist definition of "a subject" as "not the speaking consciousness, not the author of the formulation, but a position that may be filled in certain conditions by various individuals" (115). It is not difficult to translate Foucault's approach to subjectivity into a general theory of reading. For example, we might ask: what are the various positions a reading subject may occupy? How are these positions constructed? Are there possible distributions of subject-positions located in the text itself? Can a reader refuse to take up a subject-position the text constructs for him/her? Does the text construct the reading subject or does the reading subject construct the text? In "Imperialism and Sexual Difference," Spivak concludes that "the clearing of a subject-position in order to speak or write is unavoidable" (229). Now it is not clear exactly what Spivak means by this claim; is she referring to a clearing *away* of a previously held subject-position or a clearing the way *for* a particular subject-position? The ambiguity is instructive here, for when reading, speaking, or writing, we are always doing both at once. In reading, for instance, we bring (old) subject-positions to the text at the same time the actual process of reading constructs (new) subject-positions for us. Consequently, we are always engaged in a "double reading"–not in Naomi Schor's sense of the term,[10] but in the sense that we are continually caught within and between *at least* two constantly shifting subject-positions (old and new, constructed and constructing) and these positions may often stand in complete contradiction to each other.

Nothing intrinsic to the notion of subject-positions suggests that it may constitute a specifically *feminist* approach to reading; it is, however, especially compatible with recent feminist reconceptualizations of the subject as a site of multiple and heterogeneous differences. This work seeks to move beyond the self/other, "I"/"not-I" binarism central to Lacan's understanding of subject constitution and instead substitutes a notion of the "I" as a complicated field of multiple subjectivities and competing identities. There is some disagreement over whether or not this new view of the subject as heteronomous and heterogeneous marks a break with Lacan or represents the logical outcome of his theory. Teresa de Lauretis persuasively argues the former case:

> *It seems to me that this notion of identity points to a more useful*
> *conception of the subject than the one proposed by neo-Freudian*
> *psychoanalysis and poststructuralist theories. For it is not the*
> *fragmented, or intermittent, identity of a subject constructed in division*
> *by language alone, an "I" continuously prefigured and preempted in*
> *an unchangeable symbolic order. It is neither, in short, the imaginary*
> *identity of the individualist, bourgeois subject, which is male and*
> *white; nor the "flickering" of the posthumanist Lacanian subject, which*
> *is too nearly and at best (fe)male. What is emerging in feminist*
> *writings is, instead . . . a subject that is not divided in, but rather at*
> *odds with, language.* (Feminist 9)

Mary Gentile, another feminist film critic, agrees, arguing that it is precisely a woman's "tentative" subjectivity (a result of ambivalent positioning as a castrated object in the Symbolic order of the subject) which allows us to see subjectivity as a nexus of possibilities "where there is no clear split between 'I' and 'not-I,' but rather a range or continuum of existence" (19). My own position on the question is more closely aligned with Constance Penley's reasoning that the seeds of a theory of the subject as dispersed, as multiple, can already be found in Lacan's notion of the subject as a place of contradiction, continually in a state of construction. This view holds that without Lacan's concept of the "split subject," divided against itself, these new feminist theories of identity would not be possible (145). In any case, what we can take away from this specific debate on Lacan's theory of subjectivity are the strategy of positing the reader as a site of differences and the notion of the reading process as a negotiation amongst discursive subject-positions which the reader, as social subject, may or may not choose to fill.

For Foucault, which subject-positions one is likely to read from is less a matter of "choice" than "assignation." Spivak's work clarifies for us that these "I-slots" are, in fact, institutional subject-positions– "social vacancies that are of course not filled in the same way by different individuals" (*Other* 304). Though it is always dangerous to speak in terms of "choice" within a post-structuralism which deconstructs such notions as agency and free will, Spivak still provides us with a modicum of movement between institutional subject-positions. Her own reading of Mahasweta Devi's "Breast-Giver" moves carefully and deliberately among the "I-slots" of author, reader, teacher, subaltern, and historian. I see two major difficulties in applying Foucault's notion of subject-positions to either a strategy or a theory of reading. First, it leads to an inclination to taxonomize, to list one's various categorical positions in linear fashion as if they could be easily extracted and unproblematically distinguished from each other. Second, such a reading can easily lend itself to stereotyping, that is, to labelling "kinds" of readers and predicting their institutional responses as Modleski does with her hypothetical male and female reader in "Feminism and the Power of Interpretation." Spivak seems to anticipate this objection when she rightly insists that "all generalizations made from subject-positions are untotalizable" (304); yet her discussions of "the Indian reader," "the Marxist-feminist reader," and especially "the non-Marxist anti-racist feminist readers in the Anglo-U.S." who, "for terminological convenience," she categorizes under the label "liberal feminism" (254) all seem to point to a totalizing picture supporting and upholding each "I-slot."[11] Perhaps it is inevitable that we turn to such labels "for terminological convenience" (after all, how else are we to make any distinctions at all between readers?), yet the phone book compiling of "I-slot" listings can be unsettling if what we wish to emphasize is not the fixed differences between subject-positions but the fluid boundaries and continual commerce between them.

What is particularly surprising to me about the recent men in feminism debates is not the preoccupation with essence and place but the immobility, the intractableness of the privileged terms "men" and "feminism." Robert Scholes and Tania Modleski both work to *reinforce* the bar between men/feminism, each in effect erecting a defense against the incursions of the other. For although the goals of their critical projects are much the same, if not identical (to rescue feminism from the mastering impulses of deconstruction), these critics who are more allies than combatants nonetheless position them-

selves on opposite sides of the asymmetrical binarism: Scholes electing to read
"like a man," and Modleski choosing to read like a "female feminist." Stephen
Heath, on the other hand, has argued that "female feminism" can only be
viewed as a contradiction in terms. Building on Elaine Showalter's influential
"Critical Cross-Dressing: Male Feminists and the Woman of the Year," Heath
concludes that a man reading as a feminist always involves a strategy of
female impersonation (28). But is there not also a mode of impersonation involved when a woman reads as a feminist, or, indeed, when a woman reads as
a woman? Heath tentatively suggests that "maybe the task of male critics is just
to read (forget the 'as') . . ." (29), but Scholes is right to insist that we never
"just" read, that we always read *from somewhere*. The anti-essentialist "where"
is essential to the poststructuralist project of theorizing reading as a negotiation of socially constructed subject-positions. As its linguistic containment
within the very term "displacement" might suggest, place can never be entirely displaced, as it were, from deconstruction.

Let me return, in conclusion, to the question I deferred at the beginning of this consideration of gender and reading: upon what grounds can we
base the notion of a class of women reading? Both "class" and "women" are
political constructs (on this question I am most influenced by Monique Wittig)
but what, we might ask, is "politics"? Politics is precisely the self-evident
category in feminist discourse–that which is most irreducible and most indispensable. As feminism's *essential* component, it tenaciously resists definition; it
is both the most transparent and the most elusive of terms. The persistent
problem for feminist theorists of locating a suitable ground for a feminist politics finds perhaps its most urgent articulation in Donna Haraway's impressive
work on "cyborg politics": "what kind of politics could embrace partial, contradictory, permanently unclosed constructions of personal and collective selves
and still be faithful, effective?" (75). Her answer: a class of women linked
together "through coalition–affinity, not identity"–affinity based on "choice"
rather than on "nature" (73). My own inclination is to tackle these same questions of identity, politics, coalition, and feminism from the opposite direction.
Whereas Haraway posits a coalition of women as the basis of a possible feminist
socialist politics, I see politics as the basis of a possible coalition of women. For
Haraway, it is affinity which grounds politics; for me, it is politics which grounds
affinity. Politics marks the site where Haraway's project begins and where mine
ends. In both cases, politics operates as the privileged, self-evident category.

The slippage in the above paragraph from "class" to "coalition" is not merely accidental. I intend to suggest by this shift an anti-essentialist reading of "class" as a *product* of coalition. Coalition precedes class and determines its limits and boundaries; we cannot identify a group of women until various social, historical, political coalitions construct the conditions and possibilities for membership. Many anti-essentialists fear that positing a political coalition of *women* risks presuming that there must first be a natural class of women; but this belief only masks the fact that it is a coalition politics which constructs the category of women (and men) in the first place. Retaining the idea of women as a class, if anything, might help remind us that the sexual categories we work with are no more and no less than social constructions, subject-positions subject to change and to historical evolution. I am certainly not the first feminist to suggest that we need to retain the notion of women as a class for political purposes. I would, however, wish to take this conviction to its furthest conclusion and suggest that it is politics which feminism cannot do without, politics that is essential to feminism's many self-definitions. It is telling, I think, that anti-essentialists are willing to displace "identity," "self," "experience," and virtually every other self-evident category *except* politics. To the extent that it is difficult to imagine a *non-political* feminism, politics emerges as feminism's essence.

Notes

1   Adapting Kamuf's strategically reiterative formulation of "a woman writing as a woman," Culler concludes that "for a woman to read as a woman is not to repeat an identity or an experience that is given but to play a role she constructs with reference to her identity as a woman, which is also a construct, so that the series can continue: a woman reading as a woman reading as a woman" (64).

2   For example, the nominal essence of gold (Locke's favorite example) would be "that complex idea the word gold stands for, let it be, for instance, a body yellow, of a certain weight, malleable, fusible, and fixed"; its real essence would be "the constitution of the insensible parts of that body, on which those qualities, and all the other properties of gold depend" (Locke, 13.6). Locke discusses real versus nominal essence in numerous passages of *An Essay Concerning Human Understanding*, the most important of which are 2.31; 3.3; 3.6; 3.10; 4.6; and 4.12.

3   For Scholes's project to "save the referent," see "Reference and Difference" in *Textual Power* (86–110).

4 *Thinking through the Body* is the aptly-chosen title of Jane Gallop's recent collection of essays which includes a particularly discerning piece on the question of Irigaray's essentialism (see "Lip Service" 92–99).

5 See Paul Smith, "Men in Feminism: Men and Feminist Theory" (33–40); Stephen Heath, "Men in Feminism: Men and Feminist Theory" (41–46); Cary Nelson, "Men, Feminism: The Materiality of Discourse" (153–72); and Rosi Braidotti, "Envy: or With My Brains and Your Looks" (233–41), all in Jardine and Smith.

6 For a more detailed reading of the constitution of the sexed subject, see Lacan's "Mirror Stage" in *Écrits* (1–7).

7 For a summary statement of the collective's theoretical positions, see Guha (esp. vii–viii).

8 For Spivak's full critique of essentialism in the Subaltern Studies group, see *Other* 202–207.

9 The phrase is Naomi Schor's: "what is it to say that the discourse of sexual indifference/pure difference is not the last or (less triumphantly) the latest ruse of phallocentrism?" ("Dreaming" 109). This is implicitly a critique of Foucault's anti-essentialism, suggesting that both essentialism and anti-essentialism can have reactionary effects.

10 For Schor's helpful definition of "reading double" as reading both for and beyond difference, see "Reading" (250).

11 Spivak insists hers is merely a reading strategy and not a comprehensive theory. The distinction she makes between these two notions is not entirely clear; is it possible to employ a reading strategy outside a larger theoretical framework?

Works Cited

Culler, Jonathan. "Reading as a Woman." *On Deconstruction: Theory and Criticism after Structuralism*. Ithaca: Cornell UP, 1982. 43–64.

de Lauretis, Teresa. *Alice Doesn't: Feminism, Semiotics, Cinema*. Bloomington: Indiana UP, 1984.

_____, ed. *Feminist Studies/Critical Studies*. Bloomington: Indiana UP, 1986.

Derrida, Jacques. "Deconstruction in America: An Interview with Jacques Derrida." *Critical Exchange* 17 (1985): 1–33.

Devi, Mahasweta. "Breast-giver." Spivak, *In Other Worlds* 222–40.

Foucault, Michel. *The Archaeology of Knowledge*. Trans. A. M. Sheridan Smith. New York: Pantheon, 1972.

Gallop, Jane. *Reading Lacan*. Ithaca: Cornell UP, 1985.

_____. Thinking through the Body. New York: Columbia UP, 1988.

Gentile, Mary C. Film *Feminisms: Theory and Practice*. Westport, CT: Greenwood, 1985.

Grimshaw, Jean. *Philosophy and Feminist Thinking*. Minneapolis: U of Minnesota P, 1986.

Guha, Ranajit, ed. *Subaltern Studies: Writings on South Asian History and Society*. Vol. 3. Delhi: Oxford UP, 1984. 5 vols. to date. 1982–.

Haraway, Donna. "A Manifesto for Cyborgs: Science, Technology, and Socialist Feminism in the 1980s." *Socialist Review* 80 (1985): 65–107.

Irigaray, Luce. *Speculum of the Other Woman*. Trans. Gillian C. Gill. Ithaca: Cornell UP, 1985.

_____. *This Sex Which Is Not One*. Trans. Catherine Porter with Carolyn Burke. Ithaca: Cornell UP, 1985.

Jardine, Alice, and Paul Smith, eds. *Men in Feminism*. New York: Methuen, 1987.

Kamuf, Peggy. "Writing like a Woman." *Women and Language in Literature and Society*. Ed. Sally McConnell–Ginet, Ruth Barker, and Nelly Forman. New York: Praeger, 1980. 284–99.

Lacan, Jacques. Écrits: *A Selection*. Trans. Alan Sheridan. New York: Norton, 1977.

_____. *Feminine Sexuality: Jacques Lacan and the école freudienne*. Ed. Juliet Mitchell and Jacqueline Rose. New York: Norton, 1982.

Locke, John. *An Essay Concerning Human Understanding*. London: Elizabeth Holt for Thomas Bassett, 1690.

Modleski, Tania. "Feminism and the Power of Interpretation: Some Critical Readings." De Lauretis, *Feminist Studies*. 121–38.

Penley, Constance. "Teaching in Your Sleep." *Theory in the Classroom*. Ed. Cary Nelson. Urbana: U of Illinois P, 1986. 129–48.

Scholes, Robert. "Reading like a Man." Jardine and Smith 204–18.

_____. *Textual Power: Literary Theory and the Teaching of English*. New Haven: Yale UP, 1985.

Schor, Naomi. "Dreaming Dissymmetry: Barthes, Foucault, and Sexual Difference." Jardine and Smith 98–110.

_____. "Reading Double: Sand's Difference." *The Poetics of Gender*. Ed. Nancy K. Miller. New York: Columbia UP, 1986. 248–69.

Showalter, Elaine. "Critical Cross-Dressing: Male Feminists and the Woman of the Year." Jardine and Smith 116–32.

Spivak, Gayatri Chakravorty. "Imperialism and Sexual Difference." *Oxford Literary Review* 8.1–2 (1986): 225–40.

_____. *In Other Worlds: Essays in Cultural Politics.* New York: Methuen, 1987.

Wittig, Monique. "One Is Not Born a Woman." *Feminist Issues* 1.2 (1981): 47–54.

_____. "The Category of Sex." *Feminist Issues* 2.2 (1982): 63–68.

Éperon Strings

Apron. An article of dress . . . worn in front of the body, to protect the clothes from dirt or injury. A similar garment, worn as part of a distinctive official dress, as by bishops, deans . . .

Apron-string. The string with which an apron is tied on. *Apron-string hold* or *tenure*: tenure of property in virtue of one's wife or during her life-time only. *Tied to the apron strings* (of a mother, wife, etc.): unduly controlled by her, wholly under her influence. (*OED*)

A fortuitous conjunction of sounds brings together a French word and an English one: *éperon*, or spur, the phallic hook upon which Derrida hangs his discussion of Nietzsche and the feminine–and *apron*, an English word for a garment with a span broad enough to cover manual labor, male pride of rank, tenure that depends upon the feminine, female domestic labor, and feminine power over men. Derrida himself has taught us how to take such fortuitous gifts of language and weave them into a text of many colors, as in his treatment of the French pronunciation of Hegel and the French word for eagle. Following his brilliant example, one could readily produce a pseudo brilliant rhapsody on spurs and aprons–but such a text would never escape the tedium of the pseudo. You can see without my guidance, I am sure, how the word "apron," with its marvelous slippage across class and gender, power and powerlessness, could be used to cover and to uncover or open a discussion of essence and difference, of the relationship between feminism and deconstruction. Will you allow me to avoid trying to guide you? Can we pretend that we are like the prisoners in the famous metajoke, who knew their fixed canon of jokes so well that they could refer to them by numbers without the tedium of telling them? Can I just say, "Here are the pieces for a deconstructive game–apron and *éperon*–play it yourself"? I am going to assume that I can do just this, that you and I share a discourse in which such gestures are possible. This will not only save some time and possibly avoid some tedium, but it will also make a point that I think is crucial.

The point is this. We are in a situation that is neither static nor reversible. To the extent that we can "do" Derrida, to the extent that we have learned his lesson complete (as Walt Whitman says), we cannot go on doing it. We have got to go beyond it. (Derrida, *of course*, would respond that you cannot learn his lesson "complete" because it is not complete, and that he himself is always already aware of the necessity of going beyond it. Yes, but my point lies in the *of course*. How Derrida can escape it is his problem. How we can, is ours.) I think this is especially true of feminist discourse–of which it should be admitted at once, I am a student rather than a practitioner. In saying why I believe we must go on, and in suggesting what I might mean by going on, I shall have to return and look more closely at the text of Derrida's *Éperons* itself. But before doing that I must say what I hope to accomplish here and why I am attempting it. I have argued in other essays such as "Reading like a Man" (the relevant portions of which appear in my book *Protocols of Reading*) that deconstruction is (a) founded on some untenable assumptions about language, (b) often makes its critical effects by holding others to a rigor that it abandons itself at crucial moments, and (c) falters when faced with the need to take action in the ethico-political realm, because it cannot shake its "de" in order to make constructive moves. The present essay is meant to contribute to this on-going critique and to invite others into the process as well. I welcome, for instance, such critical responses to "Reading like a Man" as that of Diana Fuss (in this volume). I should say at once that I think her criticism is well founded. I have no desire to go back and defend those positions but to press on and try to reshape them in the light of such criticism as hers. In the present essay I shall be doing that in two ways: by criticizing the notion of "anti-essentialism" itself and by accepting Fuss's view that we need to reduce or weaken the bar between maleness and feminism as privileged concepts. But let me put on my apron and get to work.

My topic here will be the relationship of feminism to essentialism and its "anti" (or aunty?), as this matter is brought into focus by Derrida's treatment of it in *Éperons*, an influential text which I shall try to present as exemplary of certain difficulties in the anti-essentialist position. Derrida's importance to feminism need not be argued, I assume, since there is evidence of it in many places, as, for instance, in Toril Moi's gesture of giving him the last words in her excellent overview of feminist literary theory: *Sexual/Textual Politics*. In the quoted passage, taken from his interview, "Choreographies," he mentions his dream of a world which is not "a-sexual" but "sexual otherwise: beyond the binary difference that governs the decorum of all codes" (Moi 173). I say he "mentions" his dream because he does not describe it, and, in my view, could never describe it, since what it might mean to be "sexual otherwise" cannot find expression in our language–and if it could, this "otherwise" would hardly be recognizable as "sexual." The impossibility of textualizing such an "otherwise" is enacted for us in *Éperons*. Let us consider it.

The dream of a world in which we might be "sexual otherwise" is equivalent in Derrida's thought to the wish for an end to the regime of metaphysics, an event which, like the Second Coming, is sometimes held to be at hand but resolutely refuses to occur. In Moi's reference to it, for instance, the event appears to be impending: ". . . if, as Derrida has argued, we are still living under the reign of metaphysics . . ." (139). I like the "still." It suggests that sometime, maybe not tomorrow, maybe not next week, but sometime or other, this reign will be over. Until then, we can perhaps hope to shelter ourselves under that umbrella lost (or forgotten) by Nietzsche and found again by Derrida at the end of *Éperons*. But I doubt if there is room for more than one under that umbrella, and even that one is going to get wet. Nietzsche seems to have believed that the end of metaphysics had arrived. In fact, he sometimes thought he had delivered its coup de grace himself, putting "the real world" out of its misery, and demolishing the world of appearances along with it. The reign of Plato was over. The sun would shine anew: "Mid-day; moment of the shortest shadow; end of the longest error; zenith of mankind; INCIPIT ZARATHUSTRA" (41). That was over a century ago, however, and Derrida is much more circumspect in his claims. More than once he has indicated that metaphysics, like the poor, will always be with us, which means, of course, that deconstructors will always have work to do.

Despite his nostalgia for the "mythogram" (*Grammatology* 84–87), Derrida seems not to fear that the metaphysical regime will fall from power during his own period of loyal opposition. Indeed, he has done much to help us see the impossibility of a human existence free of metaphysical suppositions. Reduced to its stark, enthymemic outline, what he has helped us understand goes something like this: No world without things. No things without differences. No differences without language. No language without nouns. No nouns without categories. No categories without metaphysics, logocentrism, and all the mechanisms of subjection. The outline of this position is already there in Nietzsche, as in his little narrative, "How the 'Real World' Became a Myth" (40–41), which plays a crucial role in Derrida's *Éperons*. Nietzsche suggests, in this brief text, that the chain linking the world to metaphysics has finally been worn down to the point where a bold word may break it–and he, or Zarathustra, will utter that word. What he doesn't quite go on to say is that the minute Zarathustra speaks his first word–whatever it is–metaphysics will be reinstated. Even paradox, self-contradiction, and all the "on-the-one-hand-on-the-other-hands" you please cannot totally undo the power of language to bring a world into being around it: a world ineluctably marked by the metaphysical power of that very language.

Derrida may dream of a world that is "sexual otherwise" but the minute he tries to describe it, it will either fail to be purely "otherwise" or become unrecognizable as sexual. The problem here is not uniquely connected with sexuality. It is a problem of language and the grounding of language in experiences that are common to a group of people. Without common color perceptions, for instance, humans would have been unable to generate a terminology of color. That is, as Wittgenstein pointed out, if we encountered a race that perceived colors that we do not, we "would still not be forced to recognize that they see *colours* that we do not see. There is, after all, no *commonly* accepted criterion for what is a colour, if it is not one of our colours" (sect. 1, prop. 14). "Sexuality otherwise" is "otherwise" only because it is outside our text, our shared nexus of language and perceptions. If it is textualized, it will cease to be otherwise, and if it is not connected to already textualized sexuality, we will not recognize it as sexuality at all. If to hold concepts in common is to essentialize, then language always essentializes. Whenever we speak or write, we are, willy nilly, essentialists. Derrida, for instance, in his actual discussion of gender in *Éperons*, proves unable to avoid essentializing notions himself, even as he tries to undo essentialism. In this he simply embodies the problems of anti-essentialism in general, which is a position that cannot be articulated, cannot even name itself, without embarrassment. These problems appear in his text at the level of both the subject and the object. His difficulties at the sub-jective level become acute when he employs the first person plural in addressing his audience. As usual–and it is one of the things that makes him attractive as a writer–he is aware of these difficulties the moment they arise, and he directs our attention to them. Mentioning a problem, however, is not the same thing as solving it. The problem surfaces during his discussion of "woman" and castration:

> La "femme"–le mot fait époque–ne croit pas davantage à l'envers franc de la castration, à l'anti-castration. Elle est trop rusée pour cela et elle sait–d'elle, de son opération du moins, nous, mais qui, nous? devrions l'apprendre–qu'un tel renversement lui ôterait toute possibilité de simulacre, reviendrait en vérité au même et installerait plus sûrement que jamais dans la vieille machine, dans la phallogocentrisme assisté de son compère, image inversée des pupilles, élève chahuteur c'est-à-dire disciple discipliné du maître. (60)

> "Woman"—that epoch-making word—no longer believes in the simple opposite of castration: anti-castration. She is too wily for that and she knows (from her—or at least from her way of operating—we, but who, we? should learn) that such a reversal would strip from her all the possibilities of performance, would return her to the truth of sameness and install her more certainly in the old machine of phallogocentrism, along with her peer, the student who rebels by a merely optical inver-sion, which is to say the disciplines disciple of the master.[1]

Who is it that can learn from "woman"? Derrida asks the question even as he is urging "us" to learn what "he" must already know, since he tells us what it is. If "he" already knows this, of course, he cannot fully belong to the group desig-nated by "us"–the group of those who do not know what "woman" knows. In what sense, then, is he one of "us"? Are "we" those who are not "woman"? Are "we" those who are "man"? Or is there a gap between these categories into which a "rusé" non-woman may slide? Derrida implies that he is not "woman" though he knows what "woman" knows. He is nothing if not "rusé" himself. Less obviously, he may indeed think of himself as "woman" but be pretending here, for rhetorical purposes, not to be. If this is so, then we need to follow his question ("qui, nous?") and ask, "Who is not 'woman'?" Under the regime of the old logic, who is not "woman" must be "man." Derrida seems to suggest, however, that it is possible to escape the play of this binary system altogether and be something else–be "sexual otherwise," perhaps, but what is it that could make this "otherwise" sexual at all? Here and elsewhere, the masters of deconstruction act as if they–and only they–could escape the play of textuality, as if they could turn the binary and referential qualities of language on and off like a light switch. This escape from textual sexuality is indicated here in the form of that question: "qui, nous?" But any attempt to answer the question, to *name* this unnamed being, to describe some genderless sexuality, will bring us back to our metaphysical world.

It could be said, even, that deconstruction is founded upon this impossible move outside of language. In his early and important lecture on "Différance," Derrida insisted that this neologism (or neographism)–*différance* with an "a"–was "neither a word nor a concept," but in the discussion that followed the lecture (in the Michelet Amphiteatre of the Sorbonne) Jean Wahl observed that this term that could not be spoken of had nevertheless been discussed in a fascinating way for over an hour (*Speech*). The claim that one's own terminology escapes the metaphysical polarities of language has something in it of the magical, or the rules of children's games. "I had my fingers crossed when I said it. . . ." Many believers in deconstruction accept this principle (*credo quia absurdum est*)–Rodolphe Gasché for instance, in *The Tain of the Mirror*–but Richard Rorty (and rightly, I believe) has observed that, "Paying these compliments to Derrida's words seems to me whistling in the dark– saying that it would be nice if there were words which had this impossible combination of properties without explaining how the combination is supposed to have been made possible" (124 n.6). As T. S. Eliot's Sweeney says, "I've gotta use words when I talk to you" and Derrida's gotta too. But let us return to the overwhelming question, "qui, nous?" which was left hanging by Derrida at the end of his lecture on "The Ends of Man" (*Margins*) only to be reinserted into his discussion of the essence of woman. Let us return to that question and the other questions posed by his writing.

Every question implies its answer, and we cannot read Derrida without supplying names and concepts for the spaces generated by his text. That is, we cannot enter the play of his text without seeking a code that will render it intelligible to us. We cannot respond to him thoughtfully without bringing his text, however tentatively and judiciously, within some common frame of language. Which means that we must persevere in probing his terms and concepts, asking, for example, what he means in the present instance, by "woman." Who is this "woman" who is wily and possessed of important knowledge? What has "woman" to do with "gender"? And what is the gender, if any, of "we"? If "we" means "we who are not 'woman,'" which is surely one of the things it is most likely to mean, then we must ask who these non-women may be. Men? All men? Some men? Men and women, too, who do not belong to the category "woman"? Is "woman" even a "category"? What does Derrida mean by this word that, as he suggests, generates its own brackets, its own quotation marks, a word that may be, in fact, not even a word in the usual sense of the word "word." This word or non-word, and what it does or does not refer to, are actually the subject of *Éperons*: "la femme sera mon sujet" ("woman will be my subject"–which may mean that his topic will be woman, or that he will feminize his own subjectivity, or that he will subjugate woman [36]).

As it emerges, the view of "woman" presented by Derrida turns out to be closer than one would have expected to the old clichés, the old "truths" about "woman." "La donna e mobile," says tradition, and so says Derrida. "Il n'y a pas une femme, une vérité la femme en soi" ("there is no woman, a truth of woman as such" [100]) says Derrida, and he says that Nietzsche *also* says this, and he also says this *about* Nietzsche: "Il n'y pas une vérité de Nietzsche" ("there is no truth of Nietzsche" [102]). By this logic, which is an illogical argument–a syllogism of the form known as Barbara, but with an undistributed middle term, a bad Barbara–Derrida argues that, because all women are inconsistent, and Nietzsche is inconsistent, Nietzsche is a woman. Specifically, he is this castrated woman that he feared, this castrating woman that he also feared, and this affirmative woman that he loved:

> Il était, il redoutait telle femme châtrée.
> Il était, il redoutait telle femme castratrice.
> Il était, il aimait telle femme affirmatrice. (100)

Are women essentially illogical, destined biologically to participate in the "higher" logic or anti-logic of deconstruction? If so, does this make Derrida, too, a "woman"? Let us leave these questions open, for the moment. We shall return to them, and to the question of "who, we?" before concluding this discussion, but first it is necessary to explore further the picture of "woman" that

Derrida is drawing here. Discussing the power, the need, of "woman" to operate at a distance, he describes "woman" in terms closely analogous to those he
uses elsewhere to describe "différance":

> . . . *"la femme" n'est peut-être pas quelque chose, l'identité déterminable
> d'une figure qui, elle, s'annonce à distance, à distance d'autre chose, et
> dont il y aurait à s'éloigner ou à s'approcher. Peut-être est-elle, comme
> non-identité non-figure, simulacre, l'*abîme *de la distance, le distance-
> ment de la distance, la coupe de l'espacement, la distance elle-même si
> l'on pouvait encore dire, ce qui est impossible, la distance* elle-même.
> *La distance se distance, le loin s'éloigne. (48)*

> . . . *"woman" is perhaps not a thing, not the determinate identity of a
> shape that presents itself at a distance from some other thing, a
> distance that might be increased or reduced. Perhaps she is, as non-
> identity, non-shape, simulacrum, the gap in distance, the distanciation
> of distance, the gash of spacing, distance itself, if one could still say
> that, which is impossible, distance herself. Distance distances, the
> remove removes.*

This is very close to allegory, as when, in *The Faerie Queene*, the shamefast or
modest knight of Temperance, Sir Guyon, is outblushed by Shamefastness herself. Here "woman" is seen as the very principle of Derridean *différance*, the
dimensionless cause of dimension, the shapeless cause of shapes. *La donna e
mobile* with a vengeance. Woman is the antithesis of essence. She is essentially
anti-essential:

> *Il n'y a pas d'essence de la femme parce que la femme écarte et s'écarte
> d'elle même. Elle engloutit, envoile par le fond, sans fin, sans fond,
> toute essentialité, toute identité, toute propriété. Ici aveuglé le discours
> philosophique sombre–se laisse précipiter à sa perte. Il n'y a pas de
> vérité de la femme mais c'est parce que cet écart abyssal de la vérité,
> cette non-vérité est la "vérité." Femme est un nom de cette non-vérité de
> la vérité. (50)*

> *There is no essence of woman because woman splits and divides
> herself from herself. Limitless, baseless, she engulfs, distorts*

fundamentally, all essentiality, all identity, all property. Here blinded philosophical discourse founders–allows itself to fall into ruin. There is no truth of woman but this is because the abyssal split in the truth, this untruth, is the "truth." Woman is a name for this untruth of truth.

"Woman," as we must be aware by now, is indeed a name–in Derridean discourse–for a whole lot of things that are mobile, divided, differential, split, engulfing. What, if anything, does this name have to do with women, with human beings who are bio-culturally categorized as female? The properties of "woman"–as Derrida describes them–are not freely invented, *ex nihilo*. As I have suggested, they come partly from a repertory of gnomic wisdom which insists that *la donna e mobile*. They also seem to come partly from feminine biology or anatomy. Surely it is not by chance that woman "s'écarte" and "engloutit": opens herself and engulfs. Derrida connects "woman" to writing, which he opposes to "style," to the *éperon*, the spur, the ram that pierces the side or bottom of an enemy ship–figures, that carry their own traces of male anatomy and male behavior as coded in our cultural repertory ("si le style était . . . l'homme, l'écriture serait la femme"; "if the style were . . . the man, writing would be the woman" [56]). The ellipsis in that quotation connects man and style with the penis, as what Freud calls "the normal prototype of the fetish." "Woman" escapes from the binarisms of true and false and from the whole field of castration–in order to be reinserted in the new binarism of style versus writing. Freud is invoked lightly here, between the imperfect and the conditional, but one cannot touch Freud without becoming implicated in biology. An essentializing tradition hovers around Derrida's thought, lending it support at crucial moments. And where, in all this, are women, as opposed to "woman"?

The plural of this noun hardly appears–except in citations–in *Éperons*, which makes its rare appearances interesting. It is especially interesting, of course, that this plural form should appear most insistently just when the question of feminism arises.

C'est "l'homme" qui croit à la vérité de la femme, à la femme-vérité.
Et en vérité les femmes féministes contre lesquelles Nietzsche multiplie le sarcasme, ce sont les hommes. Le féminisme, c'est l'opération par laquelle la femme veut ressembler à l'homme, au philosophique, revendiquant la vérité, la science, l'objectivité c'est-à-dire avec toute

*l'illusion virile, l'effet de castration qui s'y attache. Le féminisme veut
la castration–aussi de la femme. Perd le style. (64)*

*It is "man" who believes in the truth of woman, in woman-truth. And in
truth the feminist women against whom Nietzsche multiplies his
sarcasm, are men. Feminism is the operation through which woman
wants to become like man, to be philosophical, to reclaim truth,
science, objectivity; which is to say the entire virile illusion and the
castration effect that goes along with it. Feminism wants castration–of
women as well. Loss of style.*

This passage, in which women, as opposed to "woman,"–and specifically feminist women at that–are mentioned, must be considered at length. Here Derrida
argues that to want the phallic spur is to lose it, to enter the system of castration, and to enter this system is to lose one's status as "woman"–already defined
as the being who avoids the phallogocentric field of castration and anti-
castration. How different is this argument from that put forward a century ago
by those who told women that they were losing their femininity by agitating for
the vote, by seeking a share of power? In its handsome deconstructive sheep-
skin, isn't this the same old wolf after all?

The problem that arises here is partly a problem of reference. That is,
what–or who–is Derrida talking about? In his famous lecture on "Différance,"
he said many times that "différance" was neither a word nor a concept, though
it became more like both every time he mentioned it. The difficulties of "différance" are multiplied, however, when the word "woman" is substituted for it
in the same verbal structures. This is so partly because "différance" was at least
a new spelling and therefore in a technical sense not yet a word recognized by
any dictionary, and also because under its old spelling it had been used to mean
rather similar things–by Hegel, for instance. Let us stop on this point, for a
moment, since it is relevant to our larger concern with essentialism. Hegel
begins his discussion of Difference in the *Lesser Logic*, with the following statement: "Essence is mere Identity and reflection in itself only as it is self-relating
negativity, and in that way self-repulsion. It contains therefore essentially the
characteristic of *Difference*" (sec. 116; emphasis in original). In lecturing on this
section of the *Encyclopaedia*, he added, "Identity is undoubtedly a negative–not
however an abstract empty Nought, but the negation of Being and its character-

istics. Being so, Identity is at the same time self-relation, and, what is more, negative self-relation; in other words, it draws a distinction between it and itself."

Hegel suggests, here and elsewhere, that Essence, the hidden truth of Being, is always a matter of Difference, or negative self-relation. To establish the precise connection between Derridean "différance" and Hegel's "Difference" would require more space and greater powers than are at my disposal. I introduce the passage from Hegel, nevertheless, partly as a way of suggesting that the current debate over essentialism probably assumes too simple a notion of essence to begin with (and Derrida himself is guilty of this in the passage on essentialism quoted above), but also to indicate that Derridean "différance" is intelligible to us because it has a philosophical pedigree that connects it to the mainstream of Continental thought. What I am contesting here is not that term in itself but the move from that term to "woman," which, I believe, attains the powers of allegorical freeplay only by abandoning those of philosophical rigor. Whereas Derrida at his best keeps rigor and play together with great skill, in this case, as in certain others, he allows his rhetoric to overwhelm the rigor of his thought. Only by doing so can he rewrite "différance" as "woman."

In the passage that we are considering, Derrida argues that feminist women become men by trying to think like "man" instead of thinking the womanly (which is to say, deconstructive) thoughts appropriate to them. In this passage he stops short of saying that the thinking of properly deconstructive thoughts will turn men into women, but that is certainly his conclusion about Nietzsche. "Man" and "woman" figure in this discourse not as referential categories designating two human genders, but as–what? As ideal types. Allegory is always tinged with Platonism, and every attempt to get away from essence in the form of the categorical nouns required by language leads back to essence in the form of unutterable ideas that lie beyond human understanding. In the present case we have the ideal types of "man" and "woman" operating in the same context with the referential categories of men and women. It is only by using both the ideal and the referential binarisms that Derrida can say that to be a feminist is to think like a "man."

What he actually says, however, goes beyond this. He says that feminist women *are* men. That is, he slides from his ideal types to referential categories, and, as he does so, he invokes "truth" himself: "en vérité les femmes féministes . . . ce sont les hommes" (64). Is this a blunder, or is it ironic self-parody, in which Derrida proclaims himself a member of the truth-seeking, style-haunted class of men, relying on "us" to acquit him of this charge, knowing, as we do, that he is too "rusé" to use the word "truth" seriously? To "save" Derrida we may call it irony, but we shall have to face the fact that he has made similar statements less ironically on other occasions. Furthermore, if this is all ironic play, we must then ask how it is to be connected to our lives, our hopes, and our fears. Is there no way to act in the world except by putting on spurs and becoming "man"? I think there is. We can consider it in terms of another figure, the putting on of that bisexual garment of labor and power, the apron. But we shall have to put something on. We shall have to enter language and accept the responsibility of its inevitable binarism and dialecticity.

Once upon a time, "essentialism" was opposed by an "existentialism" that emphasized the priority of actions over concepts in human affairs. The position that is now called "anti-essentialism," however, is just as opposed to existentialism as to the essentialism that it claims to repudiate. In particular, to the extent that the anti-essentialist position is a deconstructive one, it is especially opposed to choice, preferring always to remain on both sides of crucial questions, and to undo ironically every statement it seems to be making. This position of fastidious invulnerability is very tempting at the present time to intellectuals of all genders. But it is not a good position for those who would change our present state of affairs. If "we" are those who want patriarchy replaced with gynarchy, anti-essentialism is clearly the wrong tool for that job. If, "on the other hand," "we" are those who are tired of all invidious gender distinctions, we had better not succumb to the flattering notion that "woman" is designed for the play of writing while only "man" is stupid enough to pursue the illusions of truth and power.

To put it another way, if "woman" is defined as the being without an essence, where does that leave "man"? Is Derrida implying that "man" has an essence while "woman" does not? If so, this is merely a rewriting of the phallic opposition of presence and absence, with the signs reversed. To have an essence is bad and to lack one is good. Those who have them will thus envy those who lack them and will try to get rid of the nasty things. If deconstructionists were priests, castration would be a sacrament. If, on the other hand, both "man" and "woman" lack essences, then to say that "woman" lacks an essence is to say nothing at all. Such a lack can be significant only if it is supported by its opposite. Absence needs presence in order to be meaningful as absence. If one denies all essences, if, that is, one claims to be a thorough-going anti-essentialist, then one cannot make meaningful distinctions on the basis of the absence and presence of essence. Put more specifically, if "woman" and "man" both lack essences, if, indeed, there is no such thing as essence, then we cannot distinguish between man and woman in terms of such an abso-lute and had better stop using those terms as the names for ideal types. If, on the other hand, it is the essence of man to have an essence, and the essence of woman to lack one, we are back in the familiar structure of the castration system once again. Maybe the problem is not that of spurs at all. Maybe there's something wrong with the horse. Or maybe there isn't any horse there at all, making spurs the image of some impossible retro/macho dream of power. Why don't we take off our *éperons*, put on our aprons, and take a look together at what is and isn't there in our selves and in our world?

Note

1   Translations from *Éperons* in this essay will be my own. I have not quoted Barbara Harlow's translations here because they are very free, often omit things, and sometimes just plain get it wrong, as when she translates "n'enfante pas" as "begets nothing" (64/65) instead of "gives birth to nothing"–thus missing a crucial metaphor of gender. In all fairness, it must be admitted that this is a text so full of word play as to be nearly untranslatable. Certainly, I do not claim perfection for the translations I have supplied.

Works Cited

Culler, Jonathan. On Deconstruction: Theory and Criticism after Structuralism. Ithaca: Cornell UP, 1982.

Derrida, Jacques. *Margins of Philosophy.* Trans. Alan Bass. Chicago: U of Chicago P, 1982.

_____. *Of Grammatology.* Trans. Gayatri Chakravorty Spivak. Baltimore: Johns Hopkins UP, 1976.

_____. *Speech and Phenomena, and Other Essays on Husserl's Theory of Signs.* Trans. David B. Alison. Evanston: Northwestern UP, 1973.

_____. *Spurs: Nietzsche's Styles/Éperons: Les Styles de Nietzsche.* Trans. Barbara Harlow. Intro. Stefano Agosti. Chicago: U of Chicago P, 1978.

Gasché, Rodolphe. *The Tain of the Mirror: Derrida and the Philosophy of Reflection.* Cambridge: Harvard UP, 1986.

Hegel, G. W. F. *Hegel's Logic. Being Part One of the Encyclopaedia of the Physical Sciences.* Trans. William Wallace. Oxford: Oxford UP, 1975.

Moi, Toril. *Sexual/Textual Politics: Feminist Literary Theory.* London: Methuen, 1985.

Nietzsche, Friedrich. *Twilight of the Idols.* Trans. R. J. Hollingdale. Harmondsworth: Penguin, 1987.

Rorty, Richard. *Contingency, Irony, and Solidarity.* Cambridge: Cambridge UP, 1989.

Scholes, Robert. Protocols of Reading. New Haven: Yale UP, 1989.

Wittgenstein, Ludwig. *Remarks on Colour.* Linda L. McAlister and Margarete Schättle. Ed. G. E. M. Anscombe. Bilingual ed. Berkeley: U of California P, 1978.

Essentialism and Its Contexts: Saint-Simonian and Poststructuralist Feminists

*A*n historical affiliation between the Saint-Simonian feminists of the 1830s and French poststructuralist feminists links two groups of sexual radicals who analyze the repression of women's bodies as fundamental to the socio-symbolic order. It is therefore not surprising to read the Saint-Simoniennes celebrating a feminine essence even more unqualified than that for which Hélène Cixous, Luce Irigaray, and Julia Kristeva have been criticized.[1] This criticism sees their celebrations of Woman and the Maternal as flaws in otherwise valuable theories. Yet if this essentialism is viewed not essentially, but through an historical and structural perspective, it can instead appear as an unavoidable and unstable element of a more encompassing feminist discourse. Instead of resting in fixed opposition to each other, essentialism and anti-essentialism would work as interdependent, unstable terms of one necessarily heterogeneous and oscillating feminist strategy.

The Saint-Simonian Feminists

A study of the Saint-Simoniennes' writings can offer such an historical perspective on feminist essentialism. But first, let me identify briefly this remarkable group of young proletarian women, who gathered in Paris in 1832 to organize the first consciously separatist feminist movement in history and to publish a journal, *La Tribune des Femmes* (The Tribune of Women), which in its first issue announced: "We will include articles only by women" (1.8).[2] They had been recruited to the Saint-Simonian socialist movement by the charismatic Prosper Enfantin, who rose to leadership after the death of Claude Henri, comte de Saint-Simon, in 1825.

Enfantin transformed the founder's rationalist doctrine of socio-economic justice, in which the emancipation of women played a minor role, into a romantic utopianism centered around a mystical feminism. According to him, the dominant socio-economic order produced social misery by repressing what the gender system of the time coded as feminine–sentiment, love, peace, harmony. Enfantin proposed a new Religion, dedicated to a bi-sexual god "Dieu Père et Mère," a new form of the Family, cemented by bonds of love rather than property inheritance, and a "new morality." This latter would overcome the spirit/matter hierarchy through the "rehabilitation of the flesh." Since the dominant symbolic system associated women with the body, the new morality would center around the emancipation of woman, but, according to Enfantin, it was the men who would emancipate woman.[5]

As Father, Enfantin needed a Mother to join him at the head of this new movement. After an abortive attempt to place in the role of mother bourgeois women, like Claire Bazard, the wife of his co-leader Saint-Amand Bazard, or Aglaë Saint Hilaire, an old family friend, Enfantin redefined the Mother as an absent ideal, a "Woman-Messiah" whose coming would bring about equality and love between men and women, as between bourgeois and proletarians. In 1832, he declared that the Saint-Simonian movement had entered "the wait for the woman" (qtd. in Démar 120), and encouraged his sons to enter on a fervent quest for her.

Transposing romantic desire from literature to the realm of social activism, Enfantin made Woman into an absence so that She could function as the eroticized object of the quest for economic, social, and sexual justice. Speaking at a Saint-Simonian meeting, in November 1831, Enfantin pointed to the empty chair next to his as the symbol that "Woman is lacking to the doctrine" (Démar 120). In the same speech, declaring that he could no longer speak for women, and that they had to be free and equal to speak for themselves before they could be equal with men, Enfantin excluded the women from the Saint-Simonian organization: "Women will no longer, outside of the doctrine, form part of the Saint-Simonian family." "The call of woman," said Enfantin, "is an apostolate of men" (Démar 120), and so, the (absent) Ideal Woman replaced real women.

Like many of today's male poststructuralists, Enfantin's "Apostolate of the Woman" made woman into an object of male theory. Through the feminine, men would liberate themselves, and also, they thought, liberate women. But although these theories use Woman to exclude women, they also inspire women to reappropriate for their own theories what the men have taken. The young embroiderers, seamstresses, laundresses, and prostitutes of 1832, like the women philosophers and critics of the 1970s and '80s, developed their own theory and practice engendered by the Mother, a practice that brought them into ambivalent relations with the Saint-Simonian men. Many of the writers of *La Tribune des Femmes* expressed this ambivalence by continuing to identify themselves as Saint-Simonians but at the same time insisting on their independence and often angrily criticizing the men and their theories.

A Tradition of Feminist Essentialism

An analysis of the Saint-Simoniennes, if it can tell us anything about the signs of feminist essentialism in different historical contexts and in different signifying structures, would need to establish, with respect to this problem, certain rudimentary similarities and differences between the women writing in two different periods of one historical tradition. The two essentialist expressions will be defined here, in accord with Domna Stanton's critique of Cixous, Irigaray, and Kristeva, in terms of the "ontotheologic" (162), as an innate, unchangeable nature, originating in biology and/or God. Stanton shows that contemporary feminist essentialism rests ultimately on a claim to the maternal as an actuality or potentiality in every woman. This is also the case for the Saint-Simoniennes. The gender division that, according to them, makes women "creatures of sentiment" (*Tribune* 70) has its basis in the capacity for motherhood. Seamstress Jeanne-Desirée Veret writes in the *Tribune*: "The banner of women is universal, for . . . are they not all united by the same bond, that of MATERNITY" (38).

This biological image becomes a principal metaphor, in both groups of feminist texts, for a practice that seeks to liberate the feminine body through a feminine writing, but with historical differences. Conceived as a poststructuralist dislocation of the phallocentric "law of meaning in language," Cixous's "écriture féminine" inscribes feminine bodily drives as text (*With* 76). The direct inscription of a heterogeneous *jouissance* can, according to her, multiply the unitary relation between signifier and signified through a maternal explosion of language.

Since we would not expect the Saint-Simoniennes' writing, conceived in terms of romantic organicism, to harbor such poststructuralist resonances, it is all the more striking that one writer in the *Tribune* describes the mythic Mother that all women embody as "the Mother with her thousand voices"

(2:154), and that Claire Démar in her essay "Ma Loi d'avenir: ("My Law of the Future") calls her own writing a "parole de femme" ("word of woman" [63]). Like Cixous, she conceives it as a feminine revolt against masculine unitary law by means of multiplicity and sexual pleasure. The infinite variety of sexual natures, according to her, cannot be "enclosed in the same circle, the same constant law," and therefore, "the word of the WOMAN REDEEMER WILL BE A SUPREMELY REVOLTING WORD, because it will be the broadest, and consequently the most satisfying to every [sexual] nature, to every humor" (67; capitals in original).

Instead of seeking to undermine phallocentric systems of meaning, this earlier writing seeks to bring about the kind of organic unity and "harmony" (*Tribune* 235) that male law, according to the Saint-Simoniennes, has so dismally failed to provide. In an argument influenced by Charles Fourier, the *Tribune* claims that "the Code of law which men impose upon us," based as it is on a double standard of rigid repression for women and freedom for men, has brought about "disorder" (123–24). The new codes would recognize that "this mobility which you [men] claim to banish exists everywhere" (202). In the absence of the mythic Mother, the pages of the *Tribune*, by bringing together the multifarious voices of the women's varied sexual tendencies, will construct the organic harmony based on difference and mobility that cannot exist in society.

The Historical Context

This celebration of an innate, unchanging essence, rooted in the body, takes its meaning from an historical context in three senses. First, the essentialism of contemporary French poststructuralist feminism, which has puzzled and disconcerted many American feminists, can be in part explained by its belonging to an historical tradition in which the Saint-Simonian feminists also fit. The latter's own essentialism comes from a whole complex of socio-historic forces. These include the deliberate insistence on the separation of male and female spheres in the debates of the French Revolution, and the Napoleonic Code's rigid, schematic, and total polarization of gender in a written code.[4] They also include a newly developed medical science in which, according to Thomas Laqueur, "the old model . . . gave way by the late eighteenth century to a new model of difference, of biological divergence" between men and women (3).

Although, as Laqueur and also Londa Schiebinger show, this scientific model is itself a product of ideology, the young proletarian women, excluded from formal education, could hardly contest the axioms of an established science. They instead used this biology of difference to contest the very ideology of separate spheres and male supremacy it had been developed to serve. The difference that divided men and women meant, according to the Saint-Simoniennes, not that men should govern in the public sphere while women retired to the private sphere, but that men were, by their nature, incomplete, and therefore inadequate to govern alone: "Let them thus cast an observant glance upon the past, upon the present, the fruit of their vast conceptions in politics and morality. . . . Let them consider the impotence, even the vice of the mode of moralization they have used up to now, by seeing its deadly effects. . . . What they are doubtless waiting for is that woman unite with man to formulate the new law" (3.5).

In so turning the tables, the Saint-Simonian feminists did not promulgate what might be called, in the case of contemporary feminists, a strategic essentialism. Where in so-called strategic feminism, the "ontotheologic" is a by-product of a conscious quest for a new, non-phallocentric symbolic practice founded on a metaphorics of the feminine body, in Saint-Simonian feminism, essentialism takes the form of a profound, unquestioned belief articulated within their theory. Although not consciously deployed as a weapon in a strategy to change the symbolic order, it could not help but influence the women's strategy to change the course of history. Here, then, is the second meaning this essay gives to the notion of historical context. Women's unchanging nature is not, according to them, historical, and therefore history itself must change to bring this feminine nature into a new position within a different historical period: "The phase of scholars is over; all the theories have been made; let the phase of sentiment, of women, in a word, arrive . . ." (*Tribune* 106).

This strategy can use essentialism to justify historical change because of an historical determination in yet another sense. The Saint-Simoniennes' belief in an unchanging nature can underlie a progressive strategy because of their position in the July Monarchy as marginalized, oppressed, and repressed. If this feminine "nature" were to achieve a centralized, powerful, and liberated position in the new structure and law they proposed, such a belief would serve a conservative or reactionary function. The celebration of an unchanging nature, whether deeply believed or strategic, can have only a temporary status, since its function in a strategy depends on the ever-changing relations enmeshing the individual within a changing socio-symbolic structure.[5]

In the 1830s, as now, the interrelations of the gender structure enter a configuration that evokes feminist essentialism, from certain men as well as women. Because in both periods the dominant gender code as a whole has entered a state of crisis, both social-romantic and poststructuralist male theories valorize the feminine pole not so much for any intrinsic quality it might have but precisely because it is the marginal term, and therefore the corrective for the excessive rationalism and power hunger of the central male term. Where in both cases the traditional, ruling code has made feminine qualities negative, whatever they may be, male romanticism and poststructuralism undermine the code by making these qualities positive. Male writers then claim them for men. Margaret Waller and Marlon B. Ross have analyzed this phenomenon in male romantics, and in the present period, one example among many is Derrida's much analyzed reading in *Spurs* of Nietzsche's inscription of "the feminine 'operation'" in his writing: "He was, he loved this affirming woman" (57). In like manner, Enfantin identified himself with the Woman. He dismissed the efforts of the *Tribune*, saying "all that is a preparation for the public work of woman, but it is not a work of woman" (qtd. in Adler 59), and arrogated that work to himself: "it is we who give birth in pain to woman" (qtd. in Adler 33).

As a response to this move, both Saint-Simonian and poststructuralist feminists reclaim this radically revalued feminine by arguing that it is actively embodied in women. Both groups of women assume the risk of essentialism in order to alter a hierarchical power relation with male theorists, and this context also determines the feminists' theoretical vocabulary in two intertwined ways. The first is that they do not speak this vocabulary in a vacuum but in the concrete socio-historic process of a debate whose very course will change the meaning of the vocabulary, as it changes the power relation between the participants.[6]

The second determinant of this feminist vocabulary concerns the signs connoting essentialism in the context of the "symbolic order." Understood here in the Lacanian sense of an all-pervasive system of signification that pre-exists the individual and speaks through him, the symbolic order is organized around analogously hierarchical bi-polar oppositions–such as center/margin, subject/object, man/woman, mind/body, originary/derivative–all substitutable for each other. In the Lacanian system, the speaking subject is not the autonomous agent of a language he controls but exists only within that order as an effect of the "subject" position within its bi-polar structure, where he is subject to the Law of the Father. This Law decrees that in order to enter the subject position, the son repress an immediate relation to the mother's body and to his own corporeal drives, replacing it with the mediation of names and signs. Woman thus functions as the necessarily absent referent of this symbolic order and of the subject's discourse.

When the subject utters his discourse, the symbolic order speaks through him, and, as Enfantinian and Lacanian writings have amply illustrated, it speaks its structured relations of hierarchy and power, since within it the subject position is masculine and the object position feminine, whether its speaker is biologically male or female. In psychoanalytic discourse, for instance, according to Luce Irigaray, "the feminine occurs only within models and laws devised by male subjects" (86). Deconstructive and Marxist discourses on woman, according to Gayatri Spivak in "Displacement and the Discourse of Woman," produce the same effect. In "Desire in Narrative," Teresa de Lauretis has analyzed the effects of paradox produced when women attempt at once actively to embody woman and to speak as subjects, as do, in different ways, the poststructuralist and the Saint-Simonian feminists.

Their resulting discourses of feminist essentialism cannot be isolated from this multi-leveled context. Simply changing the vocaulary of a discourse may do nothing to change the symbolic order, while changing another element in its network of symbolic relations may reverberate throughout. Thus the poststructuralist feminists change not the *object* of philosophical discourse on woman, but its *subject*, by "playing at mimesis" of male discourse to show its hidden implications in the case of Irigaray (76), or by "stealing" it, in the case of Cixous, to delegitimize it (*Newly Born* 96). The texts of the Saint-Simonian women enmesh the discourse they adopt from their male colleagues in these interacting contextual relations.

The Structural Context

A critique of an essentialist vocabulary in feminist discourse can fall into an essentialist view of language, where words, disengaged from socio-historic relations, have fixed, inalterable meanings. This study will read the words that would seem to signify a feminine nature not as having an essential *meaning*, but first as having a *function* of transformation in a social debate, and second as having their own "différance" as differential signs in combination with other signs, both textual and social.

Like any signifying system, the one in which the Saint-Simoniennes write is double, operating on both the symbolic and the social levels. Although the social is always symbolic and the symbolic always social, the symbolic order operates on two distinguishable levels at once. One level consists of the words spoken and the other of the speaking subjects themselves whose bodies also function as social signs of gender, class, age, ethnicity. Meaning derives from the interaction of these two levels; it arises not only from *what* is said but also from *who* speaks to whom in a network of power relations; not only from the object of discourse but also from its subject. When the gender of the speaking sign-body changes, the meaning of the words spoken can also change.

If women, and especially women as formally powerless as the Saint-Simoniennes, appropriate as subjects the discourse which men have used to turn them into objects, they can under certain circumstances disrupt both levels of language as well as the fit between them. The hierarchies of developing capitalism mark the Saint-Simonian feminists not only as women, but as young, unmarried proletarian women, and therefore as actual or potential prostitutes. They are doubly and triply distanced from the position of the speaking subject. When, within this historic context, they take the unprecedented step of occupying the position of the masculine speaking subject to take up actively the discourse of women, their writings unsettle the rigid gender system of the July Monarchy, so that the terms of the double-layered symbolic system shift.

The Saint-Simoniennes' texts practice three forms of this disruption. One form makes visible the gaps and conflicts between the signs of gender and the social referent they supposedly signify. A second brings the differences of sexual and class struggle into the workings of the sign. A third recombines the gender positions of the dominant symbolic system into new patterns. On a very elementary level, the women's version of the search for the Saint-Simonian Mother changes it in the following way: Claire Démar responds to the idea that the men alone will go on the quest for the Mother by writing to a friend: "Never had I risen to this thought that it's up to women to call the Mother, to discover her. Yours is the honour and glory of this revelation . . ." (51). Here she seems merely to be taking over unaltered the masculine search for the absent Woman. But in her essay "Ma Loi d'avenir," Claire, scolding the editors of the *Tribune* for their timidity, says: ". . . I have doubts about us, poor women, who believe ourselves strong, and who, weak, timid, and Christian, would perhaps remain silent and insensitive to the call of the *Redemptive Woman* . . ." (66; emphasis in original). An almost imperceptible shift drastically transforms the "call of the Woman": from object of the men's call, She becomes the subject of a call to the women, and as such the model for the women as subjects.

The Social Struggle Embedded in the Sign

By replacing Enfantin's ideology in a different textual and social context, the feminists use his strategy of turning bourgeois ideology against itself, specifically the ideology of the family. Suzanne Voilquin and Pauline Roland open up the conflict hiding in the idealist sign "Mother," making visible, as mentioned above, both the gap between the sign and its supposed referent, and the social struggle embedded in the sign itself. The Saint-Simoniennes sharply separate their social mother from an extravagantly idealized symbolic mother. Far from idealizing their own mothers, the feminists feel stifled by their mothers' passivity and their insistence that the daughters imitate them.

Roland, vehemently rejecting her own mother while responding fervently to Enfantin's symbolic family, begins her correspondence with the Aglaë Saint Hilaire she has never met by writing: "It's to my mother I want to write today, it's to her I want to reveal my horrible sorrows, it's to her that I come to ask solace, certain that she will not abandon her daughter. . . ." (Jan. 1832; 1).[7] Pauline writes to a "mother" because in nineteenth-century ideology the "solace" and "consolation" she needs are archetypically summed up by the word "mother." Yet her "sorrows" themselves result from an "eternal separation [between Pauline and her beloved tutor M. Desprez] pronounced five days ago by the caprice of my mother" (Jan. 1832; 1).

With apparent disregard, Pauline uses the same word "mother" in the same letter with two entirely different, and even opposed denotative and connotative meanings. About using the title "mother" for Saint Hilaire, she says: "don't you believe that this word moves me to the depths of my soul?" (18 June, 1833; 23). But she can only be moved by this word when it is purely a word and nothing more. She is not at all moved by the word when it names her own, bodily present mother.

The Saint-Simoniennes' writings intensify an "intersection," as V. N. Voloshinov has said, "between differently oriented social interests" (23) within the single sign "mother." The sign apparently designates the metaphysical transcendence of an ideologically loaded term, but they make it signify the social conflict embedded within it. In bourgeois ideology, the ideal representation filters our relation to a sordid reality so that lived experience seems to reflect the ideal. Pauline's contradictory use of the term "mother" opens up the conflict within the sign and between the sign and its referent. It designates the reality in its sordidness and steals the ideal representation away from its intended use of social control toward a liberation from that control.

The writings of embroiderer Suzanne Voilquin intensify even more the conflict between different interests embedded within the sign "mother." Her contradictory texts embrace an idealized image of the mother and at the same time offer the most acute critique of both bourgeois and Enfantinian maternal idealisms. In an article in the *Tribune* that recalls Frederick Engels's *Origin of the Family, Private Property and the State*, but was written more than fifty years earlier, Voilquin discusses the relation between women's sexuality, maternity, and patriarchal property inheritance. The passage strangely juxtaposes motherhood as an eternal essence and motherhood as a changing social role.

> *Oh, justice of men! truly the time is near when you will be declared impious; soon the mother will no longer be martyred in her spirit and her body.* God *has entrusted to the mother* alone *the* certainty *of the family. In the maiden's bosom lies the* living link *which ceaselessly ties the generations that succeed to those that pass away; a mystery without end that concludes in the bosom of* God *in the great name of* humanity. *(127; emphasis in original)*

Here an analysis that criticizes a patriarchal social construction of women's biology and seeks to reconstruct it differently in a different social and moral order, slides into celebrating that biology, the "living link" within the maiden's breast. This passage illustrates the general Saint-Simonian strategy outlined earlier, that of positing an unchanging feminine essence, in order to argue that the socio-symbolic structures which repress and distort it must change.

This strategy, as it appears in Voilquin's article "Les deux mères" ("The Two Mothers"), also bears upon the contemporary criticism that feminist essentialism universalizes all women, cannot recognize differences of class, race, and culture. But what if the writer is a member of the marginalized class, struggling not only to occupy the subject position in a class-determined subject/object polarity, but also to dismantle the hierarchical structure itself?

"The Two Mothers" combines bourgeois idealist connotations in the signifier "mother," the feminist-proletarian speaker who speaks it, and the bourgeois-masculine subject position she occupies as speaker to create a dramatic clash. Voilquin apostrophizes a rich mother and a poor mother, encouraging the poor mother: "Like you, this woman is a mother. . . . Poor woman, hasten to present your motherly petition" (117). Maternal essence lies in each woman, but the rich mother's failure to recognize it in the poor mother epitomizes, for Suzanne, class oppression. Under its pall, that essence lies moribund. Neither woman can realize it, the poor mother because she cannot feed her children, the rich mother because she cannot feel motherly love. In Suzanne's proletarian perspective, essence cannot be that which unites all women, but that which *could* unite them in a different and changed network of relations. In a more conscious way than Roland, Voilquin uses the same signifier "mother" twice to show how its bourgeois idealist resonances hide the class conflict embedded within conflictual signifieds: "you, mother, you have disdained to ease the sorrows of a mother! May God grant that you, for the sake of your progress and to soften your soul, suffer through your children the anguish of hunger and of all the afflictions you did not prevent" (118).

When Voilquin later succeeds in becoming a midwife, she applies to her work with destitute unwed mothers the Saint-Simonian strategy of freeing maternal essence by changing the network of relations that contextualize it. A letter to Enfantin in 1838 describes her plans to open a home for these young women: ". . . this good will extend not only to motherhood, but also to all those feelings which go to make up life, for in no way is it the Sister of Charity of whom I want to see gathered around me some pale copies; it is rather woman that I want to see rise up in all the beauty of her nature" (29 Jan. 1838; 61).

Taking "woman" and "nature" out of their bourgeois context, and investing them with a different meaning in the context of a different discourse and speaking subject, Suzanne also inverts Enfantin's mystic mother. Instead of descending (and condescending) to the lowly lives of poor women from the lofty heights of a male ideal, she will rise up from them. The exalted Mother now finds expression through unwed mothers "in destitution and outside of legality . . . the poorest and the most abandoned" (5 Feb. 1838; 62), on behalf of whose rights Suzanne forms a "Maternal Society Founded in Favor of Unwed Mothers" (62) in 1838. She writes enthusiastically to Enfantin, about instituting a "fête de la maternité," celebrating not his shimmering (unconsciously bourgeois) ideal but these scorned unwed mothers. Along with his and Saint-Simon's birthdays, it will be one of "three feast-days consecrated by the proletarians" (62). This new context for the maternal essence would scandalously disrupt its former function in society.

Opening the Gap between the Symbolic and the Social

Contemporary criticisms of essentialism see it as necessarily conservative, making feminists complicitous with an ideology of the dominant class and race. Yet the Saint-Simoniennes' strategy of changing all the structural relations around unchanging essence produces a different effect. In their situation, essentialism provides the only means available to speak against the dominant ideology of gender. Their class position so marginalizes and silences them, that they are denied even the opportunity of fitting the society's feminine stereotype, which was, and still is, a strictly middle- or upper-class, white, European ideal. Integrating the discourse of that ideal into their own writings, while at the same time violating the gender role it describes, may provide, in the Saint-Simoniennes' historical situation, the only way of strategically intervening in the social arena to challenge and change the gender system.

By occupying the position of speaking subject, and, from within that position, applying to themselves the objectifying notion of feminine nature, the writers of the *Tribune* necessarily change the current ideological meaning of "nature." In the first issue of the journal, the young writers, without education, social recognition, or political rights, considered immoral because proletarian, couch the scandalous originality of their project in a bourgeois stereotype they could never hope to be seen as embodying:

> *Women of all classes, you have a powerful action to accomplish; you are called to spread the feeling of order and harmony to every corner. Turn to the profit of society the irresistible charm of your beauty, the softness of your alluring speech, which should lead men to march towards a common goal. (1.3)*

But even this timid first issue of the *Tribune* advocates a feminine essence in order to denounce the Christian morality it was formulated to serve.

Already in the second issue of the *Tribune*, Joséphine-Félicité, protesting against the sexual position of women in a social world which "outside of slavery . . . knows only prostitution" (2.5), declares her rejection of both slavery and prostitution in the name of a redefined feminine essence: "Now they judge according to their principles, and their *principles* have resulted in nothing but *lies* and *insolence*. Could it be otherwise, when we find weighing on us obligations which our nature makes unobservable; and how would we be false when we are no longer held criminal for being that which GOD has made us, loving women?" (2.6). For Joséphine-Félicité, woman's nature as sexual passion *cannot* change; therefore the social order *must* change to accommodate it.

Joséphine-Félicité upsets on two levels the system of analogous polarities subject/object, masculine/feminine, culture/nature, mind/body. On the level of discourse, she demands an end to the mind/body, nature/culture split.[8] On the level of her situation as a proletarian feminine sign-body, she occupies both subject and object positions. By thus defying the paternal Law of the symbolic order, the Saint-Simoniennes also defy the law of gender which decrees that the masculine and feminine poles remain separate and opposed, and assigns biological males to the masculine symbolic pole, biological females to the feminine.

Disrupting the Patterns of the Code

Instead of contesting the nature of masculinity and femininity in each pole in the opposition, the Saint-Simoniennes mix and combine the poles in new patterns that disrupt the mutually exclusive opposition in the early nineteenth century. In "Ma Loi d'avenir," for example, Claire Démar begins in a typically Saint-Simonian way by upholding the patriarchal symbolic system of analogous oppositions and using it to demand the active leadership of women in working-class liberation: "Yes, *the emancipation of the proletariat, of the poorest and most numerous class*, is possible, I am convinced, only through *the emancipation of our sex*; through the association of *strength with beauty, of ruggedness and gentleness, of man and woman*" (65; emphasis in original). Although on the level of the words written, Démar does not contest these stereotyped gender attributes, the act of writing an essay on unlimited and unrestrained sexual freedom certainly violates them, and its rhetoric soon mixes them up. The Saint-Simonian male leaders, according to her, "having thrown their new dogma in the face of the world, have called woman to fertilize [*féconder*] their work, which remains eternally sterile without her assistance . . ." (78). Although the form of gender opposition still reigns in this passage, the gender attributes have been crossed, so that the woman here has metaphorically assumed the male biological capacity to impregnate.

Démar's metaphor is not an isolated ornament but expresses on a rhetorical level a pervasive quality of the Saint-Simoniennes' radical bi-sexuality. In general, these women most strongly identify with a feminine essence when they most scandalously defy the ruling system of gender opposition. This contradictory gender identity appears in the letters of Pauline Roland after she moves to Paris in 1834, and undergoes an "important revolution" (June 1834; 30). The import of her decision to engage openly in a love affair with Adolphe Guéroult must be measured in terms of the sexual choices open to women of the 1830s as analyzed by the *Tribune*: "Women, up to now, have been submissive slaves or slaves in revolt, but never free" (1.3). Pauline can break out of the imprisoning opposition between respectable submission and exploitative prostitution only by recourse to stereotyped images of woman's nature. Writing to the Saint-Simonian leader Charles Lambert, she declares in veiled terms her sexual freedom by cloaking herself in the image of the Saint-Simonian Woman with its bourgeois "natural" attributes of nurturance: "I must nourish with my *life of woman* our young men" (Oct. 1833; 48).

Pauline uses this vocabulary of traditional femininity to violate both the sexual codes and the gender codes in a forbidden reversal of gender roles. In Guéroult she chooses a younger man and puts herself in the role of "initiatrix" (16 Sept. 1833; 46). Making explicit this reversal of gender roles and the theory behind it, she writes to Aglaë

> . . . *this wish is still that society know everything except the name of him to whom I shall give myself, I am allowing it the suspicion; but I don't want it to know for sure. And he alone who can understand and submit to this woman's wish . . . will have been swept away by me, he will have abdicated voluntarily his male role, and he will have recognized not only the equality of woman and man, but the superiority of a woman over him the man. . . . I want to be a* mother, *mother, but with a mysterious paternity. (June 1834; 30)*

Pauline thus practices in the social world the Saint-Simonian theory that the mother alone is the only true parent since fatherhood is inherently unknowable. According to this theory, man's desire to be certain of his father-hood, for reasons of property ownership, creates sexual slavery for women. By contesting this slavery in practice, Pauline opens up the conflict between the symbolic and the social, between dismantling the gender system within the symbolic practices of language and discourse and doing so through the lived practices of social experience. The idealism of an essentialist discourse here merges dangerously with the idealist belief that one can at will make the social world conform to one's ideals, as she commits herself to the life of an unwed mother.

This conflict between the Saint-Simoniennes' theoretical discourse and their social experience raises a question that we in the contemporary women's movement also confront, albeit in a different way: to what limit can one use a strategy that turns the socio-symbolic order against itself, and at what point does it backfire and turn the socio-symbolic order against the feminists of the 1830s or against us? Pauline's decision to redefine and recontextualize women's nature not only in writing, but also in a social world still governed by the double standard, marks such a turning point. Imprisoned at Saint-Lazarre in May 1851 for union organizing, and desperately seeking to place her children, she writes to her friend G. Lefrançois: "Don't you find it strange . . . that, having started off twenty years ago under the influence of that false theory that the mother alone is the family, and having recognized its error, I now see myself condemned to live this life we glimpsed for a moment, and forced to realize it in all its rigour . . ." (qtd. in Thomas 172). Other Saint-Simoniennes paid similarly for their sexual freedom with suicide or the poverty and isolation reserved for independent women of the mid-nineteenth century.

Yet in the early 1830s, the Saint-Simoniennes were able to balance themselves precariously on the productive side of that turning point, and so in-vented forms of discourse which can still offer a clarifying perspective on contemporary feminism. Their play with the poles of gender, for instance, offers a perspective on *écriture féminine* not only in its disruption of phallo-centric meaning, as discussed earlier, but also in its inscription of a feminine subjectivity. This subjectivity differs from phallocentric subjectivity as the illu-sion of a stable, autonomous center and generator of language.

The Saint-Simoniennes imitate not only a bourgeois ideal of feminine nature which they could never be seen as embodying, but also the masculine position which they had even less hope of occupying. In a certain sense, the gender code excluded them entirely. Their discourse that plays, to be sure rather grimly, with the terms of this code, turns that double exclusion into a strategy for power, or as Cixous will say in using with more success a similar strategy, allows them to "reap a return on the exclusion to [their] profit" (*Souffles* 166).

Poststructuralist feminist theory recognizes that within the symbolic order woman functions as a lack, and in fact as two different forms of lack. As man's reified other, she acts as the negative term within the system and so guarantees his status as the positive term. But the feminine also functions as that which cannot be symbolized within the closure of the phallocentric symbolic order, as the metaphor for the lack that founds the symbolic order itself.

Not recognized as occupying either pole of the gender system, the Saint-Simonian feminists imitate both positions, and on the level of social practice turn their own stigmatized lack into a play that articulates this energy which challenges the symbolic order. While their imitation of the feminine pole exposes their lack in terms of class, an imitation of the masculine pole exposes their lack in terms of gender. By imitating both poles, they oscillate between two forms of presence/absence, and also demonstrate that both gender positions are a form of lack, a fiction that everyone in fact imitates.

Instead of perpetuating conservative essentialist ideals of womanhood, their discourse opens the jarring contradiction between the meanings of its vocabulary and the social meanings attached to its speakers, while, in addition, calling attention to the yawning gap between the social world and its ideal representation.

Our History

As feminist theorists living a century and a half after the Saint-Simoniennes, we do not, fortunately, face their isolation, but instead belong to a large international movement. Our problem in bridging the gap between symbolic structure and social structure is not that of risking a precarious material survival but rather that of seeing our discourse recuperated into the elitist and oppressive institutions we set out to undermine. Yet, as we have seen, essentialism can play a similar, and similarly unstable, role in poststructuralist feminist strategies as it does for the Saint-Simoniennes.

In our own context, the feminists attracted to a French feminine writing that risks falling into essentialism have been engaged with other feminists in an intense and ever-changing debate which cannot be contained in the traditional form of opposing sides, as the following examples will show. On the one hand, Christine Makward, writing about a variety of French feminine writers, maintains that their "theory of femininity is dangerously close to repeating in 'deconstructive' language the traditional assumptions on feminine and female creativity" (96). But on the other hand, Alice Jardine, describing these theories, says: "For these women, feminism is hopelessly anachronistic, grounded in male metaphysical logic" (64). It is no wonder that many feminists, including Makward and Jardine, have attempted to go beyond the opposition between these two positions, since each accurately criticizes the other for sliding into a dominant and traditional male discourse in one way or another. Perhaps no feminist discourse could avoid this particular instability. Since the phallocentric symbolic order constitutes language and thought themselves, any attempt to formulate a discourse "outside" of it would have to speak within its terms, and slide into either mirroring it or being recuperated back into it.

This sliding suggests that essentialism along with all feminist discourse faces the impossibility of finding a language adequate to represent fully a feminist vision. If feminism unavoidably harbors the non-representable of its irresolvable but productive contradictions, why not assume and integrate consciously the conflicts and the sliding between their terms? While speaking either the discourse of difference or that of equality, it would make visible the impossibility of adequately representing the position it espouses, and thus point to the non-representable.

Although without the effort to represent as adequately as possible the oppression of all women (and its multiple solutions) feminism would be nothing more than a frivolous game, a language could make this effort and also try to demonstrate its birth out of the situation described by Cixous in *The Newly Born Woman*. She describes the contradictions faced by women in progressive political movements with sexist men, but her passage could also express the contradictions of women of color in feminist struggles with Anglo-European women:

> But it never becomes intolerable to me until it hurts me as it passes
> through my own body, and drags me into this spot of insoluble
> contradictions, impossible to overcome, this place I have never been
> able to get out of since: the friend is also the enemy. All women have

lived that, are living it, as I continue to live it. 'We' struggle together,
yes, but who is this 'we'? . . .

I, revolt, rages, where am I to stand? What is my place if I am
a woman? (75)

The social conflicts refracted by this signifier "we" might be consciously integrated into a feminist language. In addition to *referring* to these insoluble
contradictions, this language could also *dramatize* them. An essentialist
writing that dramatizes the conflicts between the different levels of language
and discourse (as do the writings of the Saint-Simoniennes and, at their best,
the writings of poststructuralists like Cixous) could dramatize this "nowhere-
to-stand" on which feminism grounds itself.

Notes

1 See Stanton and Moi. There is a vast difference, however, between the approaches of these
   two essays. While Moi tends to create a rigid opposition between (good) deconstructive
   and (bad) essentialist writing by the three feminists in question, Stanton's complex treatment analyzes the way in which "the tensions between a conscious repulsion of the
   ontotheologic and its enduring lures or traps are dramatized" (162) in these texts, and ex-
   plores the "constraints of a global bind" (164). She points out that "any inscription of
   difference is (over)determined by the indifferent dominant discourse" (173).

2 The issues of the *Tribune* are not dated, and are numbered only for the first three issues.
   Subsequently, the pages are numbered consecutively without reference to issue number.
   In 1833, the name of the journal was changed from *Apostôlat des femmes* to *La Tribune des
   femmes*. Translations of the Saint-Simonian texts are mine; all cited texts appear in Moses
   and Rabine.

3 For more information on the Saint-Simoniennes, see Adler, Charlèty, Moses, and Thibert.

4 According to Moses, the Napoleonic Code provided "a rallying point for feminine protest"
   (18). As it did so, it determined the particular kind of feminism it inspired.

5 In her critique of essentialism, Stanton makes a similar point: "This is not to deny the importance of an initial countervalorization of the maternal-feminine . . . as an enabling
   mythology. But the moment the maternal emerges as a new dominance, it must be put into
   question before it congeals as feminine essence" (174).

6   For a similar argument, see Scott.

7   Throughout this essay, quotations from a letter in the Fonds Enfantin will be followed by its date and the number assigned to it within its dossier at the Bibliothèque de l'Arsenal.

8   For a contemporary example of an analysis of the horrible effects of the mind/body split, along with an attempt to think it differently, see Gallop (2–3).

Works Cited

Adler, Laure. *A l'aube du féminisme: Les premières journalistes* (1830–1850). Paris: Payot, 1979.

Charlèty, Sébastien. *Histoire du Saint-Simonisme*. Paris: Gonthier, 1931.

Cixous, Hélène. "The Laugh of the Medusa." *Signs: Journal of Women in Culture and Society* 1 (1976): 875–93.

_____. *The Newly Born Woman*. Trans. Betsy Wing. Minneapolis: U of Minnesota P, 1986.

_____. *Souffles*. Paris: des Femmes, 1975.

_____. *With, ou, l'art de l'innocence*. Paris: des Femmes, 1981.

de Lauretis, Teresa. "Desire in Narrative." *Alice Doesn't: Feminism, Semiotics, Cinema*. Bloomington: Indiana UP, 1984. 103–87.

Démar, Claire. "Lettres." *Textes* 23–58.

_____. "Ma Loi d'avenir." *Textes* 61–94.

_____. *Textes sur l'affranchissement des femmes* (1832–1833). Ed. Valentin Pelosse. Paris: Payot, 1976.

Derrida, Jacques. *Spurs: Nietzsche's Styles/Éperons: Les Styles de Nietzsche*. Trans. Barbara Harlow. Intro. Stefano Agosti. Chicago: Chicago UP, 1979.

Engels, Frederick. *The Origin of the Family, Private Property and the State*. Ed. Eleanor Burke Leacock. New York: International, 1972.

Fourier, Charles. *Le Nouveau monde amoureux*. Paris: Anthropos, 1967.

Gallagher, Catherine, and Thomas Laqueur. *The Making of the Modern Body: Sexuality and Society in the Nineteenth Century*. Berkeley: U of California P, 1987.

Gallop, Jane. *Thinking through the Body*. New York: Columbia UP, 1988.

Irigaray, Luce. *This Sex Which Is Not One.* Trans. Catherine Porter with Carolyn Burke. Ithaca: Cornell UP, 1985.

Jardine, Alice. "Gynesis." *Diacritics* 12 (1982): 54–65.

Kristeva, Julia. *Revolution in Poetic Language.* Trans. Margaret Waller. Intro. Leon S. Roudiez. New York: Columbia UP, 1984.

Lacan, Jacques. *Écrits.* 2 vols. Paris: Points, 1971.

Laqueur, Thomas. "Orgasm, Generation and the Politics of Reproductive Biology." Gallagher and Laqueur 1–41.

Makward, Christine. "To Be or Not to Be . . . A Feminist Speaker." *The Future of Difference.* Ed. Hester Eisenstein and Alice Jardine. Boston: G. K. Hall, 1980. 95–105.

Moi, Toril. *Sexual/Textual Politics.* New York: Methuen, 1985.

Moses, Claire Goldberg. *French Feminism in the Nineteenth Century.* Albany: State University of New York P, 1984.

_____, and Leslie Wahl Rabine. *Feminism, Socialism, and French Romanticism.* Bloomington: Indiana UP, 1993.

Pelosse, Valentin. "Symbolique groupale et idéologie féministe saint-simoniennes." In Démar 169–226.

Roland, Pauline. Letters to Aglaë Saint Hilaire and Charles Lambert. Fonds Enfantin 7777. Bibliothèque de l'Arsenal, Paris.

Ross, Marlon B. "Romantic Quest and Conquest: Troping Masculine Power in the Crisis of Poetic Identity." *Romanticism and Feminism.* Ed. Anne K. Mellor. Bloomington: Indiana UP, 1988. 26–51.

Schiebinger, Londa. "Skeletons in the Closet: The First Illustrations of the Female Skeleton in Eighteenth-Century Anatomy." Gallagher and Laqueur 42–84.

Scott, Joan W. "Deconstructing Equality-Versus-Difference: Or, the Uses of Post-Structuralist Theory for Feminism." *Feminist Studies* 14 (1988): 51–66.

Spivak, Gayatri Chakravorty. "Displacement and the Discourse of Woman." *Displacement: Derrida and After.* Ed. Mark Krupnick. Bloomington: Indiana UP, 1983. 169–99.

Stanton, Domna C. "Difference on Trial: A Critique of the Maternal Metaphor in Cixous, Irigaray and Kristeva." *The Poetics of Gender.* Ed. Nancy K. Miller. New York: Columbia UP, 1986. 157–82.

Thibert, Marguerite. *Le Féminisme dans le socialisme français.* Paris: Giard, 1926.

Thomas, Edith. *Pauline Roland: Socialisme et féminisme au XIXe siècle.* Paris: Marcel Rivière, 1956.

La Tribune des femmes (The Tribune of Women). Ed. Marie-Reine Guindorf. Journal of the Saint-Simonian feminists. 2 vols. Paris: 1832–1834.

Voilquin, Suzanne. Letters to Prosper Enfantin. Fonds Enfantin 7627. Bibliothèque de l'Arsenal, Paris.

Voloshinov, V. N. *Marxism and the Philosophy of Language.* Trans. Ladislav Matejka and I. R. Titunik. Cambridge: Harvard UP, 1973.

Waller, Margaret. "*Cherchez la femme*: Male Malady and Narrative Politics in the French Romantic Novel." *PMLA* 104 (1988): 141–51.

GAYATRI CHAKRAVORTY SPIVAK
WITH ELLEN ROONEY

In a Word. *Interview*

*T*o *undertake to place contemporary debates on essentialism in "context" is perhaps already to take sides in the controversy those debates have engendered. In some lexicons, at least, context is an anti-essentialist slogan; to contextualize is to expose the history of what might otherwise seem outside history, natural and thus universal, that is, the essence.*

As an idiom, "in a word" signals a moment of compressed and magically adequate expression. To summarize a matter "in a word" is to locate or hit upon its proper form, to capture its essential quality and thus to say all that need be said. The problem of essentialism can be thought, in this way, as a problem of form, which is to say, a problem of reading. Context would thus emerge as a synonym for reading, in that to read is to demarcate a context. Essentialism appears as a certain resistance to reading, an emphasis on the constraints of form, the limits at which a particular form so compels us as to "stipulate" an analysis.

In "Rape and the Rise of the Novel," Frances Ferguson glosses stipulation as "trying to put a limit to ambiguity by defining the understanding of a term or a situation" (109); to put it in a word, perhaps. She argues that the "intense formality of the law of rape seems designed to substitute the reliability of invariable formulae for the manipulable terms of psychological states" (95); these "invariable formulae" ("rape," in a word) serve to foreclose the question of consent and to define rape in terms compatible with phallocentrism. For the law and for some feminists as well, the victim's "body is thus converted into evidence, having become [a] text" (91). But while the body is formally legible, individual psychological states, specifically concerning consent and its absence, go unread. In a phallocentric context, this "intense formality" functions to exclude the victims entirely from the definition of rape; for example, "for ancient Hebrew law, the act of sex carries with it the inevitability of consent. For Brownmiller and Dworkin, it carries with it the impossibility of consent" (94). The significance of form is thus stipulated in advance, an effect of the morphology of the body. Context is swal-

lowed whole, and women, as subjects, disappear with it, absorbed entirely into their bodies.[1]

The body is of course essentialism's great text: to read in its form the essence of Woman is certainly one of phallocentrism's strategies; to insist that the body too is materially woven into social (con)texts is anti-essentialism's reply. But feminism's persistent return to the body is only in part a rejoinder to the resilience of anti-feminism's essentialism. Caught between those who simply "read off" the body and those who take its ineluctable power to be a fragmentary social relation is the feminist who speaks "as a woman."

Feminisms return to the problem of essentialism–despite their shared distaste for the mystifications of Woman–because it remains difficult to engage in feminist analysis and politics if not "as a woman." Within every feminist reading practice, for example, essentialism appears as a problem both of the text and of the critic who reads "as a woman." Elizabeth Spelman calls this phrase the "Trojan horse of feminist ethnocentrism," inevitably dissembling the differences among women (x). The body can figure here as a trump card, seeming literally to embody the woman-ness of woman, obscuring the fact that "only at times will the body impose itself or be arranged as that of a woman or a man" (Riley 103). We seem to desire that what unites us (as feminists) pre-exist our desire to be joined: something that stands outside our own alliances may authorize them and empower us to speak not simply as feminists but as women, not least against women whose political work is elsewhere. In the U.S., this is an old dream of "non-partisanship" at the heart of politics, as well as what Donna Haraway calls "the feminist dream of a common language . . . a perfectly faithful naming of experience" (92). In a word.

Yet simply to label this political dream of women essentialism is to layer another political refusal over the rifts among us. The word essentialism can also work to conceal political divisions among women, insofar as it represents them as purely theoretical, a question of enlightenment. Political failures, if it be a failure not to unite all women under a single banner, are read as wholly intellectual failures–easily corrected. The original evasion is repeated; political difference is reduced to a matter of bad form, in a word, to essentialism.

In reading the body, to find "woman"; in "women," to secure feminism; to capture in a word the essence of a thing: essentialism is a dream of the end of politics among women, of a formal resolution to the discontinuity between women and feminisms. Anti-essentialism may mimic this formalism, even as it

*seeks to diagnose it. Gayatri Spivak suggests–by turning repeatedly to the ques-
tion of the word: which word to choose? to what end?–another reading. E.F.R.*

*This interview was held in Pittsburgh on December 9, 1988. The ques-
tions were crafted in consultation with Naomi Schor and Elizabeth Weed. We
thank Erika Rundle for her heroic work of transcription and Nicole
Cunningham for producing the final text.*

ER: As you know, some current discussions of the topic of essentialism
have resulted in calls for a new willingness to take the "risk of essentialism,"
and these calls include citations from some of your most recent remarks. I'm
thinking here of Alice Jardine's comment in *Men in Feminism* that "one of the
most thought-provoking statements of recent date by a feminist theorist [is]
Gayatri Spivak's suggestion (echoing Heath) that women today may *have* to
take 'the risk of essence' in order to think really differently" (58), or of Bruce
Robbins's interview with Edward Said, where Robbins asks: "One idea that has
been much repeated in conversations about intellectuals and their relation to
collectivity, especially among feminists, is the necessity to accept 'the risk of
essence,' a phrase associated with Gayatri Spivak and Stephen Heath. Does it
seem at all generalizable or useful in the case of the Palestinians?" (51).

You've examined the question of essentialism throughout your work,
and you've said a number of different things about it, at times warning against
defining women in terms of woman's putative essence and stressing the possibility that essentialism may be a trap, and, at other times, most recently in
working on the text of the Subaltern Studies Group, talking about the "*strategic*
use of a positivist essentialism in a scrupulously visible political interest." I'd
like to talk about the necessary risks of taking what may seem to be essentialist positions; about how we can signal the difference between a strategic and a
substantive or a real essentialism; about the possibility of mobilizing people to
do political work without invoking some irreducible essentialism; ultimately,
how we can determine when our essentializing strategies have become traps,
as opposed to having strategic and necessary positive effects?[2]

GS: To begin with, I think the way in which the awareness of strategy
works here is through a persistent critique. The critical moment does not come
only at a certain stage when one sees one's effort, in terms of an essence that
has been used for political mobilization, succeeding, when one sees that one

has successfully brought a political movement to a conclusion, as in the case of revolutions or national liberation movements. It is not only in that moment of euphoria that we begin to decide that it was strategic all along, because generally it doesn't work that way, although that is important, too. It seems to me that the awareness of strategy–the strategic use of an essence as a mobilizing slogan or masterword like *woman* or *worker* or the name of any nation that you would like–it seems to me that this critique has to be persistent all along the way, even when it seems that to remind oneself of it is counterproductive. Unfortunately, that crisis must be with us, otherwise the strategy freezes into something like what you call an essentialist position.

Having said this, let me also emphasize the importance of who it is that uses the strategy. When I speak of the Subaltern Studies Group, for example, I'm not speaking of, let us say, a group situated within a very privileged institution of learning in one of the most powerful neo-colonial countries. The Subaltern Studies Group is working as a counter-movement within Indian history as written even by politically correct Indians trying to fabricate a national identity in decolonization; to an extent, it is in a different structural position from someone working from within, not only the University of Pittsburgh but certainly Brown University. You and I are in a different position in terms of the production of neo-colonialist knowledge, so you can't simply take the example of one group and their historians. And if you use the word positivism, you have to take into account the importance of positivism in the discipline of history in the nineteenth century; some of the best history is written under acknowledged or unacknowledged positivist impulses. So, to an extent, we have to look at where the group–the person, the persons, or the movement–is situated when we make claims for or against essentialism. A strategy suits a situation; a strategy is not a theory.

Finally, since you have, I think, quite correctly, spoken of my moving from one position to another, I think I will say that I have also reconsidered this argument about the strategic use of essentialism which I know has caught on, quite to my surprise, since it was really only mentioned in an interview which came out in an Australian journal which I don't see cited in many other contexts in the U.S. (Spivak with Grosz). I don't know the Heath passage, so I can't contextualize that one, but this one I have had played back to me many times, and perhaps even that fact has made me want to reconsider it. Because it seems to me that just as we saw within mainstream feminism the extremely good insistence that "the personal is political" transform itself within class alliances in a very personalist culture (and I like the word personalist a lot better than the word essentialist) into something like "*only* the personal is political," so, I would say that one of the reasons why the strategic use of essentialism has caught on within a personalist culture is that it gives a certain alibi to essentialism. The emphasis falls on being able to speak from one's own ground, rather than on what the word strategy implies, so I've reconsidered it. I think it's too risky a slogan in a personalist, academic culture, within which it has been picked up and celebrated. Now I think my emphasis would be more on noting how we ourselves and others are what you call essentialist, without claiming a counter-essence disguised under the alibi of strategy. And I'll repeat that: noting how ourselves and others are what you call essentialist, without claiming a counter-essence disguised under the alibi of a strategy. I would even say that these days, seeing with a good deal of surprised humility how these things do catch on, my interest as a teacher and in some ways as an activist is to build for difference, in other words to think of what we might be doing or saying strategically, sometimes tactically within a very powerful institutional structure. Given the way these things work–the collaboration between techniques of knowledge and strategies of power–given where we are, my project is to take account of the fact that, in spite of my personal benevolence, these things are used as if they were theories. And therefore one has to be careful to see that they do not misfire for people who resemble us so little that we cannot even imagine them in the strong sense. It seems to me that that vigilance, what I call building for difference, rather than keeping ourselves clean by being whatever it is to be an anti-essentialist, that has taken on much greater emphasis for me at this point. I think I probably have said enough in answer to this question. There's a great deal more to be said, but . . .

ER: Could I ask one further thing? When you spoke just then about noting our own essentialism, that sounded to me as if it were a reassertion of the need for the critique of essentialism. I think your description of the way in which your remark has been taken up in discourses that are produced from sites of influence and power is absolutely true. And the marking of the critical moment–what you call the strategic moment–is erased. What's reasserted then is actually the need for a kind of naiveté in the assertion of personal identity.

GS: You know, when I started teaching in '65, no, even before, when I was a teaching assistant at Cornell, someone, I forget who it was, gave us teaching assistants the task of telling our students to write without using the word "however" and see what they would use in its place. I feel that very strongly about the word essence, or anti-essentialism or essentialism. What I am very suspicious of is how anti-essentialism, really more than essentialism, is allowing women to call names and to congratulate themselves. If one begins to see what words one could use in the place of essentialism or essence many, many words would come in. You yourself chose the word identity a minute ago; identity is a very different word from essence. Why do I mind this? I mind this because after all, if I understand deconstruction, deconstruction is not an exposure of error, certainly not other people's error. The critique in deconstruction, the most serious critique in deconstruction, is the critique of something that is extremely useful, something without which we cannot do anything. That should be the approach to how we are essentialists.

You know, some young man, an analytical philosopher who was in my class, was very dissatisfied with the way I was teaching Derrida because it seemed to him, since he knew Nietzsche better than he knew anything else, that I was claiming that Derrida was a poor man's Nietzsche, to use his phrase. And, to an extent, what I told him was that the way I taught Derrida might make him seem like a poor man's everything, you know, so that if you knew Heidegger best, he would seem to be a poor man's Heidegger; if you knew Plato best, he would seem to be a poor man's Plato. So if I took that angle, I would say that perhaps what I'm saying here is that Derrida is a poor man's Althusser. In Althusser's most naive essay, "Marxism and Humanism," he talks about the fact that if you know an ideology, it doesn't dissipate the ideology. I think one of Derrida's most scandalous and greatest contributions is to begin with what is very familiar in many radical positions and to take it with the utmost seriousness, with literal seriousness, so that it transforms itself. This Althusserian position on ideology is one which one could very easily criticize–Althusser himself in his auto-critique suggested this–as mired in a theoreticism, mired in an absence of auto-critique, etcetera. But if you forget all of that and see that Derrida teaches us to re-read it, you can rescue this, too. I would remind the feminists who want so badly to be anti-essentialists that the critique of essence *à la* deconstruction proceeds in terms of the unavoidable usefulness of something that is very dangerous.

So I have certainly reconsidered my cry for a strategic use of essentialism because it is too deliberate. The idea of a *strategy* in a personalist culture, among people within the humanities who are generally wordsmiths, has been forgotten. The strategic really is taken as a kind of self-differentiation from the poor essentialists. So long as the critique of essentialism is understood not as an exposure of error, our own or others', but as an acknowledgement of the dangerousness of what one must use, I think my revised statement–that we should consider how ourselves and others are essentialist in different ways–I think I would stand by it. The critique of essentialism should not be seen as being critical in the colloquial, Anglo-American sense of being adversely inclined, but as a critique in the very strong European philosophical sense, that is to say, as an acknowledgement of its usefulness.

ER: Could we pick up on the references that you have made to deconstruction and talk about what you have called "the greatest gift of deconstruction: to question the authority of the investigating subject without paralyzing him, persistently transforming conditions of impossibility into possibility" (*Other* 201). I think that one of the things that's most striking about your arguments about essentialism and about your work generally is the way you both assert the importance of positionality and refuse to essentialize it. How much would you say that your general thinking about essentialism is shaped by your conceptualization and your own practice of self-positioning or self-identification? What kind of relationship is there between the broad project to deconstruct–in the very precise sense that you were just invoking–identity, not to refuse identity but to deconstruct identity (a project you've participated in) and your own frequent concern to identify yourself, to position yourself, to refuse what you have pointed to most recently in "Can the Subaltern Speak?" as a tendency on the part of supposed critics of essentialism to make their own positions transparent and unproblematic?

GS: If I can go back to something we were talking about before we started the interview, I'm interested in a sort of deconstructive homeopathy, a deconstructing of identity by identities. What we were talking about was the fact that it's quite often claimed that "Spivak talks too much about herself." I'm saying that if I really gave the story of my life, it would sound rather different. Assuming that there is such a thing as the story of a life (about which more later), it would sound rather different from all the other talkings about myself that I engage in. I believe that the way to counter the authority of either objective, disinterested positioning or the attitude of there being no author (and these two opposed positions legitimize each other) is by thinking of oneself as an example of certain kinds of historical, psycho-sexual narratives that one must in fact use, however micrologically, in order to do deontological work in the humanities. When one represents oneself in such a way, it becomes, curiously enough, a deidentification of oneself, a claiming of an identity from a text that comes from somewhere else. In order to explain myself, I want to use a passage from *Grammatology* (47) about which I've written elsewhere ("Poststructuralism"). I'm not going to give an exact account of that passage, I'm going to turn it into a slightly crude analogy and I'm going to turn it into the analogy of a mother tongue. A mother tongue is something that has a history before we are born. We are inserted into it; it has the possibility of being activated by what can be colloquially called motives. Therefore, although it's unmotivated, it's not capricious. We are inserted into it, and, without intent, we "make it our own." We intend within it; we critique intentions within it; we play with it through signification as well as reference; and then we leave it as much without intent for the use of others after our deaths. To an extent, the way in which one conceives of oneself as representative or as an example of something is this awareness that what is one's own, supposedly, what is proper to one, has a history. That history is unmotivated but not capricious and is larger in outline than we are, and I think this is quite different from the idea of talking about oneself. I'd like to acknowledge a debt to *Anti-Oedipus* here, too, a book that I have often spoken against. In *Anti-Oedipus*, Deleuze and Guattari talk about the way in which a socius is produced and then becomes a "miraculating" agency operating like a quasi-cause (10). The example that they use is capital, but, in fact, culture, ethnos, sexuality, all of these things become miraculating agencies like this, so that one feels that as if by a miracle one speaks as an agent of a culture or an agent of a sex or an agent of. . . . A body without organs has inscribed on its recording surface this miraculating agency, which seems like a quasi-cause. Now, what you take as representing, what your self represents, is that kind of a miraculating agency, a history, a culture, a position, an institutional position. But, via that persistent critique that I was talking about, you are aware that this is miraculating you as you speak, rather than that this is what is speaking. Another concept that one can bring in here which is very, very interesting is the concept of biography. You know that you graph your bio in order to make sense of it. These are uses of essence which you cannot go around, and you are written into these uses of essence. This is the strategy by which history plays you, your language plays you, or whatever-the-hell the miraculating agency might be. It's not a question of choosing the strategy. You are, to an extent, distanced from it with humility and respect when you "build for difference," as I was saying. In that sense, I would say that being obliged to graph one's bio is very different from the attitude of claiming anti-essentialism, and I think even if the difference is not great, it's a crucial difference in terms of how you do your work. Is that an answer to your second question?

ER: Yes, and given what you have said in response both to that question and another, I'd like actually to skip to some things I thought we would talk about later, namely, why has anti-essentialism been so powerful in the way you were just referring to, as a kind of term of abuse, and how important are the questions of the disciplines, the institutional constraints of the U.S. academy, and the interventions of cross- or counter-disciplinary discourses like women's studies or area studies? What is the purchase the essentialism debate has on the academy? How does its inflection differ from discipline to discipline? Is anti-essentialism an effect of anti-disciplinary or cross-disciplinary work? Within feminism and within some other discourses, essentialism seems to be a kind of blind spot that won't go away. It hasn't, by and large, been historicized or related to the history of high philosophical essentialisms, but has been invoked to distance and disallow certain kinds of discourses. Why hasn't the response to that been a kind of philosophical essentialism that fights back, that resists this abuse, and the ahistorical and in some ways not very informed use of the word essentialism?

GS: And why there hasn't been a philosophical essentialism?

ER: In response, yes.

GS: Because essentialism is a loose tongue. In the house of philosophy, it's not taken seriously. You know, it's used by non-philosophers simply to mean all kinds of things when they don't know what other word to use. This is why I–not being a philosopher, but being auto-didactic enough so that I taught myself to read, I can't philosophize but I've certainly taught myself to read certain kinds of philosophy–this is why it shames me a little, the use of the word essentialism. It seems to me that within analytical philosophy, people like Hilary Putnam seem to be much more astutely coping with the problem of the irreducibility of essences without any of the fanfare; but they don't look, they don't sound like poststructuralist feminists or anything like that. In fact, when the question of essences is philosophically considered it doesn't seem very sexy, hmmm? For example, non-foundationalist ethics, which from the analytical ground cannot proceed very far, so that, let's say, the work of a Thomas Nagel, or the slightly more interesting work of a Bernard Williams, is actually trying to cope in a philosophical way with the problem of essence and deontological practice in the humanities. In other words, moral philosophy doesn't look a bit like all the noise about anti-essentialism outside of philoshy. The question of anti-essentialism and essentialism is not a philosophical question; that's why there isn't any rebuttal from the house of philosophy. It takes place elsewhere. And, as to why it's taken on so much importance, I don't know, frankly, that one should assign reasons in that way. But I'm happy to fabulate. You ask if this is an effect of anti-disciplinary or cross-disciplinary work, and, as a kind of very old-fashioned teacher, who has been teaching full-time now for nearly twenty-five years, I would say that sometimes this is the case in the worst way. Whereas I find that the construction of an object in an investigation need not be the acceptance of essences; you know, in these cases, small "a," small "e," anti-essentialism is a way of really not doing one's homework. And it seems to me now, looking at what all this has wrought, that it would be much more interesting to try to infiltrate the old disciplines that deal with these things, like psychology, history, anthropology, the area studies, than to give way to a kind of globalism which wants to do all of these things, calls its impatience with academic homework anti-essentialism and really repeats one of the greatest dangers of the cross-culturalism that came hand-in-hand with imperialism. One cannot forget that the knowledge venture of imperialism, which was absolutely spectacular–the establishment of anthropology, comparative literature, comparative philology, comparative religion, world history, etcetera–the knowledge venture was, in its inception, Eurocentric cross-culturalism, and that's what we are, in fact, looking at, watered down and diluted in the house of a so-called interdisciplinary anti-essentialism in the humanities and the social sciences. As a person very deeply involved with the institution of tertiary education in the United States, I would say, as I have said before, that if one establishes an interdisciplinary space which does not engage with the most important arena (a silent, unemphatic arena) of warring power in the disciplines themselves, where the people who don't publish much, who don't teach very well, engage day after day, as with distribution requirements, let us say, if one doesn't budge them, but proliferates interdisciplinary, anti-essentialist

programs, in fact one provides an alibi, once again, for the ruthless operation
of neo-colonialist knowledge. So if I seem to be speaking in a slightly old-
fashioned voice . . . advisedly so.

ER: Your invocations of the knowledge venture and the philosophical
discussion of the irreducibility of essences reminds me of a passage from "A
Literary Representation of the Subaltern," which speaks, I think, to the relationship between essentialism and the production of knowledge. It's one of
your takes on the argument that "only a native can know the scene" and you
say: "The position that only the subaltern can know the subaltern, only women
can know women, and so on, cannot be held as a theoretical presupposition
either, for it predicates the possibility of knowledge on identity. Whatever the
political necessity for holding the position, and whatever the advisability of attempting to identify with the other as subject in order to know her, knowledge
is made possible and sustained by irreducible difference, not identity. What is
known is always in excess of knowledge. Knowledge is never adequate to its
object. The theoretical model of the ideal knower in the embattled position we
are discussing is that of the person identical with her predicament. This is
actually the figure of the impossibility and non-necessity of knowledge. Here
the relationship between the practical–need for claiming subaltern identity–
and the theoretical–no program of knowledge production can presuppose identity as origin–is, once again, an interruption that persistently brings each term
to crisis" (*Other* 254). This passage touches upon a number of issues I'd like to
talk about: the first is deconstruction and what it's taught us about identity and
difference, the proper and reading, and their relationship to the production of
knowledge. How would you say your interests in deconstruction have fed your
thinking about essentialism? What's the importance of deconstruction in dismantling essentialism? How are essentialism and anti-essentialism related in
Derrida's text?

GS: In terms of the first bit that you read, there is a further problem in
there, which today I call "clinging to marginality." These things happen very
fast under micro-electronic capitalism, and the institution of tertiary education
in the United States is an extraordinary thing, with nearly 4,000 degree-granting
institutions, incredible telematic contact; it's something. Unless you have
worked within other systems with equally intelligent colleagues and students,
you don't realize how much all the dogma on anti-essentialism is supported by

this political and economic structure. Now, within that context, within the last decade, we have seen that this "clinging to marginality" is being fabricated so that the upwardly mobile, benevolent student (the college is an institution of upward mobility; it would be ridiculous to deny that, and it would be ridiculous to say that upward mobility is necessarily bad), in an upwardly mobile situation, the young student, the so-called marginal student, claiming validation, is being taught (because we don't have the sense of strategy that I was speaking of, so that what was good in strategy has now become a slogan, and we don't look at the years passing) is being taught this idea of speaking for oneself, which is then, in fact, working precisely to contain the ones whom this person is supposed to represent. In other words, the miraculation is working as if it truly is a miracle. Thus the constituency that this person is supposed to represent when she says that "only I can speak about the Chicana," that is forgotten.

Going back to the question of deconstruction, I would say that what deconstruction has taught me right from the beginning is the necessity of essentialism and how careful we must be about it. As I have often said, deconstruction considers that the subject is always centered and looks at the mechanisms of centering; it doesn't say there is something called the decentered subject. When I say this, what people say is "Well, you just centered the subject in Derrida." This shows, it seems to me, a real desire to take one kind of political position over against another, not to see that a way of thinking is about the danger of what is powerful and useful, and instead simply to think that that way of thinking is talking about how that dangerous thing doesn't exist. The former is the lesson of deconstruction for me. I'm not saying that Derrida is necessarily claiming exactly this, but this is what I learn from it. Every reading is transactional. You run with what you have, and you become something else. So deconstruction also teaches me about the impossibility of anti-essentialism. It teaches me something about the conditions of the production of doing, knowing, being, but does not give a clue to the real. The real in deconstruction is neither essentialist nor anti-essentialist; the real . . . difficulty with deconstruction is that if you like it, you have to think through the extraordinarily counter-intuitive position that it might be essences and it might not be essences. Again, if you like, a "poor man's" agnosticism, all right? That "poor man's"—words given to me by this rather officious student, who comes and goes in my class—that "poor man's" there means, taking literally, trivially, what is implicit in the radical moment in other kinds of lessons. Deconstruction is not an essence. It's not a school of thought; it is a way of re-reading. Deconstruction itself can be an essentialism. I was just reading a book called *Enlightened Absence* (Salvaggio). It is an example, I think, of essentialist, humanist, deconstructivist feminism. I think it can certainly become a viewpoint in deconstruction, a description of what it is to be feminine, how the anti-essential feminine is the essence of the feminine. It can be an essentialism, I think; it doesn't come packaged with either one thing or the other.

ER: Moving in the other direction, off the same passage, and this is related to what you were saying earlier about how one talks about oneself: can you talk about your own history, or the trajectory of your own work, your earliest intellectual and political history, and its impact on your thinking about essentialism? Is your recent work and its partial focus on the problem of essentialism a reinscription of earlier concerns, concerns that perhaps predate your work on Derrida?

GS: I don't really know. I mean, I'm sorry. Many of these answers to questions are: "I don't know." On the other hand, what I welcome is the chance of graphing myself through your questions. So if it is understood that that's what I'm doing, accounting for something about which I really have not stopped to think and that this is simply an accounting, in that spirit of a *parvenue*, I think one of the lessons learnt early for a child in a colonial context, who comes from a background which has the full share of the ambivalence toward the culture of imperialism, is related to the fact that the native language operated very strongly in my particular class; we still read, write, speak in our native language when we are by ourselves. We certainly were brought up within that context. There was a certain kind of nationalism on the rebound. In that situation, also, to learn through the percolation of the epistemic violence of imperialism . . . in school, strangely enough, mostly my teachers were tribal Christians. Now, I'm a caste Hindu. A caste Hindu child, in her native language, hegemonic Calcutta Bengali, which is quite different from the tribal languages which are not known by Bengalis, being taught by tribal Christians, who are, if one knows anything about the history of India, in certain senses outside of the religions of India, dehegemonized millenarian Christians. They were not Christianized, they became Christians, in a certain sense. They were, of course, Christianized, but I'm using it in that sense. To be in that situation, to have them as one's teachers . . . I still cannot think about my school days without an immense sense of gratitude to my parents for having thought to send me to such a school rather than to a more fashionable Western-style school or a less fashionable native-type school. In a situation like that, one begins to realize without realizing the extraordinary plurality of the source of enlightenment; in the very long haul, the sources of enlightenment were our race enemies in every sense. On the other hand, my direct teachers, who were not co-religionists, who were caste-wise lower, in some senses, outcasts, and yet my teachers, respected teachers, Christians. The sense of what a division there is in one's own making came early.

Now it's that sense of division, and then the involvement with left thinking . . . In a situation where, after independence, the idea of internationalism is under fire from the national party, the lines between socialist internationalism and the fabrication of national identity were finessed by the left. That again is an idea that gets into one's way of. . . . You know, forty years later, thirty years later, graphing one's bio, one is asked why there is some sympathy for that word that I don't like–anti-essentialism–in one's make-up, those are the things that one still thinks of. It seems to me that that's the experience of the planned emergence into post-coloniality on a middle-class child in that part of India. The word experience would have to be understood in the way in which I was talking about, the mother-tongue, insertion, representation, example, anti-miraculation. . . . The experience of that, I think, is perhaps the strongest bond and also the strongest impatience with anti-essentialism as a battle cry.

ER: Your reference to the left suggests another way of asking a question similar to the one I asked about deconstruction, a question about marxism. That is, how has your interest in and your work on Marx influenced your thinking about essentialism? How does the marxist tradition of anti-essentialism fit into your own practice and thinking? Could you talk about a dynamic of essentialism and anti-essentialism within marxism?

GS: Well, I tell you, my relationship to marxism is like anything else; because I'm such a re-reader, it moves a great deal, and in Marx it is the slow discovery of the importance of the question of value that has opened up a lot of things for me. And it does seem to me that in Marx there is a very strong sense that all onto-political commitments (just as in our neck of the woods, all onto-cultural commitments) that is to say, ontological commitments to political beings, historical agents, are seen as negotiable, in terms of the coding of value.

I would draw your attention most strongly to, let's say, those chapters in *Capital*, Volume III, where Marx is talking about the trinity formula and mocking the idea that there is anything–in your terms–essentialist about class. And then the final chapter on class, which, of course, we know is unfinished. That's not just one moment in Marx, if one attends carefully to the way in which he develops the idea of value. Unfortunately, the "Englishing" of Marx in this case has been the translations which have almost uniformly obliterated the trace of the counter-intuitive nature of Marx's exhortation to his implied reader–that is to say, the worker–and how counter-intuitive he wants the worker to be in order to realize that the worker is agent rather than victim, so that the entire idea of agency is structurally negotiable. The relationship between the realm of freedom and the realm of necessity in Marx, right from the *Economic and Philosophic Manuscripts*, displaces itself in a million ways after the discovery of value, and finally comes to lodge in that famous section in *Capital III* which is often quoted by people without their quite noticing what's going on there.

Those senses, the senses of the negotiability of commitment and the extraordinary elusiveness of value, are lost. You know, Marx calls value, let me see if I can get this straight, "contentless and simple" (*inhaltlos und einfach*). The English translations *always* call this "slight in content" (*Economic*). There is a great difference between "contentless and simple" and "slight in content." Value is not a form. Pure form is not something that Marx is talking about. Marx is talking about what in today's language we would call an "almost nothing," a *presque rien*, which cannot appear but which. . . . It's not mediation, it's the possibility of the possibility of mediation, as it were, which establishes exchange and then its appropriation and extraction, etcetera, as surplus and so on. Now this is of course a very, very complicated thing in Marx, but I would say that this way of understanding Marx's project would certainly not underestimate the importance of class, but would not see it as a trafficking in essences. That's something which goes much further than just what I've been able to say. I've written something rather recently where I take the various forms of value that Marx talks about, and it is in that piece, "Poststructuralism, Marginality, Post-coloniality, and Value" that I've tried to relate this to analyses other than economic, but I think at this point this is probably enough.

ER: Could we move, then, to the relationship between the current and growing interest in materials from the so-called third world and essentialism? Is there a perception of a strategic essentialist moment that's located "out there" in the "third world," perhaps in the form of liberation struggles, which is related to the renewed interest, specifically among U.S. critics and scholars, in essentialism and in that–that benevolent, as you have called it, but problematic–desire for translations of "third world" texts and the production of new forms of knowledge about a "third world" which is also often rendered monolithically, both within feminism and outside of feminism? How much of the difficulty that academics in the U.S. have avoiding certain essentialist traps has to do with the displacement of questions of race and ethnicity into this monolothic and safely distanced "third world" and the consequent effacement of imperialism as such?

GS: Well, you know, it works both ways. You displace it into the third world, but, on the other hand, you again reconstruct the third world as people of color and marginalized people in the United States, like all of the other syndromes, you know, like "little Italy" and "little Ireland" and now, increasingly, "little India," which becomes more real than the original cultures to the great irritation of the original cultures. Again, the word "original" is shorthand. In fact, I have an argument, which I have learned to make after reading Robin Blackburn's book rather carefully, that even New England, to an extent, with all of the rabid anglomania in the United States and its difference from the breakup of Britain and so on, that it is this relationship of a constructed space, a simulacrum in the United States, which then comes to take the place of Britain. No one speaks about the repeated emergence of this difference between the simulacrum in the United States, "realm of the hyper-real," to quote from a critic whom I don't usually endorse, and the so-called original places which have their histories (Baudrillard). So, to an extent, it's not just displacing it into the third world, but displacing it, as you have very properly suggested, within the "third world." If one looks at the so-called 'third world' as such (I'm now really quoting from something that I have written), between two texts like Frobel Folker's *The New International Division of Labor* and Nigel Harris's *The End of the Third World* there is a decade. And between these two books, one begins to realize that that very definite new economic program, after the Second World War and the accompanying change in global outlines after that, has really undergone a change. To use that as a sort of culturalist description is rather shabby academically, frankly. If the "third world" is used as a sort of mobilizing slogan for . . . call it non-aligned nations or whatever, I think it's fine, but that is rather different from essentialism. If you look at the conferences, etcetera, where this language is seriously used, you will see that each one of the countries has come asserting its difference. They really do know that it's strategic because they're not sitting in humanities departments trying to be different from others. That is a strategy that changes moment to moment, and they in fact come asserting their differences as they use the mobilized unity to do some specific thing. And that's where you see strategy at work. That has nothing to do–when the third world claims unity as a block–nothing to do with essences. And I think we should keep that as a reminder.

On the ground of cultural politics, the third world is a postcolonial world. Consider, for example, the idea that magical realism is the paradigmatic style of the third world. What is (and this is a point I've made elsewhere) the hidden ethical, political agenda behind claiming that that part of the third world which relates most intimately to the United States, namely Latin America (just as India used to relate to Britain in the nineteenth century), that a style practiced most spectacularly by some writers there, is paradigmatic of a space which is trying to cope with the problem of narrativizing decolonization, whereas, in Latin American space, one of the things that cannot be narrativized is decolonization, as the Ariel-Caliban debate that I have written about clearly articulated for us?[5] What's the agenda behind this kind of thing?

So it seems to me if one looks at the larger third world as basically post-colonial, basically making catachrestic claims. . . . Political claims are not to ethnicity, that's ministries of culture, or, you know, people getting degrees, the political claims over which battles are being fought are to nationhood, sovereignty, citizenship, secularism, all that kind of stuff. Those claims are cata-chrestic claims in the sense that everybody knows that the so-called adequate narratives of the emergence of those things were not written in the spaces that have decolonized themselves, but rather in the spaces of the colonizers. That is a catachrestic situation. There the question of essences becomes the question of regulative political concepts. I mean, I don't really think about essentialism or anti-essentialism when I look at what's going on in the third world. I see either block unity, highly strategic in the strictest political sense, or these catachrestic claims where people are having to negotiate questions like national language, nationhood, citizenship, etcetera. The question of essence really doesn't come in there because it is catachrestic. And, in fact, if one wanted to give an example here, one could find a wonderful one from the sixty-three million tribal people in India, as to how the idea of nationship, unity, et cetera, are being negotiated within that arena, but that would take a very long time.

Let me end this long and impassioned answer briefly by saying that one could look at it another way, too. Again, I want to acknowledge some debt to a re-reading of *Anti-Oedipus*. Maybe if I read *A Thousand Plateaus* again I will like it. In the old days I didn't like *Anti-Oedipus*, but I've been rereading it. One can put it this way: capital is anti-essentializing because it is in the abstract as such. There's no doubt about it. I'm not talking about capital*ism*, I'm talking about capital, and, against it, the essence of nations, cultures, etcetera, deployed for the political management of capital. And today, to an extent, the "politics of overdetermination" is the newest twist in that management, even including the idea of an anti-essentialist multiplicity of agents. I'm speaking obviously of the wake of Laclau and Mouffe's book. That's the newest twist in this management of the basically anti-essentializing movement of capital as the abstract as such. Let's stop here. This is a good answer.

ER: I take the force of your point, that when you think about the third world, especially politically, the problem of essentialism doesn't arise. But in what you have written, for example, about the Subaltern Studies Group, their practice, and their pursuit of an essential category or definition . . .

GS: . . . subaltern consciousness . . .

ER: . . . you describe a certain kind of project: they produce, in the process that you unpack, an anti-essentialist encounter with radical textuality; I think that is the way you put it.[4]

GS: Yes.

ER: That was part of what my question was directed at, the way in which your work on *their* work has gotten, at least in some ways, articulated in terms of the debate around essentialism and anti-essentialism.

GS: I should say something about this perhaps. I haven't ever really said anything. You know, I'm still part of the collective (Subaltern Studies Group) and I hope to attend the next workshop, but my intervention has made them somewhat uncomfortable. I think I turned out to be more . . . well, I will use your word, anti-essentialist . . .

ER: . . . in quotation marks . . .

GS: . . . than they had figured. So that, to an extent, I work with them. I'm not monumentalizing them. They are not a group of third world historians who are just wonderful and correctly strategically essentialist, etcetera. I think they, at least some of them, had more invested in the subaltern consciousness than I had thought when I was welcomed in the group. So it seems to me that rather than think of it as my work *on* them, it should be seen as my work *with* them as a kind of gadfly, a persistent critic among them. So that is the peculiar position that I seem to occupy in spite of the, to me, rather unfortunate opening sentence of Colin McCabe's introduction to my book. The position I occupy is such that most deconstructivists think that I'm too vulgar; most marxists think that I'm too elitist and too much in love with Parisian fads; many feminists, mainstream feminists, are beginning to feel, in fact, they have said so, that I am, in some way, anti-feminist. And, in the same way, in the Subaltern Studies Group, I'm a closet elitist perhaps. So, I like that, I don't know how, why this happens, but it keeps me home-free (laughter from ER) to an extent, it keeps me vigilant. You know Benita Parry recently has accused Homi Bhabha and Abdul Jan Mohammed and me of being so enamored of deconstruction that we're not able to let the native speak. She has forgotten that we are natives, too, eh? The postcolonial is the old colonial subject. In the same way, I *am* one of the subalternists; I don't work *on* them. And as a subalternist, not a sub-alternist historian, but a subalternist critic, I'm against their grain as I am against the grain of the anti-essentialist. You know, in fact, a group of ex-tremely committed anti-essentialists in Australia once described me in a journal, I'm sorry I've forgotten the name of the journal, and the name of the person who actually was the representative of this group who described me as such, but I wear it like a crown–as representing the decline of the real. So, you know, I'm not going to stand by that claim to the essentialism, as you put it, of the subaltern consciousness forever, saying "watch this wonderful strategic use of essentialism." There, too, the scene changes as things move.

    ER: You have made several references to the problem of theory, whether it's marxists accusing you of being too attached . . .

    GS: Not accusing–thinking of me . . .

    ER: Thinking of you . . .

    GS: I'm not so important that people are accusing me. . . . One of the subalternists did indeed accuse me of various things but I've written about that in my book.[5]

    ER: (laughing) Okay . . .

    GS: . . . but that's an exception–no, when they think of me they think . . .

    ER: (laughter)

GS: . . . if my name comes up, let's put it that way . . .

ER: (laughing) Okay . . . in any case, there is one reading of essentialism in the U.S. context that suggests that it tends to be empirical, that it's a kind of practical rather than a theorized essentialism, or that it's an essentialism by default. I wonder what you think of that reading, and that would return me to an earlier question about the absence of a kind of a philosophical rejoinder to anti-essentialism. We've already talked about that, but I wonder if you think it's possible at present to construct a kind of self-consciously theorized essentialism, or if there would be any point in even trying to do that. There are, of course, discourses perhaps in the biological or the genetic sciences that seem to be seeking to isolate universal or essential human traits. Is the reductiveness that tends to characterize those kinds of moves a primary strategy of essentialism? Do those kinds of reductions go against the grain or against the disciplinary prejudices and investments of literary and philosophical discourse and thus disable a substantive theoretical essentialism in the debate?

GS: Now, sociobiology, cognitive studies, artificial intelligence, which take something as the ground, they are exaggerated cases of most such discourses, hmmm?

ER: Right.

GS: These things become politically offensive, a way, precisely, of differentiating oppressive behavior. I have no problem there; I'm against that. And I don't particularly want to wait to theorize essentialism in order to say that; I really do believe in undermining the vanguardism of theory. I really do think that that persistent effort is very important for people to talk about in anti-essentialism. So, to an extent, I don't want a theory of essences. We have enough of those. We have nothing but the practice of essences, either. So, when I said strategy, I meant strategy. I don't even think I'm capable of thinking theory in that sense. With essences, at least I feel that they're so useful that they can become dangerous. With theory, I feel that, for the moment, for me, at least, it's best to keep it at a distance. So, I would say, coming from my own sort of odd position, I don't see why we would want a substantive essentialism. It seems to me that there is no reason. What a person like me wants to look at is why essentialism is confused with the empirical. Why do people make this terminological confusion? Earlier, in my school-teacherly voice, I said that this confusion is a way of not wanting to infiltrate the disciplines, the vested interests, the real problems. Instead, one says that the careful construction of an object of investigation in a field is essentialism. This is the same as confusing essentialism with the empirical. All we really want to claim is that there is no feminine essence; there's no essential class subject; the general subject of essence is not a good basis for investigation. This is rather different from being empirical.

If we base our ontological commitments on various forms of coding, you know, and there are people like, let's say, Gayle Rubin, whose essay I, again, have re-read recently. It is, to me, spectacular that someone coming from a Freudian/Lévi-Straussian structuralist humanism should in fact get into the idea of value in so important a way, and it's hardly picked up–that part of it–people talk about sex-gender systems, etcetera. It seems to me that if, whether we declare ourselves as essentialists or anti-essentialists, we work hard enough to see that our own ontological commitments (and they must be there, even if it's only to anti-essentialism) are dependent on various forms of coding, if we base our ontological commitments on various forms of coding, and now I'm basing myself on stuff that I've said before, we can presuppose a variety of general catachrestic names, you know, as a grounding. I've taken examples from postcoloniality, but one can, in fact, find these kinds of examples all over the place. In fact, Richard Rorty speaking about the nominalism in poststructuralism is right on target there. What he does with it is something else. But to see that, to base one's ontological commitment on an examination of value coding and then to take, to presuppose, a catachrestic name in order to ground our project, our investigation, allows us to be thoroughly empirical without necessarily being blind essentialists, essentialist as such. Ultimately, if you will forgive me for saying so, but then you need some kind of a voice, you know, in your journal, that will speak from the other side, I have to say that a lot of self-consciously anti-essentialist writing seems to me a bit useless and boring. You know what I'm saying? It's often very derivative, resembling other and better models that are not as scared of essences. It seems to me that to be empirical in this way would be a much greater challenge, require much harder work, would undermine . . . would make people read different things, you know. I mean, if you're reading development economics or old-fashioned ethnography that's still coming out . . . in order to be able to re-fashion it this way, it takes up all your time; you don't read Cixous's latest thing. In fact, I'm very out-of-date on much of the, you know, "with-it" writing because it takes time to read the other stuff and then *do* this thing that I'm talking about, and I don't even do it well. So that's what I would say. I think to confuse empirical work with the pursuit of essences is, in itself, something that should be examined, and I don't see any need for a substantive theory of essentialism.

ER: We've been talking about feminism all along, but to address it very directly, how would you say feminism, as such, which is already problematic . . . (laughs) . . . *feminisms*! . . . how have feminisms influenced your thinking about essentialism? Did feminism or women's studies put essentialism on the agenda in the U.S. academy? And what would you say–you just now mentioned Cixous–about the way essentialism and anti-essentialism are intertwined in the practice of feminist theory and women's studies, in the U.S. or in France, in the work of the anti-feminist feminists like Cixous or Kristeva?

GS: I think in general women's studies philosophy is humanist. There is a piece by Jean Grimshaw in the current *Radical Philosophy* on Mary Daly's humanism. Of course, Mary Daly is not representative of U.S. feminism, but I think some lessons can be learned there about essentialist or anti-essentialist debate.

When I began to write as a feminist, the idea of differences being unjustly made and differences unjustly not being recognized needed the presupposition that what was self-same or identical was an essence. It was okay as a strategic presupposition; it certainly allowed me to learn and teach. But it does seem that like most strategies, for me at least, it has served its purpose, and at this point I can't go on beating that horse anymore. And as I say, my feminism now takes a distance from that debate.

As you know, anti-feminist means something else in France. I really don't have much to do with it because that's very situation specific. I like reading Irigaray, but I read her within the tradition of the French, foregrounding rhetoric. I see many of my students, who accuse her of being essentialist as she's talking about women, not reading *in that way*. They're saying, "well, she's saying this about women, this about. . . ." If you read her, in the way that, from the surrealists on down, we've been taught to read the best in French writing, without taking for granted her own sometimes irritatingly declared ruptures . . . but you know that Hegel has to be read that way, you know, Marx has to be read, Derrida has to be read that way. Why do we become essentialist readers when we read someone like Irigaray? I take a great deal of pleasure reading her because she writes within that tradition and . . . it's good.

I'm repelled by Kristeva's politics: what seems to me to be her reliance on the sort of banal historical narrative to produce "women's time": what seems to me Christianizing psychoanalysis; what seems to me to be her sort of ferocious Western Europeanism; and what seems to me to be her longstanding implicit sort of positivism: naturalizing of the chora, naturalizing of the pre-semiotic, etcetera. I'm so put off by this that I can't read her seriously anymore, so it's more my problem. I mean, I'm not generous and catholic enough to learn from her anymore. Cixous, I should pick up on again, and perhaps I will do so since I'm going to teach. . . . I've put some stuff by Cixous on the reading list so that I'm obliged to really take a look at her.

I think the kind of anti-essentialism that I like these days–again, every time I use that word, I'm using it because it is your word–is (I've already talked about Rubin), is, let's say the work of someone whom I've used a lot, a woman called Kalpana Bardhan. But, if you read her, you probably wouldn't see what I was talking about. Again, as I was saying, one has to do that work of learning how to honor empirical work. In her work, she talks about how stratified, let's say, the whole idea of women is in a place like India. In Bardhan's work (she's a development economist), you begin to see how impossible it is to focus on, even within endogamous or exogamous marriage lines, how impossible it is to focus on something called a space out of which you will define and articulate something called a woman. She even diversifies in this way the radicals who can join in their struggle. Then, in another space, she diversifies the people who study them–good people, herself, Barbara Miller. . . . I find, in that kind of a work which is not against essentialism but which completely pluralizes the grid, it is my task as a reader, as it is with deconstruction, to read it and run with it and go somewhere else. It is my task as a reader to see where in that grid there are the spaces where, in fact, woman oozes away, you know? That's the kind of stuff that really excites me these days, you know? So that's what I read. Essences, it seems to me, are just a kind of content. All content is not essence. Why be so nervous about it? Why not demote the word "essence," because without a minimalizable essence, and I'm now thinking of Derrida's notion of a minimal idealization, without a minimalizable essence, an essence as *ce qui reste*, an essence as what remains, there is no exchange. Difference articulates these negotiable essences. So, I have no time for essence/anti-essence. It seems to me that there's so much work to be done that demoting the notion of essence, minimalizing, looking at these minimalizable essences, seeing that that's how it works, one can go ahead and do something else. You know what I'm saying?

ER: Yes, but it seems to me that the reason that that can't be done across the board is teaching. I always have to "do" essentialism/anti-essentialism with my students because in the first flush of feminist thought they become the most energetic essentialists, or personalists, perhaps. And that's, of course, a quite different thing from a research program or the kinds of books that one wants to write, but in my experience that's part of the reason that the question won't go away. It's a kind of initial question, politically and intellectually, when students discover the possibility of a feminist discourse.

GS: Well, of course that's a problem. What I'm trying to suggest, because this is not a problem I don't have, what I'm trying to suggest is that rather than make it a central issue, work it into the method of your teaching so that the class becomes an example of the minimalizing of essences, the impossibility of essences; rather than talk about it constantly, make the class a proof of this new position. If we're talking strategy, you know as well as I do that teaching is a question of strategy. That is perhaps the only place where we actually get any experience in strategy, although we talk a lot about it. And it seems to me that it's a change that strategy has called for. I think talking about essentialism and anti-essentialism and making students take sides–they're not yet ready, they don't, they know nothing about the real meaning–essence is a grand word, you know? They know nothing about how much has been achieved in the name of essences. In that context, it seems to me that one can make a strategy of taking away from them the authority of their marginality, the centrality of their marginality, through the strategy of careful teaching, so that they come to prove that that authority will not take them very far because the world is a large place. Others are many. The self is enclosed; the concrete is fabricated. One can do it in true teaching rather than talk about it *ad infinitum* because they're not even ready to take sides. We have to assume that we, as dogs in office (*King Lear*, you know, "a dog's obeyed in office"), are teaching them, hmmm? That's what I would say.

ER: How would you make a distinction–obviously you would make a distinction–between specificity and essence, so that it's possible to articulate specificities without moving in the direction of totalization and therefore without lapsing into essentialism? Perhaps one of the things that has happened in the debate in the U.S. is that critics have been attacked as essentialists when in fact they've been talking about specificity.

GS: Well you know, I'm not saying that there isn't a problem of freezing one's little arena of expertise into a global model. That problem cuts across so-called essentialists and so-called anti-essentialists. Remember I was saying "what would you do if you had to use another word?" I think that problem should be attacked. I don't know whether it should be diagnosed as essentialism because at this point that word has become really . . . it's been overworked. I don't even know if it was originally ready to be worked, but now, it seems to me, it's doing nothing there except signalling what color cockade you're wearing in your hat.

ER: There has been, at least in literary studies, a kind of consensus that feminist critics have done exactly what you describe, taken a very small sample and then generalized about a "feminine aesthetic" or a "woman's tradition"–produced ahistorical misrepresentations of things as feminine, feminine, you know, the Feminine, with a capital "F." Insofar as this criticism has been generally accepted, there's a kind of consensus in favor of pursuing specificity, multiplying differences. Is there a way in which multiplication can become pluralism? What are the consequences of that?

GS: The real problem, one of the reasons why it becomes pluralism, is that we live in a country which has pluralism–the pluralism of repressive tolerance–as the best of its political credo. That's why it becomes pluralism, you know? I mean, none of us is particularly interested in changing our social relations, so the real answer is that. What to do about it? Certainly not chat about essentialism. I think we should shelve that question there and then talk about it a bit more within those limits. It seems to me that the proliferation of multiplicity, which is always limited by what choices are allowed, is a very bad idea. It seems to me that one should focus where one can focus, make it possible for one's students to focus a bit more.

Once we have established the story of the straight, white, Judeo-Christian, heterosexual man of property as the ethical universal, we must not replicate the same trajectory. I think we certainly have to watch it, but it is not possible. . . . We are . . . we have limits, we cannot even learn many languages. This idea of a global fun-fair is a lousy idea as a teaching idea. One of the first things to do is to think through the limits of one's power. One must ruthlessly undermine that story that I was talking of, the story of the ethical universal, the hero. But the alternative is not constantly to evoke multiplicity; the alternative is to know and to teach the student the awareness that this is a limited sample because of one's own inclinations and capacities to learn enough to take a larger sample. And this kind of work should be a collective enterprise. Other people will do some other work. This is how I think one should proceed, rather than make each student into a ground of multiplicity. That leads to a pluralism. And I see so often in the U.S. student–we were talking about this miraculating agent–I ask the U.S. student: "What do you think is the inscription that allows you to think the world without any preparation? What sort of coding has produced this subject?" I think it's hard for students to know this, but we have a responsibility to make this lesson palliative rather than fully destructive. This is not a paralysing thing to teach. In fact, when a student is told that responsibility means proceeding from an awareness of the limits of one's power, the student understands it quite differently from being told "Look, you can't do all of this." You know what I'm saying? I can't do all of this. But I will share with you what I have learned about knowing, that these are the limitations of what I undertake, looking to others to teach me. I think that's what one should do rather than invoke multiplicity.

ER: How is this problem of the subject related to the relationship between essentialism and the efforts to theorize the body, or bodies, as someone pointed out to me when I showed him this question? What kind of problem is this? Can we theorize our bodies without essentializing them as the body? Is our confusion about how to theorize bodies the root of the problem of essentialism? Insofar as there is another factor that keeps the question of essentialism kind of bubbling, I think it has to do with the fact that, at least in the U.S., the effort to biologize gender is not over in the general culture, political culture, for example, the front page of the *New York Times* a few weeks ago explaining why at certain times of the month we can't find our cars because of our . . .

GS: Really?

ER: . . . hormones raging. Yes.

GS: I didn't see that. It gives me an answer to my question!

ER: (laughs) How is your own effort to address bodies in some of your work part of your thinking about essentialism? And how do race and class actually enter in here, as well as the more obvious gender?

GS: Well, you know, all of those generalizations, again, I am against universalizing in that way. I mean I would look at why they're essentializing, rather that to say that "this is bad" necessarily, because I think there is something, some biological remnant in the notion of gender, even in the good notion of gender. Biology doesn't just disappear, except it should not be offered as a ground of all explanations. So basically on that, you know, I'm a nonfoundationalist in that sense, especially when grounds are found to justify bad politics.

So it's almost as if I'm going at it the other way, a sort of deductive anti-essentialist, how is the essence being used? But apart from that I would say that biology, a biology, is one way of thinking the systematicity of the body. The body, like all other things, cannot be thought, as such. Like all other things, I have never tried to approach the body as such. I do take the extreme ecological view that the body as such has no possible outline. You know, again, *Economic and Philosophic Manuscripts*, where Marx, talking about species life, says nature is the great body without organs. You know, if one really thinks of the body as such, there is no possible outline of the body as such. I think that's about what I would say. There are thinkings of the systematicity of the body, there are value codings of the body. The body, as such, cannot be thought, and I certainly cannot approach it.

ER: This also is a question that's not in here, per se, because when I looked again at that not very well formulated question about the unconscious and death, I realized that there is no question about psychoanalysis anywhere in here.

GS: That's okay.

ER: (Laughs) Okay?

GS: Yah!

ER: (laughing) These are my last questions that didn't fit elsewhere. Is it possible to speak of a non-essential essence? Would that be a kind of gloss on strategic essentialism?

GS: I don't think so.

ER: No?

GS: I mean, one might just as well speak about an essential non-essence. It's possible to speak of everything. But an essence, if it's mini-malizable, is also cross-hatched. But in the longer question as you had it before you had asked about the relationship to death. . . . I would like to say that death for me–body, woman, worker, lover, so this perhaps applies to all words–but death as such can only be thought via essence or rupture of essence, that mother-tongue analogy that I gave you. . . . I cannot approach death as such, you see what I'm saying? To an extent it takes us back to the question of catachresis. Catachresis is a nice thing . . . better than an anti-essence.

ER: I've already asked about deconstruction as a kind of questioning of essences or of the relation between the essential and the anti-essential, and as I look back I want to ask you about de Man, as opposed . . . I was about to say as opposed to Derrida, but not necessarily as opposed to Derrida, but in his specificity as someone who can be of help.

GS: Well, you know, Derrida, from his very early work was animated by this peculiar intuition of deconstruction. Of course when I knew de Man he was a phenomenologist, interested in people like Lévi-Strauss, Poulet, etcetera, and deconstruction was a thing that appealed to him greatly and he ran with it in another direction. I see his work as lapidary and strong in its very limits. That is to say, I don't believe he ever gave away his control in the writing. He talked about giving up his control, but he never really gave away his control in the way that Derrida constantly can. De Man even writes about it in the normal way. But writing, accounting for something, can sometimes be understood in one way. It seems to me that the strength within its limits was a sort of extraordinary training in reading, which is then open for use in many ways. Just as I was saying to you that what one learns from deconstruction is the importance of essences, how useful they are. From de Man, the lesson that I learn is the extreme importance of an absolutely literal-minded reading. I think that's his strength. And that cuts across as many different manifestations.

ER: You spoke earlier, several times, about other words that might be used rather than anti-essentialist, and although I didn't know you were going to say that, as I was thinking about talking with you, I did fix on certain terms in your work, like "interruption," or "transactional," or "discontinuous." I don't mean that you were thinking of this when you made the earlier remarks, but are these perhaps other words that can serve the strategic, have strategic effects?

GS: At the expense of being repetitive, but I think it bears repetition, I'm feeling more centered or positioned by that word essence than I like, because after all essence is the word in anti-essentialism too, if you take a position vis-à-vis anti-essentialism. So I feel more positioned or centered by that word, whereas I have never developed a position of thinking its relation to the question of essences. I thought through that bit about essences as *ce qui reste* because I wanted to come forward, to answer questions that clearly positioned me as having a position on the strength of, you know, those couple of sentences I said to Liz Grosz and have somewhat regretted since then. Now, having taken that apology, as it were, if you put that together, that idea of essences as what remains, the minimalizable, something with which we negotiate (we were talking about the strategy of teaching, etcetera, and this works with students), without talking about the debate, making it a topic of discussion–if you put this together with interruption as bringing to crisis, then you can see how it can relate. It really can relate to anti-many things, bringing to crisis.

Now, in this wave, sort of in this endless wave of my thinking–and I'm talking about where I am here, now–I'm sort of soldiering on in my own way to bring anti-essentialist metaphysics to crisis. Not that that will remain the only agenda if you talk to me again. Strategic means strategic. I'm attempting to bring anti-essentialist metaphysics to crisis because I care. You see this whole business of what I began with–that you deconstructively critique something which is so useful to you that you cannot speak another way. . . . You know, I just told my graduate students what I would look for in their papers, and one of the things I said was "Earn the right to use words, your language. Never say text when book will do. Never say discourse when language will do. Never say critique when criticize will do," because this is too important for us, and I don't want my students to push it around and think that this is taught in a critique of humanism. So, to that extent, I would say, because I care, because after all this is the only way that I can speak. . . . I talked a little bit about how the post-colonial on the cusp of decolonization is almost made a paradigm of this kind of a thing. I feel it necessary to bring anti-essentialist metaphysics to crisis. What one cares about one doesn't want to see spoiled so easily. This brings us, of course, to the next question about which I've spoken before, the politics of overdetermination–looking for some way out of being marxist and still not losing credit. This idea of alliance politics, etcetera. Laclau and Mouffe's work, to an extent, is supporting the kind of very reactionary pluralism that most humanities students are into anyway. When I asked Laclau this question in London, he very painstakingly explained to me the difference between plurality and pluralism in the public arena, just as . . . he had, in fact, explained with the same kind of painstaking care the difference between contingency and randomness to a young philosopher about ten minutes before that. The philosopher had said something rather like what I had said, and so I didn't feel completely crushed because (both laugh loudly) I just thought that this was uncalled for. But it seems to me that this, the anti-essentialist metaphysics, is in fact giving support to the politics of overdetermination: "we are all overdetermined," sort of multiplicity of agents, which is really rather a reactionary position.

"Transaction": now a transaction can be a transaction between essences, so it is not necessarily anti-essentialist. And radical discontinuity cannot appear, like pure difference; remember, essences cannot appear either. I mean, theoretically, essences are not allowed to appear, so there's not much theoretical difference between pure essence and pure difference. Radical discontinuity cannot appear. So discontinuity, to relate this to what I thought through in terms of essences for your set of questions–the minimalizable, what remains–discontinuity must traffic in minimal continua. So we go back to *ce qui reste*, fragments of essences to reckon with, and that's where writing like Bardhan's is so interesting. Fragments of essences to reckon with rather than preserving myself from them. If you see this as an anti-essentialist project, I start running the other way again. (ER laughs.) Because you see, this is the whole business about strategy, asking what regulates your diagnosis, why do you want me with you, what claims me, what is claiming me? I've written about this too. I'll tell you what I am against: unacknowledged corporatism. I am anti-corporatist, and that cuts across essentialism and anti-essentialism.

ER: Can we talk, just because of the very last things that you've said, about the question of audience? When I thought about these questions, I also thought about my own work. I've been writing about pluralism. What I have been calling pluralism is partially what you were just referring to as corporatism. It's an essentialism that doesn't have to do so much with the object of study as with one's audience. The pluralist assumes not just her own transparency–in fact she may articulate her positionality–but the transparency and therefore the unity of one's audience. That's where essence resides, or is expressed, that is what pluralism doesn't acknowledge. Perhaps this isn't what you meant by anti-corporatism. . . . I guess what I'm asking is for you to say a little bit more about it. What I see as the pluralist moment is the moment when one doesn't acknowledge–and I've learned this from you, at least I think I have learned it from you–the exclusions that fragment one's audience.

GS: Yes. Now one thing that I will say is that when one takes the representative position–the homeopathic deconstruction of identity by identity–one is aware that outside of that representation of oneself in terms of a stream, there are areas that are completely inaccessible to one. That's, of course, that's a given. In the same way, it seems to me, that when I said "building for difference," the sense of audience is already assuming that the future is simply a future present. So, to an extent, the most radical challenge of deconstruction is that notion of thought being a blank part of the text given over to a future that is not just a future present, you know. So in that sense, the audience is not an essence, the audience is a blank. When I was speaking of building for difference, I was thinking of the fact that an audience can be constituted by people I cannot even imagine, affected by this little unimportant trivial piece of work, which is not just direct teaching and writing. That business displaces the question of audience as essence or fragmented or exclusivist or anything. Derrida calls this a responsibility to the trace of the other, I think, and that I find is a very. . . . It's something that one must remind oneself of all the time. That is why what I cannot imagine stands guard over everything that I must/can do, think, live, etcetera.

But when an audience, having said that, when an audience is responsible, responding, invited, in other words, to co-investigate, then positionality is shared with it. Audience and investigator: it's not just a binary opposition when an audience really is an audience. That's why, I mean I hadn't thought this through, but many of the changes I've made in my position are because the audience has become a co-investigator and I've realized what it is to have an audience. You know what I'm saying? An audience is part of one. An audience shows us something. Well, that is the transaction, you know, it's a responsibility to the other, giving it faces. It's not. . . . I don't see this de-essentializing particularly, but really deconstructing the binary opposition between investigator and audience. Radically, in that it is not a future present, it is the blankness of the future but also . . . the less radical method, the logical one, where one begins to imagine the audience responding, responsible, and invited to be co-investigator, one starts owning the right to have one's invitation accepted, given that the invitation is, like all letters, open letters intercepted and that people turn up in other places for other occasions with that invitation, so that we begin to deconstruct that binary opposition bit by bit. I don't see that particularly as de-essentializing. It's something else. But yes, I think the question you've asked is very very important.

ER: As you were answering it . . . you used the word "future"; after I had finished these questions, at the very end, I realized there was no question about history, either as a potentially essentializing discourse or as a potentially anti-essentializing discourse. Actually, now these questions, with the words essentializing and anti-essentializing . . .

GS: See what happens?

ER: . . . larded in so thickly, are no longer the right questions, but, having said that, what would you say about history?

GS: Well, I'll give you a very short answer. It depends on your view of history as negotiable determinant or fact.

ER: Thank you.

GS: Thank you.

Notes

1   Space doesn't permit me to do justice to Ferguson's extraordinarily interesting and intricate essay. Her analysis reveals that the legal system's preference for addressing "stipulated states" enabled it to evade the systemic problem of the contempt for women's testimony on rape. Ferguson points out that it also makes it extremely difficult for women who are attacked by men they know to convince district attorneys even to press charges. (See Estrich's discussion of "simple rape.") At the same time, in her analysis of *Clarissa*, Ferguson stresses that stipulation *can* be used, in particular cases, to combat phallocentric constructions of sexuality and sexual violence.

2   See Spivak, *In Other Worlds: Essays in Cultural Politics*:

> *We must of course remind ourselves, our positivist feminist colleagues in charge of creating the discipline of women's studies, and our anxious students, that essentialism is a trap. It seems more important to learn to understand that the world's women do not all relate to the privileging of essence, especially through "fiction," or "literature," in the same way (89); Reading the work of Subaltern Studies from within but against the grain, I would suggest that elements in their text would warrant a reading of the project to retrieve the subaltern consciousness as the attempt to undo a massive historiographic metalepsis and "situate" the effect of the subject as subaltern. I would read it, then, as a* strategic use of positivist essentialism in a scrupulously visible political interest. This would put them in line with the Marx who locates fetishization, the ideological determination of the "concrete," and spins the narrative of the development of the money-form; with the Nietzsche who offers us genealogy in place of historiography, the Foucault who plots the construction of "counter- memory," the Barthes of semiotropy and the Derrida of "affirmative deconstruction." This would allow them to use the critical force of anti-humanism, in other words, even as they share its constitutive paradox: that the essentializing moment, the object of their criticism, is irreducible (205).

3   See "Three Women's"; Rodó; Retamar.

4   See *Other* 202–7; see also Guha.

5   Things have changed somewhat since this interview was conducted in December 1988.

Works Cited

Bardhan, Kalpana. "Women's Work, Welfare and Status: Forces of Tradition and Change in India." *South Asia Bulletin* 6.1 (1986): 3–16.

Baudrillard, Jean. *Simulations*. Trans. Paul Foss, Paul Patton, and Philip Beitchman. New York: Semiotext(e), 1983.

Blackburn, Robin. *The Overthrow of Colonial Slavery, 1776–1848*. London: Verso, 1988.

Deleuze, Gilles, and Felix Guattari. *Anti-Oedipus: Capitalism and Schizophrenia*. Trans. Robert Hurley, Mark Seem, and Helen R. Lane. New York: Viking, 1977.

———. *A Thousand Plateaus: Capitalism and Schizophrenia*. Trans. Brian Massumi. Minneapolis: U of Minneapolis P, 1987.

Derrida, Jacques. *Of Grammatology*. Trans. Gayatri Chakravorty Spivak. Baltimore: Johns Hopkins UP, 1976.

Estrich, Susan. *Real Rape*. Cambridge: Harvard UP, 1987.

Ferguson, Frances. "Rape and The Rise of The Novel." *Representations* 20 (Fall 1987): 88–112.

Folker, Frobel, et al. *The New International Division of Labor*. Trans. P. Burgess. Cambridge: Cambridge UP, 1980.

Grimshaw, Jean. "'Pure Lust': The Elemental Feminist Philosophy of Mary Daly." *Radical Philosophy* 49 (1988): 24–30.

Guha, Ranajit, ed. *Subaltern Studies: Writings of South Asian History and Society*. 5 vols. to date. Delhi: Oxford UP, 1982– .

Haraway, Donna. "A Manifesto for Cyborgs: Science, Technology and Socialist Feminism in the 1980s." *Socialist Review* 80 (1985): 65–107. Rpt. in *Coming to Terms: Feminism, Theory, Politics*. Ed. Elizabeth Weed, New York: Routledge, 1989. 173–204.

Harris, Nigel. *The End of the Third World: Newly Industrializing Countries and the Decline of Ideology*. London: Penguin, 1987.

Heath, Stephen. "Differences." *Screen* 19.3 (1978): 50–112.

Jardine, Alice. "Men in Feminism: Odor di Uomo or Compagnons de Route?" *Men in Feminism*. Ed. Alice Jardine and Paul Smith. London: Methuen, 1987. 54–61.

Laclau, Ernesto, and Chantal Mouffe. *Hegemony and Socialist Strategy: Towards a Radical Democratic Politics*. Trans. Winston Moore and Paul Cammack. London: Verso, 1985.

Marx, Karl. *Capital*. Trans. Ben Fowkes. Vol. 3. Harmondsworth: Penguin, 1976. 3 vols.

———. *Economic and Philosophic Manuscripts of 1844*. Ed. Dirk J. Struik. New York: International Publishers, 1964.

Miller, Barbara D. *The Endangered Sex: Neglect of Female Children in Rural North India.* Ithaca: Cornell UP, 1981.

Nagel, Thomas. *Mortal Questions.* Cambridge: Cambridge UP, 1979.

Parry, Benita. "Problems in Current Theories of Colonial Discourse." *Oxford Literary Review* 9.1–2 (1987): 27–58.

Putnam, Hilary. *Meaning and the Moral Sciences.* Boston: Routledge and Kegan Paul, 1979.

Retamar, Roberto Fernández. "Caliban: Notes towards a Discussion of Culture in Our America." Trans. Lynn Garafola, David Arthur McMurray, and Robert Márquez. *Massachusetts Review* 15 (1974): 7–72.

Riley, Denise. *"Am I That Name?" Feminism and the Category of "Women" in History.* Minneapolis: U of Minnesota P, 1988.

Robbins, Bruce. "American Intellectuals and Middle East Politics: Interview with Edward Said." *Social Text* 19/20 (1988): 37–53.

Rodó, José Enrique. *Ariel.* Ed. Gordon Brotherson. Cambridge: Cambridge UP, 1967.

Rorty, Richard. "Philosophy as a Kind of Writing: An Essay on Derrida." *Consequences of Pragmatism: Essays: 1972–1980.* Minneapolis: U of Minnesota P, 1982. 90–109.

Rubin, Gayle. "The Traffic in Women: Notes on the 'Political Economy' of Sex." *Toward an Anthropology of Women.* Ed. Rayna Reiter. New York: Monthly Review, 1975. 157–210.

Salvaggio, Ruth. *Enlightened Absence: Neoclassical Configurations of the Feminine.* Urbana: U of Illinois P, 1988.

Spelman, Elizabeth V. *Inessential Woman: Problems of Exclusion in Feminist Thought.* Boston: Beacon, 1988.

Spivak, Gayatri Chakravorty. "Can the Subaltern Speak?" *Marxism and the Interpretation of Culture.* Ed. Cary Nelson and Lawrence Grossberg. Urbana: U of Illinois P, 1988. 271–313.

_____. *In Other Worlds: Essays in Cultural Politics.* New York: Methuen, 1987.

_____. "Poststructuralism, Marginality, Post-coloniality, and Value." *Literary Theory Today.* Ed. Peter Collier and Helga Geyer-Ryan. Cambridge: Cambridge UP, 1990. 219–44.

_____. "Three Women's Texts and a Critique of Imperialism." *Critical Inquiry* 12:1 (1985): 243–61.

_____, with Elizabeth Grosz. "Criticism, Feminism and the Institution." *Thesis Eleven* 10/11 (1984–85): 175–88.

Williams, Bernard. *Moral Luck: Philosophical Papers, 1973–80.* Cambridge: Cambridge UP, 1982.

Notes on Contributors

TERESA DE LAURETIS is Professor of the History of Consciousness at the University of California, Santa Cruz. She guest-edited the *Queer Theory: Lesbian and Gay Sexualities* issue of *differences* (1991). Her most recent book, *The Practice of Love*, is a deviant psychoanalytic reconsideration of lesbian sexuality as perverse desire.

DIANA FUSS is Assistant Professor of English at Princeton University. She is author of *Essentially Speaking: Feminism, Nature and Difference* and editor of *Inside/Out: Lesbian Theories, Gay Theories.*

ELIZABETH GROSZ is Director of the Institute of Critical Theory and Cultural Studies at Monash University, Australia. Her most recent books are *Jacques Lacan: A Feminist Introduction* and *Volatile Bodies: Toward a Corporeal Feminism.*

LUCE IRIGARAY, psychoanalyst and theorist, is a director of research at the Centre national des recherches scientifiques in Paris. Her recent works include *Le temps de la différence: pour une révolution pacifique* and *Je, tu, nous: pour une culture de la différence* (English trans. by Alison Martin). ROBERT LAWRENCE MAZZOLA is Assistant Professor of French and Italian at Wagner College, Staten Island. His essay "Coming to Terms: Mask and Masquerade in Marguerite Duras' *L'Amant*" appeared in *Journal of Durassian Studies* (1992), and he is currently working on fratricide in Duras's novels.

LESLIE WAHL RABINE is Professor of French and Director of Women's Studies at the University of California, Irvine. Her recent books include *Reading the Romantic Heroine: Text, History, Ideology* and *Feminism, Socialism, and French Romanticism*, co-authored with Claire Goldberg Moses.

ROBERT SCHOLES is Andrew W. Mellon Professor of Humanities at Brown University. His last book was *In Search of James Joyce*. He has just finished a book, written with Nancy R. Comley, called *Hemingway's Genders.*

NAOMI SCHOR is William Hanes Wannamaker Professor of Romance Studies at Duke University. Her most recent book is *George Sand and Idealism*. Along with Elizabeth Weed she is the founding co-editor of *differences.*

GAYATRI CHAKRAVORTY SPIVAK is Professor of English and Comparative Literature at Columbia University. Her newest book is *Outside in the Teaching Machines.* ELLEN ROONEY is Associate Professor of English and Modern Culture and Media at Brown University and Director of the Pembroke Center for Teaching and Research on Women. She is the author of *Seductive Reasoning: Pluralism and the Problematic of Contemporary Literary Theory* and is working on a book on "Criticism and the Subject of Sexual Violence."

Index

A

Alcoff, Linda: and de Lauretis on uses of essentialism in Anglo-American feminist criticism, 5, 8-12; dialogue with de Lauretis in feminist critical writing, 34n.2

allegory: in Derrida's critique of Nietzsche, 126

Althusser, Louis: Marxist critique of essentialism, 59n.4; position on ideology, 156

anti-essentialism: Beauvoir's and Irigaray's positions on compared, 45-51; and discontinuity between women and feminisms, 152-53; existentialism and essentialism as counterposition to, viii; feminism's persistent return to the body, 152; influence of Irigaray and Derrida on debate concerning, xv-xvi; and Irigaray's linking of the fluid and the feminine, 52-54; positive form of anti-essentialism as constructionism, xvii-xviii; and real/nominal distinction in essentialism, xi, 100; relationship of feminism to in Derrida's *Éperons,* 117-28; Scholes on deconstruction and, 101; in Schor's critique of Foucault, 113n.9; Spivak on Marxism and, 164-65; Spivak on use of term, 156, 160-61, 172, 173, 178-79

Anti-Oedipus (Deleuze and Guattari): Spivak's critique of concept of miraculating agency, 158-59, 168

anti-Semitism: Kristeva's critique of Sartre, 96n.3

Anzaldúa, Gloria: concept of experience in Anglo-American feminist theory, 8

Aphrodite: and feminist reconstruction of religious history, 65-66, 67; and

marriage in Schüssler Fiorenza's interpretation of Christianity, 73

Appiah, Anthony: on "classic dialectic," 47

authority: symbolic forms of female in Italian feminism, 24-26

authorship: practice of collective in Italian feminism, 36n.7

autocoscienza (self-consciousness): in history of Italian feminism, 18-20

autonomy: as goal of feminism of difference, 91-92

B

Bachofen, Johan Jacob: interpretation of development of Christian patriarchy, 81n.2

Bardhan, Kalpana: Spivak on essentialism and difference in, 173, 180

Barthes, Roland: Miller's reading of Rich and, 14

Bazard, Claire: role of mother in Saint-Simonian movement, 131

Beauvoir, Simone de: conflict between "equality" and "difference" feminists, viii-ix, 86-87; existentialism and issue of difference in feminism, viii; liberationist critique of essentialism, 43; Kristeva on anti-maternal position of, 96n.2; position on essentialism compared to Irigaray's, 45-51

Benjamin, Walter: on epistemological ruptures in course of history, 27

Bhabha, Homi: Benita Parry's critique of, 169

biologism: definition of as form of essentialism, 84-85; essentialism as distinct from, xii

Blackburn, Robin: influence on Spivak's notions of regionalism, 166

Boccia, Maria Luisa: feminist political theory in Italy, 28-29

body: as fundamental issue in essentialism, ix, 152; Spivak on essentialism, gender, and theorizing the body, 176-77

Borghi, Liana: lesbian activism in Italian feminism, 36n.9

Boston marriages: as examples of relationships of entrustment, 23

Braidotti, Rosi: on question of place in male relationship to feminism, 104-105

Brennan, Teresa: on history of critique of essentialism, ix; on rethinking of essentialism in feminist theory, xiv

Browning, Elizabeth Barrett: as example of relationship of entrustment, 23

Brownmiller, Susan: essentialism and context in defining rape, 151

Buddhism: Jesus's life compared to teachings of, 69-70

C

capital: Spivak on political management of, 168

capitalism: historical context of Saint-Simonian feminists, 137

castration: Derrida's discussion of "woman" and, 120

Catholicism: Irigaray on women and Christianity, 77-78

Cavarero, Adriana: on theory of sexual difference in Italian feminism, 15-16, 26, 32